George Husmann

American grape growing and wine making

George Husmann

American grape growing and wine making

ISBN/EAN: 9783337717117

Printed in Europe, USA, Canada, Australia, Japan

Cover: Foto ©ninafisch / pixelio.de

More available books at **www.hansebooks.com**

AMERICAN
Grape Growing
AND
WINE MAKING

BY

GEORGE HUSMANN

WITH SEVERAL ADDED CHAPTERS ON THE GRAPE IN-
DUSTRIES OF CALIFORNIA

FOURTH EDITION—REVISED AND REWRITTEN

ILLUSTRATED

NEW YORK
ORANGE JUDD COMPANY
1902

PREFACE TO THE REVISED EDITION.

Books are like men, they become old as rapidly as their authors, and unless books are revised frequently and kept abreast with the times, they fall behind and become of little value. And as we, their authors, find that toward the end of life time seems to travel with railway speed and seemingly flies faster, thus crowding us with events and their progress, we become aware that but a short space is left us in which to record it.

When I look back over life's checkered journey, at an age when many are called to join the silent army, the wish becomes but natural to leave to those of my viticultural friends (and I hope I have many throughout this broad land) who have had patience with my several efforts to become useful, especially to the beginner in grape culture, a memento of which I need not be ashamed. That even the revised and enlarged edition which preceded this has become very old, that it is far behind the times and their progress, no one knows better than I. When I think of the time when I, as a youth of twenty, planted the first small vineyard I ever took charge of, on my father's farm in the backwoods of Missouri, in 1847, and find now that my pet fruit, the grape, has spread over the whole Union, until there is not a State or Territory in which its cultivation has not been attempted in a more scientific and thorough manner than my first crude attempt; that the vineyards of this broad land now cover millions of acres; that we have hundreds of varieties instead of the three or four

iii

then known, and that the grape in some form has become an article of daily diet for millions,—the progress
seems almost incredible.   Yet with all this progress, we
are still striving for advancement.   This is as it should
be, and when we old men are gone, let us hope that our
children, inspired by the same love for the work which
urged us on, will take it as it drops from our hands and
carry it on to completion.   It would seem then but a
natural desire to round out the work of a lifetime by a
retrospect of the past ten years—the period which has
elapsed since the preceding revision—in noting the many
improvements in the way of new varieties, in pruning
and training, in marketing and in combating diseases
and insects injurious to the grape.   But living at the
western extreme of the Union, where the *Vinifera* is
almost exclusively cultivated (the American varieties
being only used as stocks for grafting), I have been compelled to draw on my Eastern friends for information,
which they have freely and kindly furnished, and have
thus made the second, the most interesting part of the
book.   To them, one and all, I tender heartfelt thanks,
coupled with the hope that the new edition may be
generally helpful in the work we are striving to
advance.

The period elapsing since 1883 has witnessed great
changes in viticulture.   At that date its friends were
almost discouraged by its manifold enemies of a fungous
nature, but remedies have kept pace with them until
now the cultivation of the *Vinifera* seems possible in
localities where heretofore only the most hardy of our
native sorts have been grown.   Of course, winter protection is necessary in these localities, but the best varieties are well worth the extra trouble.   From several
parts of Texas and New Mexico I have already the assurance that they can furnish the earlier varieties of the
Vinifera by the beginning of May; thus, when we join

North and South, we may hope for an almost continuous supply of table grapes throughout the Union.

In new varieties of American origin, we have also made remarkable progress. Prof. T. V. Munson of Denison, Texas, has accomplished wonderful results by cross-breeding and hybridizing, and also by his classification of vines. It has been my aim in this edition not to publish an immensely long list of varieties, but from the many to cull the best—varieties which have proved to be an improvement on those described in the previous edition, and which, as wine or table grapes, have been successful over the largest territory. That each of the States of this immense country will have to grow the varieties best suited either for table, market or wine, is self-evident. The times when enthusiasts may predict success for universal grapes are past, never to return. We all know now that soil and climatic conditions change the product, and that we cannot have a cosmopolitan grape. I have therefore omitted classification for localities.

Those who have the progress of humanity at heart, are apt to indulge in daydreams which are seldom realized. One of mine has been to see the American nation a community where wine drinking has supplanted the use of the more alcoholic beverages, such as whiskey, brandy etc., and thereby advanced to a state of *true temperance* I have endeavored to show, in the chapters devoted to wine making, how every one can make a pure, wholesome, light wine, and I see no cause why I should retract anything I nave said in that respect. I still believe that the pure, unadulterated juice of the grape is the most wholesome of all stimulants, a gift of God to man, too good to be abused by intemperance or excess. But while I hold this belief, I have no fault to find with that class of grape growers who consider it a perversion and a snare to use the grape for any purpose but the

table. If this be their conviction they have a right to
follow the dictates of their conscience, according to us
who entertain a different opinion, the same right.   Let
us then exercise the broadest charity to each other and
unite in the desire to do the utmost good to the community by giving them the most healthful fruit to eat
and the most innocent of stimulants to drink.

No one will question the difficulties in the way of
writing a book which shall carry some useful information to every one engaged in grape culture, in a country
so immense as this.   The information contained in Part
II will furnish many reliable data to nearly every one
here, giving him, at least, a safe basis on which to start
his experiments.   For all is as yet an experiment, and
happy will he be who, at the close of his life, can sift
from his numerous trials and experiments a few which
have been successful and which may serve as a basis for
further development of the science of viticulture.   A
lifetime devoted to this science has clearly demonstrated
to me that I could spend another in the same field, finding something new to acquire at every step.

Wishing all my viticultural brethren, far and near,
success in their efforts to advance our noble calling, and
that they may be able to glean something to assist them
from this last effort of my pen, I remain,

Theirs Fraternally,
GEORGE HUSMANN.

Talcoa Vineyards, Napa, California : 1896.

CONTENTS.

PART III.

AMERICAN WINE MAKING.

PART IV.

GRAPE CULTURE AND WINE MAKING IN CALIFORNIA.

PART I

THE CULTURE OF AMERICAN GRAPES AND VARIETIES

CHAPTER I.

CLASSIFICATION OF GRAPES.

It is only within the last twenty years that much attention has been given to the parentage and classification of our native varieties, it being thought of little or no importance whether a variety was derived from one or another of the few native species. Recent experience has shown that the varieties of a species, however widely they may differ from one another in some respects, agree in other points, and however far they may be removed from the native type, they retain certain characteristics which indicate a common parentage. On the other hand, if we know from which species a variety is derived, we can with some certainty predict its behavior in cultivation, and to a certain degree its value. Especially has this become of the first importance since the appearance of our greatest insect enemy, the *Phylloxera vastatrix*, as we know from experience that certain species are entirely exempt from, while others are to a certain extent subject to its ravages. This is so generally true that the experienced viticulturists of the present day regard the origin of the cultivated varieties as of first importance. It is not in the character of the fruit alone that our varieties differ, as they are derived from our native species. The foliage, the wood, the tendrils, the roots and other parts of the vine retain their peculiarities and hardiness, not only as to the ability to endure cold, but also to resist the attacks of parasitic plants and insects or whatever else affects the health of the plant—all these traits are now known to be transmitted with as much certainty as are the form and quality of the fruit.

3

All our numerous varieties now on the list are classed according to the species of *Vitis*, the generic name of the grape, from which they are known to be derived, and the name of the species is given to the class. So when, for the sake of brevity, we speak of a variety as an *Æstivalis*, a *Vinifera*, or *Riparia*, we simply mean that it originated from the class, and bears the characteristics of the species of that name. All the varieties of the European grape are regarded as having had their origin in *Vitis vinifera* of the old world, which, though it has been cultivated from ancient times, is found nowhere in a wild state. The varieties of this, while generally unsuccessful east of the Rocky mountains, succeed admirably on the Pacific coast and now seem to be successful in Texas and Arizona. Their greatest enemies seem to be the fungous diseases, to which they are exceedingly subject. But the many preventives and remedies discovered in the past ten years may give them a wider distribution. These varieties differ from our native species in their leaves, which are more smooth and delicate, and more deeply lobed; the flesh of the berries adheres to the skins, while the seeds have a narrower and longer beak than any of the native varieties.

That most accomplished botanist and keen observer, the late Doctor George Engelmann of St. Louis, deserves the credit of first attempting a thorough classification of our native species. It was he who first called attention to the shape and size of the seeds. He classified them into 14 species in the following order: 1. Labrusca or Northern Fox; 2. Candicans or Mustangensis; 3. Caribæa or Caloosa; 4. Californica; 5. Monticola or Mountain grape; 6. Arizonica; 7. Æstivalis or Summer grape; 8. Cinerea or Ashy Winter grape; 9. Cordifolia or Winter grape; 10. Palmata or Rubra; 11. Riparia or River grape; 12. Rupestris, Sugar or Bush grape; 13. Vinifera or European grape; 14. Rotundi-

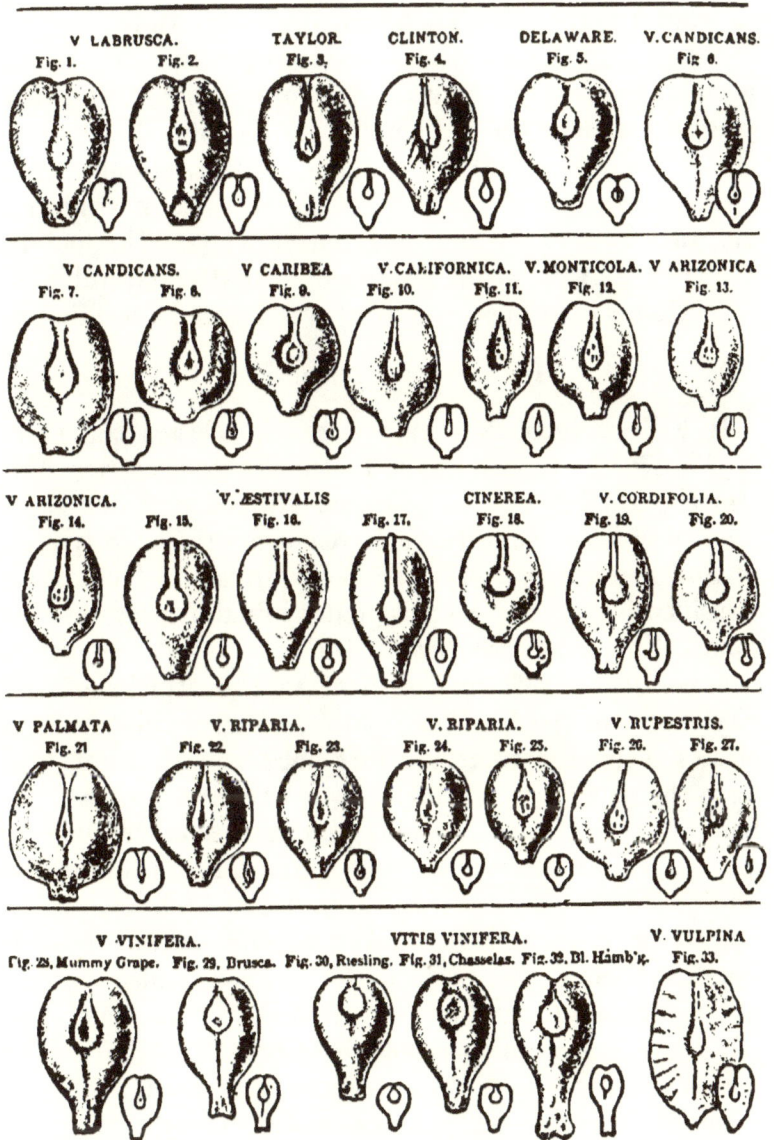

TABLE OF GRAPE SEEDS

folia, Vulpina or Southern Fox. The accompanying illustration of the seeds on the preceding page will show on what peculiarities he based his distinctions, and as he was one of the keenest observers of nature, as well as a most prominent botanist, his opinions are of great weight. This is the old classification. Mr. T. V. Munson of Denison, Texas, has made an entirely new one. To complete this, he has spent much time in studying the various species in their native wilds. He has, in addition to this work, produced an extremely valuable collection of seedlings by skillful crossing and hybridizing.

THE MUNSON CLASSIFICATION.

It will be seen that in Series 5 he classes the *Vitis vinifera* or European grape in the Æstivalis series, and also the Herbemont, Lenoir and Rulander, which have been previously classed as natives or Southern Æstivalis, as South European or Vitis Bourquiniana. The latter classification cannot be accepted as final for several reasons. First, the structure of the roots is entirely different, being very soft and subject to the attacks of the phylloxera in the Vinifera, while in Bourquiniana, as he classes them, the roots are very hard and resistant, and have the peculiarity of only one or two starting from the base of the cuttings, branching out into smaller rootlets, and striking downwards like a bird's claw ; while in the Vinifera the roots start all around the buds the whole length of the cuttings, and generally do not branch much. Second, the texture of the wood is also entirely different, as all the Vinifera grow easily from cuttings, while the Bourquiniana root with difficulty. Third, the leaves are also different in structure and ability to resist fungous diseases, being thick and leathery, while the fruit is but little (if any) subject to mildew and rot ; on the other hand, the Vinifera succumbs first of all, so much so that their culture in the open air has had to be abandoned in the Eastern States. In the structure of the roots, a greater affinity exists between Vinifera and Californica than between Vinifera and Bourquiniana, as those of the two first named are soft and spongy, while those of the Bourquiniana are hard and firm; so much so that Mr. Munson himself classes them as resistant. He claims that he has traced Bourquiniana back to Southern France. If this is correct, it seems very strange that France especially should so largely order, as they did in 1874-7, from Texas and Missouri, the cuttings of Bourquiniana, because they found them resistant.

I have thought it my duty to give the subject of classification a great deal more room than it would otherwise occupy, and to state my objections to a system which, with the exceptions named, I consider the most perfect and complete yet introduced. Professor Munson deserves the thanks of all grape growers for his systematic efforts and for the large number of valuable seedlings he has produced by crossing and hybridizing. He may well feel an honorable pride in his achievements. With these few introductory remarks, we will let his classification and synopsis speak for themselves.

GENUS VITIS (Tournefort, Linnæus, in part).

Explanation: H., hardy north; H. II., half hardy north; T., tender north.

SECTION 1. *Euvites,* Planchon.

SERIES 1. *Riparia.*

Vitis rupestris (Scheele), II.	1
Vitis riparia (Michaux), synonym palmata, Vatel.	
Vitis vulpina (Linnæus), II.	2
Vitis Solonis (Hort. Berol.), II.	3
Vitis Doaniana (Munson), II.	4
All excellent for hybridizing other species.	

SERIES 2. *Occidentalis.*

Vitis Arizonica (Engelmann), H. H. The Canon grape of Arizona; var. glabra (Munson), H. H.	5

CHAPTER II.

PROPAGATION OF THE VINES.—BY SEEDS.

While the raising of grape vines from the seed is more a labor of love, than of actual profit, yet its influence on grape culture generally has been so great, and we are already indebted so largely to its zealous followers, that it cannot be entirely omitted in a work like this. We can not gain further perfection in varieties without this, and the success which has already attended the labors of Rogers, Wylie, Campbell, Ricketts, Muench, Miller, Weydemeier, Langendoerfer, and especially Mr. Jacob Rommel, in giving to us the Elvira, and other varieties still more promising, affords hopes of even more important results.

To begin then at the beginning : choose your seed from a good stock. I am inclined to believe that only the *æstivalis* and *cordifolia* (or *riparia*, as Engelmann has it) species will give us the true wine grapes of the country, and if we can increase their size somewhat, they will also be the best table grapes. We have them already as large as the Catawba, and they are more juicy, of finer flavor, and less pulpy than the varieties from the *Labrusca* species, while they are much more healthy and hardy. Remember that we have already too many varieties, and that every new one we add should have some decided merit over any of the old varieties, or else be discarded at once.

Choose the best berries and the most perfect bunches, from which to take the seed, and either sow in autumn, and cover, or keep them over winter, mixing the seeds with moist sand, when separated from the pulp, to insure ready germination. Sow early in spring, in well pulverized clay soil, in drills one foot apart, and drop the seeds about an inch apart in the rows, covering about three-quarters of an inch deep, with finely pulverized soil. When the young plants appear, keep them clean and well cultivated through the summer; in the fall take them up carefully, and put in well drained fine soil, so as to preserve their roots in the most perfect condition. It will be well, during the summer, to look over them frequently, and if any of them show disease in the leaf, pull them up at once, as it is useless to save such as are feeble and unhealthy. It may also be well to shade the young vines for the first month or so, to prevent the sun from scalding them while yet young and tender, and if any of them grow remarkably strong, give them small sticks for support. In the following spring they may be transplanted to their permanent location in the vineyard or garden. The ground for their reception should be moderately light and rich, and loosened to the depth of at least 18 inches.

Make a hole about 8 inches deep, then throw in soil so as to raise a small mound in the center of the hole, about 2 inches high; shorten the top of the young vine to about 6 inches, and then place it on the mound, spreading its roots well in all directions; fill up with well pulverized soil, until the upper eye is even with the surface of the ground. Then press the soil lightly, place a good stake about 4 feet high with each vine, and when the buds start, allow but one sprout to grow, which is to be tied neatly to the stake. The vines may be planted in rows 6 feet apart, and 3 feet apart in the rows, as many of them will prove worthless, and have to be discarded. Allow all the laterals to grow on the young cane, as this will make it stocky and short-jointed. Cultivate well and frequently, keeping the soil loose and mellow.

The second season the seedlings will generally make from 3 to 4 feet of short-jointed growth; in the fall of that year they should be cut back to about three buds, and have the ground drawn up around them for protection in winter. Should any of them look very promising, fruit may be obtained a year sooner by grafting the wood of the seedlings upon strong vines. Young vines thus grafted will generally bear the next season (see "Grafting," on another page). Next spring, which will be their third, remove the covering, and when the young shoots appear, allow *only two* to grow. After these have grown about 18 inches, pinch off the top of the weakest of the two shoots, so as to throw the growth into the strongest shoot, which is to be kept neatly tied to the stake or trellis, treating it as the summer before, and allowing all the laterals to grow. At the end of this season's growth they should be strong enough to bear the next summer. If they have made from eight to ten feet of stocky growth, the leading cane may be cut back to ten or twelve eyes, or buds, and the smaller one to a spur of two eyes. If the vines will fruit at all, they will show it the next summer, when only the most promising ones should be kept, and the barren and worthless ones discarded. Seedlings have this peculiarity: both the berry and bunch will increase in size every year for the first three or four years; therefore, if the quality of the fruit is only good, the size may come in time. The fruit of the Elvira (of which more hereafter), which is now about as large in bunch and berry as Catawba, was at first not more than half its present size, it having increased in dimensions every year for the last eight years.

CHAPTER III.

PROPAGATION BY CUTTINGS IN THE OPEN AIR.

The easiest and most simple mode of propagating the vine is by cuttings planted in the open ground; it can be successfully followed with the majority of the *Labrusca* and *cordifolia* varieties, and a few of those from the *æstivalis*, although the latter will not take root readily, and had better be propagated by layering and grafting.

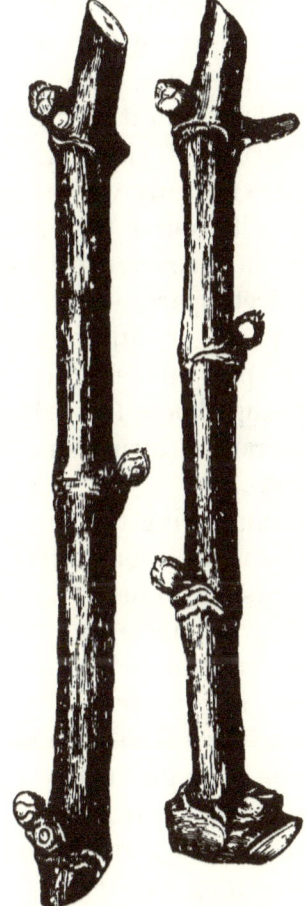

The most general method is the following: In fall, when pruning the vines, choose the best ripened wood of medium size, which is better than either the very large or very small, and cut it into lengths of from 9 to 12 inches, cutting close below the lower bud, and about an inch above the upper, as in figure 1.

Figure 2 shows a cutting with part of the old wood attached; cuttings of this kind will generally root more readily than the other. These cuttings will mostly average three to four buds each; tie them in convenient bundles of 100 to 250 each, taking care to make their lower ends even, and keep them either in a cool, moist cellar, or bury them out-doors in well

Fig. 1.   Fig. 2.

CUTTINGS — ALL NEW AND PART OLD WOOD.

drained ground, with the upper ends downwards, covering up well with finely pulverized soil. The making of cuttings may be continued during winter, although they will root more readily if cut early, and there is also no danger of frost injuring the buds.

In spring, so soon as the ground is dry enough, the cutting bed should be prepared. Choose for this a light, rich soil, pulverized at least a foot deep; if not light and rich enough, it can be made so by well-decomposed leaf mould. Make a cut along the whole length of the bed with the spade, deep enough to receive the whole length of the cuttings, and press these well down into it, so that the upper buds are even with the surface of the earth ; fill up with loose soil, and press it down firmly with the foot along the line, so as to pack it well around the cuttings. The cuttings may be put close in the row, say 1 to 2 inches apart, and the rows 2 to 3 feet apart, so as to allow of cultivation either by hand, plow, or cultivator. After the bed is finished, mulch with spent tan, sawdust, or leaf mould, so as to protect the young shoots from the sun; maintain a moist and even temperature during summer, and keep the soil open and porous.

Keep the soil of the cutting bed clean during the summer. The young vines will generally make a hard, firm growth 1 to 4 feet in length the first summer ; they will make their roots just where they ought to be, and will be by far the best plants for general use, being preferable to vines raised either from single eyes or by layers. In the fall they should be carefully taken up, and heeled-in in well pulverized soil, deep enough to cover the crowns, first assorting, so as to make them as even in size as possible for planting. They are then ready for setting in the vineyard, and a good strong one-year-old vine is, beyond a doubt, the best for that purpose.

CHAPTER IV.

PROPAGATING THE VINE BY LAYERS.

All varieties of the grape may be readily increased by layering, but it is especially valuable for those hard-wooded varieties of the *æstivalis* species, which will not grow readily from cuttings, and vines thus propagated will, if handled rightly, make very good plants. To layer a vine, shorten in the canes of the last season's growth to about one-half their length, then, early in the spring, pre-pare the ground by the use of the spade or fork, to thoroughly pulverize it. Make a small furrow about an inch deep, bend down the cane and fasten it firmly in the bottom of the furrow, with wooden hooks or pegs. The canes may be left thus until the young shoots have grown from 6 to 12 inches, then fill up around them with fine soil or leaf mould. Canes so layered will generally strike root at every joint. The shoots may be tied to small sticks, and when they have grown a foot, their tops should be pinched to make them more stocky. In the fall take them up carefully, commencing to dig at the end furthest from the vine, and separate the plants, by cutting between the joints, so that each shoot has a system of roots by itself. They are then either planted immedi-ately, or heeled in, as described for vines from cuttings, to be planted in the spring.

CHAPTER V.

GRAFTING THE VINE.

The advantages to be gained by grafting are so evident that, although it was almost an unknown art forty years ago when I began its practice, it has become a necessity to every grape grower. It is a little more difficult than the same operation on fruit trees, yet it is so simple that any one familiar with the use of a sharp knife can easily acquire the art. The experience of forty years has taught me that the simplest methods of grafting the vine are the best for common use, especially where it must be done on a large scale, as a protection against phylloxera, and where skillful hands are not always available. When whole vineyards of resistant stocks are to be grafted in a few weeks, the labor must be divided. While each operation is simple in itself, with only inexperienced labor at hand it is best to give each a special task, which he can soon learn to successfully perform.

With these few preliminary remarks, we will first consider the advantages to be gained by grafting; secondly, the best time to do it; and thirdly, how to do it to be most successful.

I. Its advantages.—The facility with which new and valuable varieties can be increased and their fruit tested: If grafts of bearing wood are worked upon strong stocks, they will bear a few bunches the same season and a full crop the next. The ease by which healthy stocks of no value can be changed into the most valuable bearing kinds: Varieties which are difficult to grow from cuttings can be propagated with the greatest ease by grafting. Increased fruitfulness: The temporary obstruction by grafting seems to have the effect upon the graft of making it produce more and finer fruit than on its own roots. Last, but not least, grafting affords us the only means by which to combat successfully the phylloxera. So far no discovery has been made entitling anyone to the large prize offered by the French government for a remedy or preventive of the ravages of that insect, yet the greater part of the destroyed vineyards have been rehabilitated by replanting with American vines; and while it seems that they are even more particular as to soil than the varieties of the Vinifera, no doubts are entertained of their power as resistants when the proper soil has been found.

II.   The best time to perform the operation.—I differ with most of the writers on this subject. I have met with the greatest success when the sap was flowing freely, which will, of course, vary according to location.   Here our best time is about the middle of April, though I have grafted with as good success up to the middle of May, provided the cions were kept dormant in a cool, shady place and were selected with the proper care. When the sap is flowing freely the junction is immediate, and the sap at once ascends the graft. At this time all bandages are superfluous, and even injurious, provided the stock is strong enough to hold the cion firmly. No matter if the stock has already made shoots a foot in length, there will be no perceptible difference, though it is safe to commence when the buds are swelling and the sap is in rapid circulation. As this involves also the question of the age of the vine, let me here say that the best success I have had was with vines from an inch to an inch and a half in diameter, strong enough to hold the cion firmly, and that absolutely nothing is gained by grafting when the vines are smaller. Wait until the vine is strong enough, then give its energies full play by inserting good strong cions, with buds sufficient to take up the flow of sap ; few failures will occur, and you can

2

count upon a few clusters the same summer, with a full crop the following season.

III. How to do it.—Necessary implements: You need a good, thin-bladed, sharp knife to cut the cions, a sharp saw to cut off large stocks,—the smaller ones can be cut with good pruning shears,—a chisel for grafting, having a blade two and a half or three inches broad in the middle and a wedge on each side (see figure 3), a wooden mallet and a few strings of raffia, or other bandage, in case a stock should need tying, which is seldom the case. Your cions should be of selected wood, the size of a lead pencil or somewhat larger, cut in time in winter, tied in bundles and bur-

FIG. 3. GRAFTING CHISEL.

ied their entire length on the shady side of a building or under a tree, to keep them dormant. Short-jointed, firm wood is to be preferred. All can be carried in a basket, if one intends to perform the operation alone. If several are to work together, of course the tools must be divided accordingly. We work here generally in gangs of three, the first man clearing away the ground from the stock, until he comes to a smooth place for inserting the cion, whether this be at the surface or slightly below. The former is preferable if resistant vines are to be grafted with non-resistant cions. He

FIG. 4.
CION FOR
GRAFTING.

then cuts off the stock horizontally about an inch and a half above a knot or joint. The next man cuts the cions to a smooth, long, sloping wedge just below a bud (figure 4), then splits the stock, either with pruning shears or chisel, according to its size. If the stock is not more than an inch in diameter

the shears are best, as only one cion is to be inserted.
Keep the blade of the shears on the side where the cion
is to join the stock, so as to prevent bruising, and make
a long, smooth, sloping cut, a little transversely if possible, as the junction will thereby become all the more
perfect. Then push the wedge of the cion firmly down
into the cleft, taking care that the inner bark or fiber
of stock and cion are well joined, as on this principally
depends the success of the operation. To open the cleft,
the wedges on the chisel are used if necessary. An ex-
pert will depend very little on these unless the stocks are
very heavy, but will open the cleft with knife or shears,
and then push down the cion to its proper place. The
inner side of the cion, opposite the bud, should be somewhat thinner, so that the stock will close firmly on it;
the cion should also be inserted far enough so that the
bud is just above the horizontal cut on the stock. The
third man follows, presses a little moist earth on the
surface of the stock, and then hills up around the junction to the uppermost buds of the cion, with well-pulverized soil, taking care not to move the cion, and the
operation is finished. It becomes necessary sometimes
to tie the stock, when it is not large enough, or from
some defect in grafting it does not firmly hold the cion.
In such a case, pass a string of raffia or some other flat
bandage firmly around the stock and tie it, but in no
case use grafting wax or clay, as the strong flow of sap
from all the pores is apt to drown and sour the cion,
while without obstructing it, it will flow around the
stock, serving to keep the junction moist and facilitate
the union. As the whole operation is covered with
earth, there is no danger of drying up, as is sometimes
the case when fruit trees are top-grafted.

A very important consideration, to insure success, is to
equalize the stock and cion. If, therefore, large stocks
are to be grafted, we must have strong, well-developed

wood for the cions, and have buds enough to take up
the full flow of sap; while small stocks, if used at all,
should be grafted with small cions of only two or three
buds. When the stocks are strong, I take two cions
and insert one on each side of the stock, of full length,
say from 14 to 16 inches, and with 6 to 8 buds each.
This has many advantages. The principal one is that
they will elaborate and work up the entire flow of sap.
Another is, that if the cions have well-developed fruit
buds they will produce quite a number of clusters from
the upper buds, and thus show the character of the fruit
the first year. I have already picked a thousand pounds
of grapes from an acre thus grafted, the first summer,
and a full crop of five or six tons per acre the following
season. Another advantage is that it establishes the
crown of the graft at the right distance from the ground,
as the three upper buds will produce the canes for the
next season's bearing. If both cions grow, cut off the
weakest above the junction the next spring, leaving only
the strongest. I generally find that the whole surface
of the stock is covered by the new growth and that the
junction between stock and cion is perfect. Another
advantage is, especially in California, where we plow
and cultivate close to the vines, and where some of the
workmen are careless, they are more apt to run over and
disturb small grafts than the large ones, which are protected by hills of earth above the surface; nor are the
young shoots disturbed and broken so easily by careless
hands, or high winds.

I have been so explicit about this method, because I
have found it more successful and easier to perform than
any other. I take it for granted that the aim of every
practical grower is to reach the best results in the short-
est possible time. There are, of course, many other
methods, but better adapted to younger vines. Foremost among these is the whip, or so-called English cleft

graft, which is familiar to most of my readers, and which the French and Germans use both on cuttings and on one-year-old plants, and which are packed away in sand or sawdust after being grafted in the shop. I have tried this method many times in former years, planting the grafts carefully in the nursery, but never had a success worth mentioning, owing, I suppose, to the time when it was done, and also because there is thus not enough circulation of sap to form an immediate junction and produce a thrifty growth.

This method is also practiced upon young vines in the vineyard with better results, if done late enough. But it is a more difficult operation, not so easily taught to unskilled hands; necessitates tying, and the cions are more easily moved out of place. So I have abandoned it altogether. I wait until the vines are strong enough to hold the cions firmly, which is generally the case the third or fourth summer, then cleft graft as described, and have at least ninety per cent. to grow, as well as a crop the next summer. This is the most economical, as well as the quickest and easiest way to obtain an even vineyard. French experts concede that by their method of grafting in shop and then planting the grafts in nursery for two years, where they are irrigated and then transplanted into the vineyard, it takes six years to produce a bearing vineyard, while we can do it in four and have but one transplanting to do. True, they claim that experts can do the work, but we can get along without experts, and must do so as they are seldom to be had, and then only at high wages.

The so-called Champin graft, called thus after its inventor, Aimee Champin, is only a variation of splice grafting, and hardly needs a separate description.

A mode of grafting much in vogue in Germany and Hungary, is the green or herbaceous, fully described and illustrated in a treatise published by Prof. Herman

Gœthe. I have not practiced it in the East, but tried it in California thoroughly and without success. The summers are too hot for it, and so it has to be done in June and July, above ground. I believe that it will never be generally practiced in America. To make it succeed at all, the grafts must be shaded in some way. As we must, in this practical country, try to reduce expenses to a minimum and plan for quickest returns, the method of cleft grafting described above will be found to alone fulfill the desired conditions. I do not, therefore, consider it worth while to describe minutely other methods of but little value to the practical grape grower. I sum up briefly in a few rules, which I have taken as my guide here, where grafting plays such a very important part in viticulture.

1. Let your stocks be chosen with a view of their adaptation to the soil, and do not graft until they are strong enough, say from an inch to an inch and a half in diameter.

2. Choose your cions with great care, of medium, short-jointed, well-ripened wood of last season's growth, and keep them dormant, in a cool place, covered with sand or earth.

3. Wait until the sap in the stock is in rapid motion, at least until the buds swell, and then perform the operation quickly, taking care that the inner barks of stock and cion fit closely.

4. Leave buds enough on the cion to elaborate and circulate all the sap, thereby avoiding black knot and all diseases which are apt to follow late frosts, excessive pruning, etc.

5. Hill up around the junction so as to protect it from drying out and to protect the graft, but do not tie or put on grafting wax or clay, as by so doing you may drown and rot the cion.

After this short recapitulation of the principles which should govern in grafting, we come to the

AFTER TREATMENT OF THE GRAFT.

This is very simple. A stake should be driven close to the graft immediately after grafting is finished, and the young shoots, when they appear, tied to it for support, as they generally start vigorously and are easily broken off, or blown off by high winds. Do not be discouraged if some time elapses before they start. I have often had them remain dormant until July or August, and then make a rapid growth. If suckers from the stock appear, as is generally the case, they should be removed at once, taking care to cut them close to the stock, so as to have no stumps or dormant buds. When young they generally come off easily. Tying and suckering should be repeated every week or ten days at least. As long as the cion remains fresh and green it may begin growing at any time. Of course, care must be taken not to disturb the cion. If everything does well, there will be from three to four canes from the upper buds, and these may be treated just as any other bearing vine, in pruning.

AFFINITY OF STOCK AND CION.

A few remarks on this subject, suggested to me by experience, may not be out of place. As a general rule, vines of the same class will readily unite. For instance, Labrusca on Labrusca, Riparia on Riparia, etc. I have also found that Æstivalis varieties will graft easily on Labrusca—for instance, Norton and Cynthiana graft easily on Concord, Catawba, or Isabella. Most of the Vinifera varieties also graft readily upon Riparia, or Æstivalis, although there is a difference. Of the varieties I have tried to graft, the easiest to take were Sauvignon Vert, Semillion, Marsanne, Green Hungarian or Vert Longue, Franken Riesling, Gamay Teinturier, Mataro and Grosse Blaue, while Sultana, Refosco and Yellow Mosler did not take as readily, though a large percentage grew. On the Rupestris and Arizonica the junction was still more difficult. I cannot recommend these for stocks on account of their propensity to sucker, and also because they show less adaptability to different soils than do Riparia and Æstivalis. The Californica takes the graft very readily, but is not entirely resistant and succeeds only on fertile, rather moist soils.

Budding has often been tried, but with scant success, and I cannot recommend it.

I have given much space to this subject, because I think it very important that every grape grower should be familiar with the most practical mode of operation, and any one who does not understand it cannot claim to be advanced in his profession.

CHAPTER VI.

THE VINEYARD—LOCATION, ASPECT AND SOIL.

That the selection of a proper location, as well as the best soil, is of great importance if the grower intends to reach the best results, no one will deny. Generally it may be said and taken as a rule, that locations free from frosts, and exposed to a free circulation of air, are best adapted to the grape, but they should also be underlaid with the most suitable soil. That this should be naturally very rich is not so important as that it should be loose and friable, so that the roots of the vine can penetrate it easily and draw nourishment as well as moisture from below. The best results will be obtained on a soil which is naturally porous, so that it will drain easily and not retain moisture on the surface. Such a soil will also retain moisture well, and thus the vines will not suffer, either from "wet feet" or extremes of drouth. Soils underlaid by hardpan, especially where they contain alkali, should be carefully avoided, as they will never produce a large or healthy crop of good grapes. Those locations which are free from malaria may generally be considered as safe for the grape, and where malaria prevails we cannot expect to grow good and healthy grapes of the best quality. This will apply in its closer sense only to those who intend to make grape-growing their business, either for market or wine. For the amateur, who only wishes to grow grapes for family use, and has already a homestead, it will be easy to choose a location somewhere on his grounds as favorable as he can find it, where he can grow grapes enough for his purpose. Some varieties are so hardy and healthy that they will succeed anywhere, and he ought to choose these, contenting himself with them, even if they are not of first quality. Steep hillsides, although they will generally produce quality, should be avoided by the professional grower, as they are difficult and expensive to work and are liable to wash with heavy rains, which soon carry off the surface soil. The aspect of the vineyard is not of so much importance here as it is in Europe, where the southern is preferred, because growers need all the sun they can get to properly ripen their grapes. On the contrary, in this country, except in the extreme north, we suffer from sun-scald during July and August, and as northern and eastern aspects generally have the richest and deepest soil, they are usually preferred to the southern and western, which are exposed to the full rays of the noon and afternoon sun. As to the quality of the soil, it may be presumed that any land which will grow fair grain is rich enough for grapes, and contains the elements necessary for their culture. I do not think, however, that an extremely poor soil can be depended upon to produce either quantity or quality. For market we want a perfect fruit—one that pleases the taste as well as the eye; and for wine we must have a product rich in sugar, of fine flavor and quality. It would seem unnatural to suppose that starved vines could produce this, and as unreasonable to expect it from a rank and therefore unhealthy growth on land which is too rich. Therefore, a soil of medium fertility. and well drained, will generally produce the best results.

CHAPTER VII.

PREPARING THE SOIL.

For the preparation of the soil, the foundation of his work, the grape grower must be guided in his operations by the condition in which he finds his ground. If it is an old field, free from stumps and stones, or a piece of prairie soil, it will be easily prepared. Break up the soil with a good large turning plow and strong team to pull it, and follow in the same furrow with a subsoil stirring plow, which merely loosens the ground; and do this as deep as possible, if 20 inches, all the better, though 16 inches in all will do if you cannot go deeper.

If, however, the land is a new piece of forest soil, the task will be much more difficult. This must be carefully grubbed of stumps and roots, and although the same implements will, in a measure, suffice, yet the turning plow should have a sharp coulter in front, and the subsoil plow should also have a strong and sharp coulter, with merely a wedge-shaped, strong share to stir the soil. Besides, much more power will be necessary. In stony soil, the pick and shovel must take the place of the plow, as it would be impossible to work it thoroughly with the latter; but I think there is no advantage in the old method of trenching or inverting the soil. If we examine the wild vines of our forests, we will generally find their roots running along in the surface soil. It is unnatural to suppose that the vine, the most sun-loving of all plants, should have its roots buried several feet below the surface, where neither sun nor air can reach them. Work the soil well and thoroughly, and as deep as you can, it will be labor well invested; will be the best preventive against drouth, and the best drainage in wet weather, but leave it in its natural position, and do not plant too deep. Rest assured if the roots find anything congenial below, they will hunt it up. Should the soil be very poor, it may be enriched by ashes, bone dust, manure, etc., but it will seldom be necessary, as most of our soil is naturally rich enough, and it is not advisable to stimulate the growth too much, as it will become rank and unhealthy, and impair the quality of the fruit.

Wet spots may be drained by gutters filled with loose stones or tiles, and then covered with earth. Surface draining can be done by running a small ditch or furrow, every sixth or eighth row, parallel with the hillside, and leading into a main ditch at the middle or end of the vineyard. Steep hillsides should be terraced or benched, but as this is laborious and expensive, they should be avoided.

CHAPTER VIII.

WHAT GRAPES TO PLANT—CHOICE OF VARIETIES.

Any one who attempts to advise beginners what varieties of grapes to plant is treading on very hazardous ground. Such advice is much more difficult to give now than it was ten years ago, when the area planted to grapes was far more limited, both East and West. Comparatively few varieties of American grapes only were cultivated east of the Rocky mountains, while to the westward of them varieties of the *Vitis vinifera* were exclusively grown. That is all changed now. The geographical boundary between the American and the Vinifera varieties is by no means sharply defined. Many of the latter are now cultivated in some parts of Texas with encouraging success, while vineyardists in the Pacific States have to rely on American stocks at least for their only security against the insidious and destructive phylloxera. Grape culture has extended into regions where it was not thought of ten years ago, and enterprising propagators have originated great numbers of new varieties. A few of these have attained popularity as standard sorts; others are more or less promising; and a still greater number are on trial, or have proved unworthy of cultivation. Only time and patient trial can determine the permanent value of these and the other new varieties which nearly every year brings forth. The nearer I approach to the boundaries of the "unseen land," the more conservative do my views become, and the greater my reluctance to offer dogmatic advice which, however well intended, may prove misleading in the end. The best advice that I can offer to beginners in grape culture is to visit the vineyards of their neighbors and learn what varieties have been successful there.

Great results have been achieved by Munson and Jaeger, in producing crosses between native varieties and hybrids of native and foreign origin. They are very promising, but have not been tried long enough to become fully established. The veteran John Burr, of Leavenworth, Kansas, produced many new varieties, some of which promise to be permanent memorials of his active usefulness as a horticulturist. There are many others who are entitled to the grateful consideration of grape growers for their ceaseless endeavors to promote the culture of our native grapes. The results of their efforts are already seen in the increased success and confidence which attend the business of grape growing and the large increase of the area devoted to it.

Under the circumstances it does not seem advisable to designate a list of varieties from the almost countless numbers recommended in the catalogues of nurserymen, but only to enumerate a few of the established varieties which hold their position in public favor, and a selection of newer varieties "promising well." It seems useless, if not preposterous, to publish a list of nearly a hundred varieties, as a firm has recently done, for the mere purpose of "giving the public the most complete list ever published." Such a list only serves to "make confusion more confounded," and be more likely to mislead than to help growers to make proper selections.

A few of the older varieties retain their ground and are regarded as standard. They are so well known that it is needless to describe them here. Persistent spraying and intelligent care have greatly increased the health and hardiness, and added to the prospect of success, of many varieties formerly regarded as too tender or too liable to disease for successful cultivation. The following are well tried and generally known, viz.: Catawba, Concord, Cynthiana, Delaware, Elvira, Goethe, Herbemont, Herbert, Lady, Lindley, Martha, Norton's Virginia, Pocklington, Triumph and Wilder. Let it be distinctly understood that I do not recommend these *everywhere*, but they have been cultivated so long and in so wide an area that every person may easily learn whether any one of them is likely to be successful in his own locality.

VARIETIES PROMISING WELL.

Many of these may have been tried and proved in some localities, while comparatively unknown in others. My aim is to describe only the *best* of them,—those which I regard as worthy of general trial. There may be others fully as good, which have either not been tried long enough or in sufficiently extensive area to determine their merits. Among the most promising of all are probably those of T. V. Munson and of Hermann Jaeger, but as they open up a wholly new field, I have preferred to let them speak for their seedlings, as they do in Part II of this volume. I can assure the reader that their statements are entitled to implicit confidence.

I have made no attempt to classify the following varieties, but indicate the origin of each in parentheses, leaving each reader to select such as may be desired for his own locality.

BARRY (*Hybrid*).—One of the best of Rogers' hybrids. Bunch full, medium, broad, mostly shouldered; berries large, round, black and tender; ripens about with Concord; vigorous and productive.

BAY STATE (*Hybrid*).—Grown by Wagener & Co., Pulteney, N. Y. Seedling of Black Hamburg crossed with Marion. Vigorous and hardy; large, retentive foliage; bunch medium, shouldered, handsome; berry oblong, red, holds well to the stem, tender, pulp sweet, sprightly and juicy; early, but a good keeper.

BLACK DEFIANCE (*Hybrid of Labrusca and Vinifera*). —Originated by S. W. Underhill, Croton, N. Y. Large and handsome; bunch large, well shouldered, loose; berries full, medium; foliage good; late, ripening about with Catawba, or even a little later.

COLERAIN (*Labrusca*).—Seedling of Concord, produced by D. Mundy, Colerain, Ohio. Very promising. Vine a strong grower, healthy and hardy, and an abundant bearer; very early but hangs well to the vine; bunches shouldered, medium, as are the berries, which are light green with delicate bloom; skin thin; very juicy and sweet yet vinous; generally but one seed to each berry.

DIAMOND (*Labrusca*).—Cross between Concord and Iona, produced by Jacob Moore, of New York. Vigorous grower, retaining its leaves well, which are large and light green. Bunch large, moderately compact, shouldered; berry about the same size as Concord, adhering well to the bunch; greenish white, with yellow tinge; flesh melting and juicy, sweet, free from foxiness. Very hardy, and has produced good crops for ten consecutive years. Considered superior to all the older white grapes.

DUCHESS.—Cross between a white seedling of Concord and Delaware, or Walter, by A. J. Caywood & Son, Marlboro, N. Y. Bunch medium to large, long, shouldered; berries medium, white, transparent, juicy, fine quality; ripens about with Concord. In its original habitat it is hardy and healthy, a strong grower, and productive; keeps and ships well.

EARLY OHIO.—Originated with R. A. Hunt, Euclid, Ohio. A chance seedling, which attracted attention by its early ripening. Earliest of all, ripening a week before Moore's Early and three weeks before Concord, and consequently brings the highest price in the Cleveland market. Bunch medium, shouldered; berry black, round, somewhat smaller than Concord, firm in texture; flavor spicy, pleasant; hangs well to the stem, and therefore ships well.

EATON (*Labrusca*).—Grown by Calvin Eaton, of Concord, N. H. Vine a strong, rank grower, resembling Concord, and the grape ripens about the same time with it. Bunch large, sometimes weighing eighteen ounces, compact; berries very large, round, black, covered with blue bloom. Very juicy, somewhat pulpy, not as sweet as Concord, but less foxy.

ECLIPSE.—Originated by John Burr, the indefatigable experimenter, to whom we owe many valuable varieties from unknown seed. Bunch large, doubly shouldered, rather loose; berry very large, white, tender and juicy, sprightly, sweet, rich and vinous; hardy and productive. Ripens about the same time as Concord.

EARLY VICTOR (*Labrusca*).—Same origin. Bunch medium, shouldered, compact; berry medium, round, black, juicy, sweet and sprightly. In quality one of the best of the earlier varieties; vigorous, hardy and productive; very early; has rotted in some locations.

EMPIRE STATE.—Appears to be one of the most valuable of the many seedlings of J. H. Ricketts. Claimed to be a cross between Hartford and Clinton. If so, it has departed strangely from its parents, as it has a slight Vinifera flavor. Bunch large and handsome, shouldered, rather loose; berry medium, white, tinged with yellow, covered with white bloom; rich, sweet and sprightly, without foxiness; productive and keeps well.

EUREKA.—Produced by Dr. Stayman, Leavenworth, Kansas, from seed of Delaware. Good grower, hardy, healthy and productive. Bunch large, shouldered, compact and handsome; berry red, medium, tender, sweet, sprightly and vinous. Claimed to be fully equal to Delaware, but with heavier foliage and bunches; medium early.

EXQUISITE.—Same origin. Medium grower, healthy, hardy and productive. Bunch medium, compact; berry below medium, red, very sweet, juicy and vinous, without pulp; ripens with Delaware.

3

GENEVA.—Produced by Jacob Moore, of New York, from a hybrid of Black Fox with Muscat of Alexandria, and this hybrid recrossed with Iona. Vine hardy and productive; bunch medium, not shouldered, rather loose; berry above medium, oblong, green, transparent, with little bloom; pure flavor, and sprightly; medium early.

GREEN MOUNTAIN.—Claimed to be at the head for earliness, productiveness, good quality and vigorous growth. It is a Labrusca, found in a garden on a slope of the Green mountains, in Vermont. As it is one of the lately introduced varieties, it needs further trial to determine its actual merits. It is claimed for it that it will mature in a wider territory than any other variety; that it resembles the Vinifera more than any other native grape, and is the grape for every one to plant, being a young and profuse bearer. Bunch full medium, handsomely shouldered; berry medium, round, greenish white; skin thin; pulp tender and sweet, slightly vinous; free from foxiness; seeds small. Very early, ripening the last week in August. Stephen Hoyt's Sons, Connecticut, are the introducers and propagators, and if it fulfills one-half they say in its favor it will be a very valuable grape.

HAYES (*Labrusca*).—Produced by John B. Moore, Concord, Mass. Same origin as Moore's Early. Bunch medium, moderately compact, shouldered; berry medium, round, greenish white changing to amber yellow; flesh tender, juicy and delicate; fine flavor, no foxiness. Foliage thick and heavy; vine vigorous, hardy and productive; ripens at least a week earlier than Concord.

HOSFORD (*Labrusca*).—Seedling from Concord, grown by Geo. Hosford, Ionia, Michigan. Vine a vigorous grower, hardy and good bearer. Bunch large, shouldered; berry very large, round, black, with fine bloom; pulp tender and juicy; sweet and pure, not foxy; skin thin; ripens a few days before Concord.

IDEAL.—This new grape has won very high praise wherever it has been tried. Grown by John Burr from seed of Delaware. Vine strong, hardy, healthy and productive; bunch large, shouldered, rather compact; berry large, red, tender, juicy, rich, sweet and vinous, without pulp. Claimed to be better than Delaware, and is much more showy.

JEWEL.—Same origin. Claimed to be the very best early grape that has ever been fully tested. Vine moderately vigorous, healthy and hardy; bunch medium, compact, shouldered; berry full medium, black, slightly pulpy, sweet, rich and sprightly, of best quality; skin rather tough. Ripens a week before Moore's Early; will hang well on the vines and ships well.

JUMBO (*Labrusca*).—Seedling from Concord, grown by Mrs. R. Rose, Marlboro, N. Y. Bunch very large, compact, shouldered; have weighed as much as twenty ounces each; berry very large, blue black, with fine bloom; good quality and sells well on the New York market. Earlier than Concord.

KEYSTONE (*Labrusca*). Produced by John Kready, Lancaster Co., Pa., and supposed to be a seedling of the Concord. Vine a strong grower, healthy, holds its foliage well. Bunches large, compact and shouldered; berry about size of Concord, black with blue bloom; skin tough; ripens with Concord, but will keep in a cool, dry place until March.

LIGHTFOOT.—Produced by W. H. Lightfoot, Springfield, Ill., from seed of Niagara. Vine vigorous and healthy. Bunch medium to large, shouldered; berry full medium, roundish and uniform, with thin but tough skin, and holding firmly to the stem; color light green, changing to yellow when fully ripe, with delicate bloom; flesh melting without pulp; pure flavor, juicy and sweet. Ripens after Concord.

MAGNATE.—Originated at Leavenworth, Kansas, and

is said to be a hybrid. Vine vigorous, hardy, and very productive. Bunch very large, shouldered, compact; berry white, large, tender, sweet, with slight native aroma. Said to be free from rot and mildew, and in every way reliable. Ripens with Concord, but keeps well on the vine.

MATCHLESS.—Originated at Leavenworth, Kansas, by John Burr, from unknown seed. Vine vigorous, healthy and productive. Bunch very large, compact, handsome; berry very large, black, pure in flavor, sweet and sprightly; hangs well to the bunch after ripening; a very promising variety.

MILLS (*Hybrid*).—Grown by Wm. H. Mills, of Hamilton, Ontario, and introduced by Ellwanger & Barry. Cross of Muscat-Hamburg with Creveling. Vine vigorous and productive; foliage large and healthy. Bunch very large, compact, shouldered. Berry round, large, black, covered with thick bloom; flesh firm, juicy, breaking, with a brisk, sprightly flavor; skin thick; berries adhere well to the stem. Ripens somewhat later than Concord and keeps well.

MONTEFIORE.—Cross of Elvira with Ives. Produced by Jacob Rommell, of Morrison, Mo. Vine healthy and hardy, very productive, and free from mildew and rot. Ripens later than Concord, and makes a fine red wine.

NIAGARA.—This is rather an old variety, introduced about fifteen years ago by Hoag & Clark, Lockport, N. Y., but reports concerning its success are so conflicting that I have thought best to class it here with newer varieties. It is largely planted in some localities, while in others it is much subject to rot. Bunch very large and handsome, mostly shouldered; compact. Berries full medium, round, white, with amber flush on sunny side; skin thin but tough; carries well; little pulp; sweet, with peculiar agreeable aroma. Ripens with Concord. Vine vigorous and very productive.

Owego.—Origin questionable. Produced by John Burr. Vine vigorous, hardy and productive. Bunch medium, compact. Berry very large, red, tender, juicy, sprightly and vinous; quality best.

Oswego (*Labrusca*).—Free from disease as far as known. Vine vigorous, healthy, productive. Bunch very large, compact, shouldered. Berry large, tender, juicy and sprightly; black, better than Concord, more showy and keeps better. Much valued in Kansas. Origin unknown.

Ozark (*Æstivalis*).—Originated with Dr. J. Stayman, Leavenworth, Kansas. Very vigorous, hardy and productive. Bunch very large, compact, shouldered. Berry large, black, rich and sprightly, with a peculiar, pleasant flavor; free from disease. Ripens later than Concord, and will hang on the vines until frost. Regarded as one of the best market and wine grapes.

Paragon.—Produced by John Burr, from unknown seed. Vine vigorous, hardy, productive and free from disease. Bunch large, compact, shouldered; berry large, black, juicy, rich and vinous, without pulp; ripens with Concord, but will hang and keep well on the vine until late frost.

Perfection.—Originated by Dr. Stayman, from seed of Delaware, and is called the best and earliest red grape in Kansas. Hardy, healthy and productive. Bunch long, shouldered, compact and handsome; berry medium, tender and sprightly, with little pulp, or native aroma; much like Delaware, but larger in bunch and berry.

Rochester.—Produced by Ellwanger and Barry, Rochester, N. Y., from seed of mixed varieties. Vine healthy, hardy and productive; bunch large, shouldered, very compact; berry full medium, round, dark purple, peculiar color, with white bloom; very sweet, vinous and tender. Ripens first week in September.

SELMA.—Produced by G. Segessmann, Amazonia, Mo. Seedling of Elvira and probably Concord. Perfectly hardy, productive and healthy. Bunches large and perfect, shouldered; berry medium, black, nearly round, adhering firmly to stem; juicy and sprightly, pleasant flavor; skin thick and firm. Ripens a few days after Moore's Early, and makes a good claret wine.

SUPERB.—Produced by A. F. Nice, Griswoldville, Ga., from seed of Eumelan, raised at Weymouth, Mass. Hardy and a good grower; wood short-jointed and stocky; leaf large and healthy. Bunch large, compact; berry medium, black, with blue bloom; quality best, sweet and rich; pulp tender and juicy; skin thin but tough. It starts late, but ripens two weeks before Concord; keeps and ships well. Liable to overbear, and needs thinning.

THOMAS (*Rotundifolia*).—Introduced by D. Thomas. Claimed to be an improvement on the old Scuppernong. Berries large, oblong, purplish violet; skin thin; transparent, tender, sweet and vinous. I simply repeat the description here without recommending any of that class.

ULSTER PROLIFIC (*Labrusca*).—Seedling of Catawba crossed with wild Æstivalis, produced by A. J. Caywood, Marlboro, N. Y. Bunch medium, shouldered; berry medium; skin thin, but tough; sweet and of fine flavor. Ripens with Concord; keeps and carries well. Vine very hardy, healthy and prolific.

VERGENNES.—Originator, William E. Green, Vergennes, Vermont. A chance seedling found in his garden. Ripens after Concord. Bunch of medium size, shouldered; berry large, skin thin and tough; good quality, fine keeper and shipper; good for late market. Vine vigorous, healthy and hardy.

WHITE BEAUTY.—Originated from Duchess, by Dr. J. Stayman. Vine vigorous, healthy, hardy and very productive. Bunch large, long, compact, shouldered and handsome; berry full medium, firm but tender, sprightly and pure flavor. Claimed to be the most perfect white grape in Kansas, ripening with Concord, and will hang until late frost. A good shipper.

WHITE JEWEL (*Riparia*).—Introduced by Dr. Stayman. Seedling of Elvira. Very early—claimed to be the earliest grape in Kansas. Vine healthy and very productive; bunch medium, long, very compact, handsome. Berry medium, oblong, very juicy, sweet, sprightly, and of good quality.

WILLIE (*Labrusca*).—Produced by Dr. L. C. Chisholm, Nashville, Tenn. Seedling of Northern Muscadine, crossed with Concord. Fruit larger than Concord, both in bunch and berry; very showy; black, with whitish bloom; skin not as thin as Concord; vinous and sprightly; not foxy; an excellent wine grape; ripens with Concord. Vigorous, healthy, and very productive.

WITT (*Labrusca*).—Originated with Mr. Witt, Columbus, Ohio. Healthy in growth and foliage; very productive. Bunch large and handsome; berry large, pure flavored and best in quality. Ripens early, but keeps well. Claimed to be the best of the white seedlings of Concord.

WOODRUFF RED (*Labrusca*).—Originated with C. H. Woodruff, Ann Arbor, Michigan. Chance seedling, and probably a cross between Concord and Catawba. Very hardy, strong grower, and healthy. Bunch large, shouldered, heavy and compact. Berry large, sweet and of fair quality, but somewhat foxy. Desirable for market.

In the foregoing selection of varieties, I have been obliged to depend mainly on Eastern sources for descriptions. I have endeavored to cull the most promising from an almost endless list, but must leave it wholly to the discretion of the reader to decide what varieties, if any, are suited to each particular locality. This is, of

course, only a partial list of American origin. There
may be others equally promising, among the seven hundred varieties now before the public. I have not touched
upon the new varieties of my friends T. V. Munson and
Hermann Jaeger, which may be the most promising of
them all, as their originators will speak for them in Part
II of this volume.

RETROSPECTIVE.

This chapter on choice of varieties refers, of course,
only to American grapes, suitable for planting and cultivation east of the Rocky mountains. It may not be
out of place here to glance backward over the last ten
years and observe the progress made in grape culture
during that period. That immense progress has been
made is beyond question. Throughout the country,
from Maine to Idaho, and from Florida to Texas, men
of skill and energy have been engaged in the work of
originating new varieties for the table, the market and
the wine-press. As a result the grape and its juices, in
some form or other, are no longer the exclusive luxuries
of the rich, but the common property of all. The
Southern States are prepared to enter the market as early
as May, and the State of New York ships its grapes until
as late as December, and as far as Denver and other
Colorado points. Fresh grapes are thus furnished for
eight months in the year. Great advance has also been
made in the quality of American grapes. What was regarded as good enough ten years ago, is so no longer.
The varieties originated by Miller, Rommell, Campbell,
Rogers, Caywood and others are nearly all either cast
aside or used only for further experiments, only a few
remaining as remembrances. But the pioneer experi-
menters labored not in vain. They made the path clear
for those who were to follow, and we can, without envy
or bitterness, step aside while the succeeding generation
follows in our footsteps, even surpassing us in the work

that we began. What we aimed to do may be accomplished by them. Let their motto be, as ours was, " Excelsior," until this country becomes in truth, what the pre-Columbian Northmen called it, a true Vineland.

CHAPTER IX.

PLANTING THE VINE.

The distance at which the vines may be planted, will, of course, vary with the different varieties. The rows may all be 6 feet apart, as this is the most convenient distance for cultivating, and gives space enough for man, horse and plow, or cultivator. Slow growing varieties, such as Delaware, Catawba, or Alvey, may be planted 6 feet apart in the rows, but Concord, Norton's, Herbemont, and all strong growing varieties, will need more room, say from 8 to 10 feet, to give the vines ample space to spread, and allow free circulation of air, one of the first conditions of success. The next question is : Shall we plant cuttings or rooted plants ? The latter are by far the best, as cuttings, even of the easiest growing varieties, are uncertain, and we cannot expect to have so even a growth as from rooted plants carefully assorted. Choose, therefore, good, strong, one-year-old plants, the best you can get, either from cuttings, layers, or single eyes. Good plants should have plenty of strong, well-ripened roots, which are smooth and firm—for excrescences and warts upon the roots are a sign of Phylloxera —and have also well-ripened, short-jointed wood. They should be of even size, so as to make a uniform growth, and not have been forced by the propagator into rank growth, for we cannot expect plants that have been petted and pampered with artificial manures, to flourish with

the every day food they obtain in the vineyard. But
do not take second or third-rate plants, if you can help
it, for they will not make the thrifty growth of first-class
plants. The best are the cheapest even if they cost a
little more. Especially important is this with such varieties as Norton's or Delaware, which do not root readily,
and are always more difficult to transplant. Better pay
double the price for them and get good plants, as they
will make healthier vines and bear sooner.

But I also caution you against those who would sell
you "extra large layers for immediate bearing," and
whose plants are "better than any one else grows them,"
as their advertisements will term it. It is time that this
humbug should cease, and the public in general should
know that they cannot, in reason, expect fruit from a
vine transplanted the same season, and that those who
pretend it can be done without vital injury to the plant,
are only seeking to fill their pockets at the cost of their
customers. They know well enough themselves, that it
cannot be done without fatally injuring the plant, but
they impose upon the credulity of their customers; sell
them large vines at extravagant prices, which these good
souls will buy, and perhaps obtain a few sickly bunches
the first season, but if they do, the vines will make a
feeble growth, not ripen their wood, and be winter-killed
next season. Therefore, if you look around for plants do
not go to those who advertise "layers for immediate
bearing," or "better grown than any one's else," but send
to some honest, reliable nurseryman whom you can trust :
one who is not afraid to let you see how he grows them,
and let him send you a sample of his plants. Choose
good, strong, healthy plants, one year old, plant carefully, and be content to wait two years for results ; but
then, if you have cultivated the vines carefully, you will
get a crop of grapes that is worth gathering. You can
not, in nature and reason, expect it sooner.

If the ground has been prepared in the fall, so much the better, and if it has been thrown into ridges, and is dry enough, it may be planted in the fall. The advantages of fall planting may be summed up as follows: The

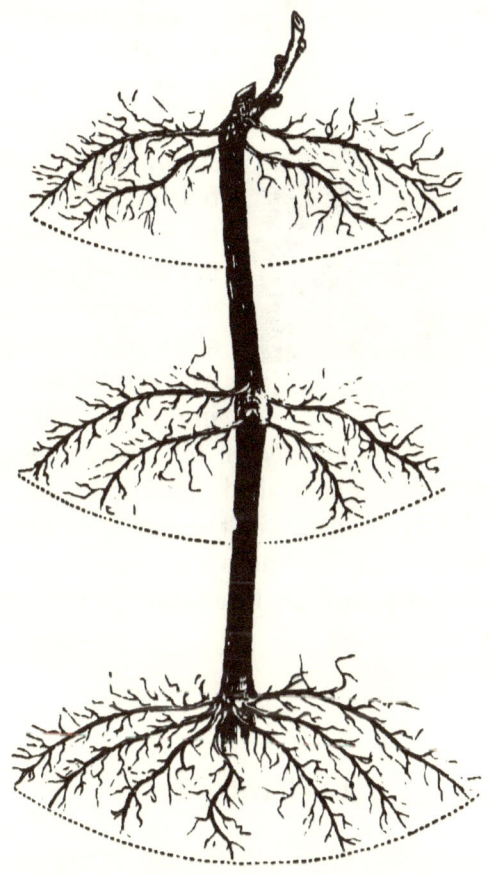

Fig. 5.—YOUNG VINE READY TO PLANT.

ground is generally in better condition than in spring and will work better, as we usually have better weather, and more time to spare; the ground can settle among the roots, which will be healed over and callused by spring, when the plant is ready to start with full vigor.

Mark your ground, laying it off with a line, and put a small stake where each plant is to be. A very convenient plan is to tie a string, or piece of bark, into your line at the proper distance for each plant, then you have an even measure every time. Dig a hole, 8 or 10 inches deep, as shown in figure 6, in a slanting direction, raising a small mound of well pulverized earth in the center;

then, having pruned your plant, as in figure 5, with its tops and roots shortened-in, as shown by the dotted lines, lay it in, resting the lower end on the mound of earth ; spread out its roots evenly to all sides, and then fill in with well pulverized earth, leaving the upper bud above

Fig. 6.—PLANTING THE VINE.

the ground. When planted in fall, raise a small mound around each vine, so as to drain off the water, and throw a handful of mulch on top of the vines, to protect them. All the work should be done when the ground is in good condition, and dry and mellow enough to be worked in well among the roots.

CHAPTER X.

TREATMENT OF THE VINE THE FIRST SUMMER.

The first summer after planting, nothing is necessary but to keep the ground loose and mellow and free from weeds, stirring it freely with hoe, rake, and plow, whenever necessary, but never when the ground is wet. Should the vines grow strong, they may be tied to the small stakes, to elevate them somewhat above the ground. Allow but one shoot to grow, rubbing off all others as they appear, but allow all the laterals to grow on this shoot, as it will make it short-jointed and stocky.

In the fall, prune the young vine back to three buds, if it has grown well ; to one or two, if it is small. A fair growth for the first season, is from 3 to 4 feet. During the winter, trellises should be provided, as this is the most convenient and the cheapest method of training ; and we expect our vines to grow from 10 to 15 feet the coming summer. Procure good posts, 7 feet long, and 3 to 4 inches in diameter, of Red Cedar where it can be had, as this is the most durable ; if that is not at hand, use Osage Orange, Mulberry, Black Locust, or Post Oak. Char the lower ends of the posts slightly, or dip them in coal tar, as far as they go into the ground, to make them more durable. Make holes with a post auger, placing the first post in each row about 4 feet outside of the last vine, and parallel with the row ; set the second post midway between the second and third vines, and so on, so that two vines always occupy the space between two posts. If preferred, every other post can be omitted this summer, and the intermediate ones may be set the next fall, as the trellis will be strong enough to bear the young growth, and that is all it will have to do the next summer. Make the holes 2 feet deep and set the posts firmly, pounding down the ground around them with a small wooden pestle or crowbar. Brace the end post firmly, by driving in a short stake 4 feet from the last post, fastening a wire to the top of the post and drawing it down and around the stake, as shown in figure 17. Procure No. 12 wire ; bore holes with a half-inch auger through the end post (which should always be rather heavier and square), one near the top of the post, and one or two others, as you wish to make the trellis of two or three wires. If the trellis is to be of only two wires, make the next hole 2 feet below the upper one ; if three wires are to be used, 20 inches below. The three-wire trellis is somewhat more convenient in tying up the young vines and lower canes, but is also costlier, while the two-wire trellis is more economical, and when the vines are once established in their proper shape, just as good, while it is more convenient for cultivation below, and allows freer circulation of air below the bearing canes. Fasten your vine to the post at one end, drawing it along the line, and pass it through the hole in the end post. Have pieces of 1 inch boards, 1½ inch broad, and a foot long, with a hole bored through the center. Draw your wire also through this, and then by turning the board, you can, in wrapping the wire around it, tighten that at your pleasure, and loosen it also, which should always be done in the fall, as the cold contracts the wire, and the strain would be too great. Now you can fasten the wire to the intermediate posts by small staples, which are manufactured for this purpose, and can be had in any hardware store. If your vineyard slopes to the south, and the rows run parallel with the hillside, fasten on the south side ; if to the east, fasten to the east. Laths will, of course, do instead of wires, but the posts must then be set much closer ; laths always need repairing ; the wires are much more convenient to tie to, and in the end much cheaper. Many train to stakes. Where timber is plenty, stakes may be cheaper, yet it is much more labor to tie to them, and the vines are always in disorder, while they will cling to the wires with their tendrils, thus doing most of the tying themselves, and the bearing canes can be distributed much more evenly, producing more and better ripened fruit. I am satisfied that the additional cost of trellis will be more than paid by the larger and better crop the first bearing season. Fill all vacancies, if any occur, with extra strong vines in the fall.

CHAPTER XI.

TREATMENT OF THE VINE THE SECOND SUMMER.

We find the young vine at the commencement of the second summer pruned to three buds. From these we may expect two or three strong shoots to ripen into bearing canes for the next year. The first work will be to cultivate the whole ground. This can be done by a common turning plow, first throwing away a furrow at each side of the row, as in the first cultivation of corn, taking care not to go too deep, so as to injure the vine or its roots. Then hoe the space under and around the vines, either with the two-pronged German hoe, or the Hexamer hoe, stirring and inverting the soil to the depth of about 3 inches. Then take the plow again and throw the soil back to the vines, using care, however, not to cover them ; stir the whole to a uniform depth, and leaving a shallow furrow in the middle. The ground should be dry enough to work well, and not clog ; rather wait a few days than to stir the soil in wet weather. Of the three shoots which may grow, leave two to grow unchecked ; the weakest is to be pinched as soon as about five or six leaves are developed, taking off the top of the young shoot with your thumb and finger. The other two, if Catawba or Delaware, you can let grow unchecked, but all the strong growing kinds, as Concord, Martha, Gœthe, etc., and all the *æstivalis* and *cordifolia* class, should also be pinched when the shoots have attained a length of 3 feet, or just above the second wire from above ; this will force the laterals into a stronger growth, so that each will attain the size of a medium cane. On these we intend to have our fruit the coming season, as the shoots from buds on these laterals will produce more and finer fruit than those on the main canes, if left unchecked ; and they can also be kept under control much better. Figure 7 will show the result of training the second summer, with the method of bracing the trellis.

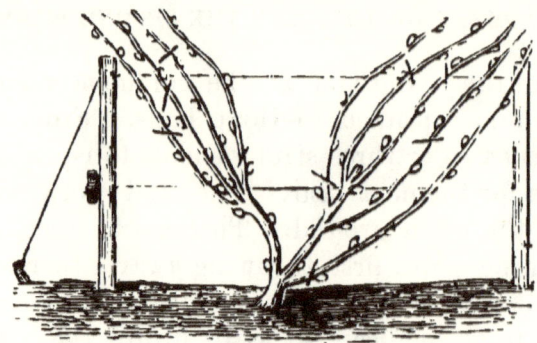

Fig. 7.—THE VINE AT THE END OF THE SECOND SEASON.

Figure 8 gives the vine, pruned and tied, at the end of the second season. Figure 9 represents the manner of training and tying the Catawba and Delaware, or other slow growing kinds.

The above method of training is a combination of the single-cane and fan-training system, which I tried first on the Concord from sheer necessity, when the results pleased me so much, that I have since adopted it with all

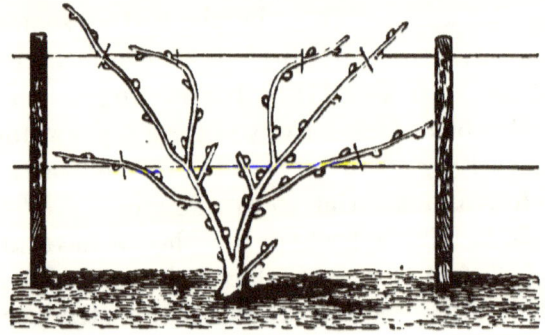

Fig. 8.—THE VINE PRUNED AND TIED.

the strong growing varieties. The circumstances which led me to the trial of this method, were as follows : In the summer of 1862, when my young Concord vines were making their second season's growth, we had, in the beginning of June, the most destructive hailstorm I have ever seen here. The vines were not only stripped of all their leaves, but the young succulent shoots were also cut down to about 3 feet from the ground. The vines, being young and vigorous, pushed out strong laterals, each of them about the size of a fair, medium cane. In the fall, when I came to prune them, the main cane was not long enough, and I shortened in the laterals to from four to six buds each. On these I had as fine a crop of grapes as I ever saw, with large, well developed bunches and berries,

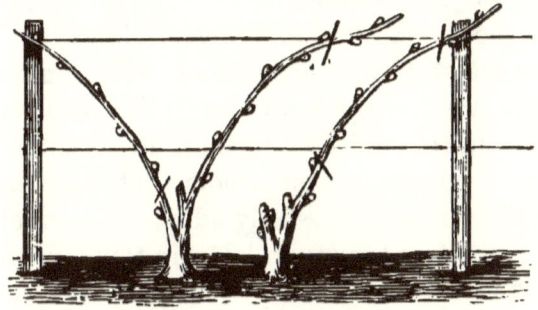

Fig. 9.—TRAINING SLOW GROWING VARIETIES.

and a great many of them, as each bud had produced its fruit-bearing shoot. Since that time I have followed this method altogether and have obtained the most satisfactory results.

The ground should be kept loose and mellow during the summer, cultivating as often as may become necessary during dry weather, and the vines are to be tied neatly to the trellis with bark or straw.

There are many other methods of training, as the old bow and stake training, so much in vogue formerly. But it crowds the whole mass of fruit and leaves so closely, that mildew and rot will follow as a natural consequence; it should have been given up long ago. But we have a class of grape growers who never learn or forget anything.

These will hardly prosper. The grape-grower, of all others, should be a close observer of nature, a thinking and reasoning being. He ought to experiment and try new methods all the time, and should he find a better, be willing to throw aside his old method, and adopt one more suited to the wants of his vines. Only in this manner can he expect to attain success.

There is also the arm system, of which we hear so much, and which certainly looks very pretty on paper. But paper is patient, and the advantages of the system cannot be denied, if every shoot and spur could be made to grow just as in drawings, with three fine bunches to each shoot. Upon applying it, however, we find that vines are stubborn, some shoots will outgrow others, and before we hardly know how, the whole beautiful system is out of order. It may do to follow with a few vines in gardens, or on arbors, but I do not think that it will ever be successfully adopted for vineyard culture, as it involves too much labor in tying, pruning, etc. I think the method already described will more fully meet the wants of the vine grower than any I have yet seen ; it is so simple that an intelligent person can soon become familiar with it, and gives us new, healthy bearing-wood every season.

Pruning may be done in the fall, as soon as the leaves have dropped, and continued, on mild days, during the winter months.

CHAPTER XII.

TREATMENT OF THE VINE THE THIRD SUMMER.

At the beginning of the third season we find our vine pruned to three spurs, of two buds each, and six short lateral arms of four to six buds each. These are tied firmly to the trellis, as shown in figure 8, for which purpose small twigs of the Golden Willow, of which every grape-grower should plant a supply, are the most convenient. In their absence, twigs of some of the wild willows, or good strong twine, may be substituted, though not near so convenient. The ground should be plowed and hoed as before, taking care, however, not to plow so deeply as to cut or tear the roots of the vines.

The vines being plowed and hoed, and, as we hope, pushing young shoots vigorously, we come to one of the most important and delicate operations to be performed on the vine, one of as great, or even greater, importance than pruning. This is summer-pruning, or pinching, i. e., thumb and finger pruning. Fall pruning, or cutting back, is but the first step in the discipline to which the vine is to be subjected ; summer pruning is the second ; and one is useless and cannot be systematically followed without the other. Look at the vine well before you commence, and begin near the ground.

The time to commence is when the young shoots are 6 to 8 inches long, and as soon as you can see all the young bunches or buds, the embryo fruit. We commence on the lower spur, having two shoots ; rubbing off, at the same time, all suckers or wild shoots that may have started from the crown of the vine below. From the two buds two shoots have started. One of them may serve as a bearing cane or reserve next summer, we, therefore, leave it unchecked for the present. The other, which is intended for a spur again next fall, we pinch with thumb and finger, just beyond the last bunch or button, taking out the leader between the last bunch and the next leaf, as shown in figure 10, the cross line indicating where the leader is to be pinched. We now rub off all the shoots between the lower spur and the next lateral cane, should any appear, as they generally produce imperfect fruit and are quite too near the ground. Next take the spur on the cane, treating it precisely like the lower one, leaving the strongest shoot unchecked for a bearing cane next year, and pinching the other. Now go

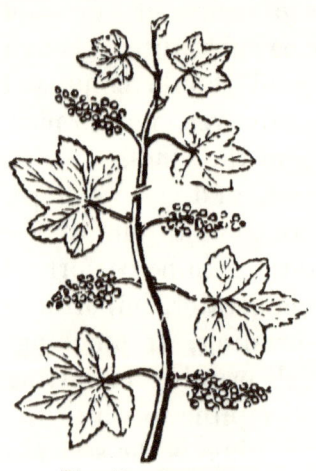

over all the shoots on the lateral canes, shortening each one to just above the last promising looking bunch. If a bud has started two, or even three shoots, rub off the weaker, leaving but one and the strongest, and if any bud has not started vigorously, rub it off altogether. Go over the other cane in the same manner, and if you think there are still too many bunches, take away the smallest. A vine in its third season, however strong it may be, should not

Fig. 10.—PINCHING.

be allowed to bear over 15 lbs. of grapes, and if allowed thirty to forty bunches it will have that quantity, provided it is not a variety which bears but small bunches. Now is the time to thin the fruit, before it has abstracted any strength from the vine. If any shoots are not sufficiently developed to show their condition, we pass them by, and go over the vine again after a few days.

This early pinching of the young shoots has the tendency to throw all the vigor into the development of the young bunches and the leaves remaining on the shoot, which now develop with astonishing rapidity. It is a gentle checking, and leading the sap into other channels, not the violent process which is often followed long after the bloom, when the shoots have so hardened that the knife must be used, and by which the plant is robbed of a large part of its leaves, to the injury of both fruit and vine. Let any one who wishes to satisfy himself, summer-prune a vine according to this method, and leave the next vine until after the bloom ; he will soon be convinced which is best Since I first practised this method, now about twenty years, it has added at least one-third to the quantity and quality of my crop, and it is now followed by most of the intelligent growers of my State. It also gives an early opportunity to destroy the small worms, a species of leaf-folder, which are very troublesome about this time, eating the young bunches and leaves, and which generally make their web among the tender leaves at the end of the shoot. The bearing shoots all being pinched back, we can leave the vines alone until after the bloom, only tying up the young canes from the spurs, should this become necessary. Do not tie them over and among the bearing canes, but lead them to the empty spaces in the middle, as our object must be to give the fruit all the air and light we can.

Fig. 11.—PINCHING THE LATERALS.

When they have bloomed, the laterals will have started from the axils of the leaves on the bearing shoots. Go over again, and pinch these back to one leaf, as shown in figure 11, the cross lines showing where the laterals are to be pinched. This will have the tendency to develop the remaining leaf very rapidly, enabling it to serve as a

conductor and elaborator of sap to the young bunch opposite, and shading that when it becomes fully developed. The canes from the spurs, which we left unchecked at first pinching, and which we design to bear
fruit the next season, may now also be stopped or pinched
when they are about 3 feet long, to start their laterals
into stronger growth. Pinch off all the tendrils unless
where they serve as supports to the young growth. This
is a very busy time for the vine dresser, and upon his
close attention and diligence now, depends, in a great
measure, the value of his crop. A vast deal of labor can
be saved by doing everything at its proper time.

This is about all that is necessary for this summer, except tying the young growth along the top wires, and
an occasional tying of a fruit-bearing branch, if it should
become too heavy. The majority of the branches will,
however, be able to bear their fruit without tying, and
the young growth which may yet be made from the
laterals may be left unchecked, as it will serve to shade
the fruit when ripening. This short and early pinching
is also a partial preventive of mildew and rot, as it admits light and air to all parts of the vine. But I cannot
caution too strongly against late cutting back, one of the
first causes of disease, and ruinous to the vine, as the defoliation of the vine in August disturbs and violates all
its functions, and enfeebles it.

The reader will perceive that fall pruning, or shortening-in the ripe wood of the vine, and summer-pruning,
shortening-in and thinning the young growth, have one
and the same object in view, namely, to keep the vine within proper bounds, and to concentrate all its energies for a
two-fold object, the production and ripening of the most
perfect fruit, and the production of strong and healthy
wood for next season's crop. Both operations are only different parts of the same system, of which summer-pruning
is the preparatory, and fall-pruning the finishing part.

If we think that a vine sets more fruit than it is able to bear and ripen perfectly, we have it in our power to thin it, by taking away all imperfect bunches and feeble shoots. We should allow no more canes to grow for next season's bearing than we need, if we allow three canes to grow where only two are needed, we waste the energies of the vine, which should all be concentrated upon ripening its fruit in the most perfect manner, and producing enough wood for next season's bearing, and of the best and most vigorous kind, but no more. If we prune the vine too long, we overtax its energies, making it bear more fruit than it can well mature, and the result will be poor, badly-ripened fruit, and imperfect wood. If we prune the vine too short, we will have a rank, excessive growth of wood and leaves, and encourage rot and mildew. Only practice and experience will teach the true medium, and the observing and thinking vine-dresser will soon learn where the true medium is, better than he can be taught by volumes of advice. Different varieties will, of course, require different treatment, and it would be folly to prune them all alike. A compact, slow grower, like the Delaware, will require different treatment from a rank grower like Concord, and much shorter pruning. The Delaware and Catawba fruit well upon single canes, while the Concord, Martha, and others, fruit better on spurs upon laterals, while most of the *æstivalis* and *cordifolia* classes, especially the Norton's, Cynthiana, and Taylor, will fruit better if pruned to spurs of two or three buds, on the old arms, than on young canes. With these latter, the old arms should, therefore, be retained as long as they are sound and vigorous, pruning all the healthy, good sized shoots to two or three buds : always, however, growing a young cane to fall back upon, should the old one become diseased. It is because so few of our common laborers will take the pains to study the habits and nature of their vines, and do a little thinking for themselves, that we find among them but very few good vine dressers.

It is hardly necessary to state that the ground should be kept mellow and clean through the summer, and especially during the ripening of the fruit, but never touch it in wet weather.

At the end of this season, we find our vines, if Concords or similar varieties, with the old fruit-bearing canes, and a spur on each side, from each of which we have a cane, as the smaller one was stopped, like all other fruit-bearing branches, and which we now prune to a spur of two buds. The other, the young cane, which was stopped at about 3 feet, on which the laterals were left to grow unchecked, we prune as last season, each lateral being cut back to four to six buds, and the old canes which had borne fruit, are cut away altogether. With Norton's, Cynthiana, Taylor, etc., the old arms are left, and the well developed shoots are cut back to two buds each, as before mentioned, while the small, weak ones are cut away altogether. This leaves us with an arm on each side, to be tied the next spring, as shown in figure 18, and ends our operations for the season. Of the gathering of the fruit, as well for market as for wine, I shall speak in another place.

CHAPTER XIII.

TREATMENT OF THE VINE THE FOURTH SUMMER.

We now consider the vine as established, able to bear a full crop. The operations to be performed are precisely the same as in its third year, only modifying the pruning, fruiting, etc., according to the strength of the vine, pruning shorter if the vine shows a decrease in vigor, longer, if it grows too rank.

Should the vines show a decrease in vigor, so as to indicate the need of stimulants, they may be manured with
ashes, bone dust, compost, or still better, with surface
soil from the woods or prairies. This will serve to re-
plenish the soil which may have been washed off, and is
much more beneficial than stable manure. When the
latter is employed, a small trench may be dug in the
middle of the row just above the vine, the manure laid
in, and covered with soil. But an abundance of fresh
soil, drawn around the vine, is the best of all manures.

Should your vineyard have vacancies, they had best be
filled with layers from neighboring vines, made as follows:
Dig a trench from the vine from which the layer is to be
made, to the empty place, about 8 or 10 inches deep,
bend into this trench one of the canes of the vine which
has been left to grow unchecked for the purpose, and
pruned to the proper length. Let the end of this layer-
cane come out at the surface, where the new vine is wanted, and fill up the trench with well pulverized earth. It
will take root at every joint, and grow rapidly, but as it
draws a great deal of nourishment from the parent vine,
that must be pruned much shorter. When the layer is
well established, it is cut from the parent vine, either the
second or third season. Such layers will fill up much
better than if the vacancies are supplied by planting
young vines, as the latter do not grow very vigorously, if set among the others, after the second season.

Pruning is best done in fall, but can be done any time
during mild weather in winter, and here even as late as
the middle of March. Fall pruning will prevent flow of
sap, and the cuttings, if to be used for future plantations,
or sold, are also better if made in the fall, and buried in
the ground over winter, with their upper ends downwards.
All the sound, well-ripened wood of last season's growth
may be made into cuttings, and if they can be sold,
will largely add to the product of the vineyard.

CHAPTER XIV.

TRAINING THE VINE ON ARBORS AND WALLS.

This has a different purpose from culture in vineyards, and, therefore, the vines require different treatment. Vineyard culture has for its object the most perfect fruit, and bringing the vine, with all its parts, within easy reach of the cultivator. Arbor culture has for its object the covering of a large space with foliage, for ornament and shade ; fruit being but a secondary consideration, though a large quantity of fruit of fair quality can also be produced, if the vines are judiciously treated.

The first aim should be to grow very strong plants, so as to cover a large space. Prepare the border by digging a trench 2 feet deep and 4 feet wide, and fill with rich soil, rotten leaves, bones, ashes, etc. Set your plants in this, in the manner already shown in vineyard planting. Leave but one shoot to grow on them during the first summer, which ought to become very strong. Cut this cane back to three buds the next fall. Each of these buds will produce a strong shoot the next spring, which should be tied to the arbor and allowed to grow unchecked. In the following fall, cut each of these three canes back to three buds, as our first aim must be to get a good basis for our vines. These will give nine canes the next summer, and as the vine is now strong enough, we can begin to demand a crop from it. We have now three different sections or branches to the vine, each one of which bears three canes. Cut one of these three canes back to two eyes, and prune the other two canes to from six to ten buds each, according to the strength of the vine. Treat each of the three sections in the same manner. Next spring tie these neatly to the trellis, dividing them equally, and when the young shoots appear, thin out the weakest, leaving the others to grow unchecked. Next fall cut back the weakest of the canes to two buds each, the stronger ones to three or four buds, the spurs at bottom to come in as a reserve, should any of the main arms become diseased.

Others prefer the Thomery or horizontal arm training, but I think it much more complicated and difficult. Those who wish to inform themselves about it, I refer to the books of Fuller and Mead, which are very explicit on the subject.

CHAPTER XV.

OTHER METHODS OF TRAINING.

These are almost without number; one of the most common is to place three stakes around the vine, about a foot from it, and to wind the canes or arms around them spirally, until they reach the top. They are then " spurred in " every season, and no young canes grown, except to replace a decaying arm. This mode is much more inconvenient than a trellis, and it crowds fruit and foliage too much, inducing mildew. Another, much in vogue in Europe, and also in California, is the so-called bush or stool method of training. The vine is made to form its crown, i. e., the part from which the branches start, from 12 to 18 inches above the ground and all the young shoots are allowed to grow, but summer pruned or checked above the last bunch of grapes. The next spring or fall all of the young shoots are " spurred-in " to two buds ; this system of spurring-in is kept up, and the vine will at last present the appearance of a bush or miniature tree, producing all its fruit within a foot from the crown, and without further support than its own stem. Very old vines, sometimes, have from a dozen to twenty spurs, and present, with their fruit hanging all around their trunks, a pleasing, but odd aspect. This method could not be applied here with any chance of success to any other than very slow and stocky growers. The Delaware, the Alvey, and also the Eumelan, would be the most suitable, as they are very close-jointed, stocky, and hardy. It would be useless to try it with strong growers.

Another method of dwarfing the vine is practised to form a pretty border along walks in gardens or along terraces, and is as follows : Plant the vines about 8 feet apart, treat them the first season as in common vineyard culture, but cut back to two buds. Provide posts 3 to $3\frac{1}{2}$ feet long, and pointed at one end ; drive these into the ground for 18 inches, and nail a lath on the top. This is the trellis, and should be about 18 inches above the ground, or 2 feet, if you prefer. Allow both of the shoots from the vine to grow unchecked, and when they have reached the trellis, tie one to the right, the other to the left, allowing them to grow at will along the lath. The next fall, cut back to the proper length to meet the other vine, and in spring, tie firmly to the lath. When the young shoots appear, all are rubbed off below the trellis, but all those above the trellis are pinched, as in vineyard culture, beyond the last bunch of grapes. The trellis, with its garland of fruit, will look very pretty. In the fall, all the shoots are " spurred-in " to one or two buds, one being allowed to grow from each spur, to produce fruit the next summer ; the same treatment is repeated every year.

During a trip among the vineyards of Western New York, on the shores of Lake Erie and Keuka, or Crooked Lake, I observed a method of training which seems to produce good results there, but which I think would not prove successful here, as our hot sun would scald the leaves, and the grapes being so near the ground would be more liable to rot. I can but think that even in these localities the method described by me, would be better, and save a good deal of labor.

Their method is as follows : They grow two canes on each vine, which are tied horizontally to the lower wire, one to the left, the other to the right, and also a spur on each arm to produce a new cane for next year. The shoots, which grow from the eyes on the two horizontal canes, are left to grow unchecked, and when they have become long enough to reach the second wire, are tied to it, and from there to the upper wire, thus bearing the fruit all between the lower and second wires. The next fall the cane, which has borne the fruit the last summer, is cut off close to the spur, and the new cane grown from it takes the place of it the next summer. It is a very simple way of renewal training, but were we to do it here, the leaves which are on the main shoots would drop off, leaving the fruit exposed · while with the system of summer-pruning I follow, the young and vigorous leaves on the pinched laterals shade the fruit perfectly, and remain fresh and green. Besides, it takes an immense amount of tying and tying material, and we can pinch four shoots in a shorter time than we can tie one. As our pinched shoots become very stocky, they will bear the weight of all the fruit without tying, and the slanting direction in which we tie will distribute the fruit more evenly. I believe, therefore, that our New York growers would do well to give this method a trial, and compare results.

I also saw the horizontal arm training in great perfection at Mr. H. E. Hooker's, at Rochester, and confess that his arms of the Brighton, with their handsome clusters, looked very handsome. He thinks he could carry an arm to the distance of 50 feet in the same way. His treatment consists simply in "spurring-in" the young shoots on his canes along the first wire to one to two eyes, growing his fruit on these, and leaving the old arm, pruning back the young shoots to spurs every year, leaving the bearing shoots unchecked, and tying them to the wires above. While it succeeds there, I have my doubts as to its applicability with us, for the reasons already given, nor do I believe that he can grow any better fruit even there, than could be obtained by our simpler method.

Prof. L. H. Bailey has written a little book on American Grape Training, a copy of which he has kindly placed at my disposal, with permission to make such extracts as may be found useful for this volume. It discusses almost every method of training practiced in this country except those set forth in the preceding chapters, which are, however, still followed, to some extent, everywhere.

The Kniffen System,—so named after its originator, William Kniffen,—or some of its modifications, is largely followed in many parts of the State of New York, at least for strong growing varieties, as Concord, Worden and Niagara. The fundamental idea underlying the Kniffen system, in all its modifications, seems to me to be the obtaining of grapes with the smallest amount of labor. The method known as the four-cane Kniffen seems to have been the original of the system. Two wires are used, and as soon as the vine becomes strong enough a spur and a cane are grown from the lower trellis; that is to say, four canes are grown from two spurs, one on each side of the vine, of which one is cut back to a spur when pruning, the other to a cane, which is carried along the lower wire and tied. If the vine is strong enough to be carried to the upper wire, it is pruned in the same manner there, so that each of the wires carries a separate load of wood and fruit. Both tiers thus carry two spurs for renewal, two canes for bearing, and the shoots from the bearing canes are allowed to droop down, without further pruning and tying. Each of the spurs is supposed to produce two canes, of which one is cut back to a spur, the other to a bearing cane, and the cane which has produced the fruit is cut off. A very simple form of renewal training, and if it produces as good fruit as some more complicated methods, it is well worth following. Modifications of it are as follows :

THE LOW, OR ONE-ARMED KNIFFEN.—In this the trellis is only three or four feet high, with a single wire. A spur and a bearing cane are left on each side, and the whole mass of bearing cane, fruit and foliage, is carried by it. The advantages urged for this are (1), the protection of grapes from wind; (2) larger size of the fruit, in consequence of the small amount of bearing wood; (3) the ease of laying down the vine; (4) the readiness with which the top may be renewed from the root; (5) cheapness of the trellis.

THE HIGH, OR UMBRELLA KNIFFEN.—In this method the vine is carried, as soon as its strength permits, to the upper wire, and the young cane cut back even with it. The top is then formed from the upper four buds, or rather, from their shoots, which appear during the summer, of which two are led along each side of the wire. In pruning them the next winter, one of them on each side is cut back to a spur, the other to a cane of a length corresponding to the strength of the vine, which cane is bent from the upper wire to the lower, forming a sweeping, or umbrella top. The renewal is the same as with the other forms.

SIX AND EIGHT CANE KNIFFEN.—In these, which require three, or even four wires, there is little if any apparent difference from common fan training, as it distributes the growth of the vine over the whole trellis.

OVERHEAD KNIFFEN TRAINING.—In this method the vine is carried to the top of the trellis as soon as it is strong enough. The trellis is made six feet high, with strong posts, to which crosspieces are attached. One wire is stretched from post to post, and one on each side, the cross-bars being three feet long. These three wires run parallel with each other, the bearing canes are tied from the middle to the sides, and the young canes along the middle of the trellis.

There are several other modifications of this system, such as cross wire training, etc.

THE MUNSON SYSTEM.—My friend Munson of Denison, Texas, has invented another method, somewhat on the same principle, which he finds very satisfactory. He sets two posts in the same place, but with their tops diverging from two to three feet. One wire is stretched from the top of each post to the next, and a cross wire a foot lower bears a third wire, to which the vines are fastened. The canes are led over and fastened to the middle wire, while the young growth from the spurs is carried over on the side wires. Thus the whole forms a V-shaped mass of foliage, the fruit hanging below. He claims for this system the following advantages :

1. The natural habit of the vine is maintained, which is a canopy to shade the roots and body of the vine and fruit, without smothering.

2. New wood, formed by a sap which has never passed through bearing wood, is secured for the next crop.

3. Simplicity and convenience of trellis, allowing passage in any direction, circulation of air without danger of breaking tender shoots, ease of pruning, spraying, cultivation and harvesting.

4. Perfect control of crop in pruning to suit the capacity of the vine.

5. Long canes for bearing, which agrees with the nature of American vines better than do short spurs.

6. Ease of laying down in winter. The vine, being pruned and not tied, being away from the posts, can be

bent down to one side, earth thrown upon it, and in spring can be easily raised and tied up.

7. Cheapness of construction ; ease of removing trellis material, and using it again.

8. Durability of both trellis and vineyard.

The following explanation is by Professor Munson : "The trellis stands six feet high. The shoots stand up at first, but soon droop over, and are supported by the side wires. After the vines have flowered the bearing laterals have their ends pinched off, and this is all the summer pruning the vine gets, except to rub off all eyes that start on the body below the head, or crotch. Two to four shoots, according to strength of vine, are started from the spurs at the fork, or crotch, and trained over the center wire for renewal canes. When pruning time arrives, the entire bearing cane of the present year, with all its laterals, is cut away at a point from where the young renewal shoots have started, and these shoots are shortened back, according to strength of vine ; some, such as Herbemont, being able at four years to fill four shoots six or eight feet long with fine fruit, while Delaware could not carry over three or four feet each way, of one shoot only. The different varieties are set at various distances apart, according as they are strong or weak growers. Thus the trellis and system of pruning are reduced to the simplest form. A few cuts to each vine cover all the pruning, and a few ties complete the task. A novice can soon learn to do the work well. The trunk, or main stem, is secured to the middle wire, along which all bearing canes are tied after pruning, and from which the young laterals which produce the crop are to spring. These laterals strike the outer wires, soon clinging to them with their tendrils, and are safe from destruction, while the fruit is thrown in the best possible position for spraying and gathering, and is still shaded with the canopy of leaves. I have now used this

5

trellis five years upon ten acres of mixed vines, and I am more pleased with it every year."

I give all these methods for what they are claimed to be worth, and for the consideration and trial of my readers. Each of them may be adapted to certain varieties and localities, and are worthy of a trial, as well as are Mr. Cashin's methods of spiral and zigzag training.

On one point, however, I take issue with Professor Bailey, and this is summer pruning, which he seems to think of very little consequence. I think it very important, especially in growing grapes for wine. I have always found, where summer pruning was neglected or done late, that the crop ripened very irregularly, the first bunch on the shoot ripening first, the second somewhat after it, and the third or fourth much later.

In growing grapes for market, several pickings may be admissible, or even profitable, but to use them for wine we want a uniformly ripened product, and this we can obtain only by very early summer pruning, as fully described in a former chapter. By late summer pruning we accomplish just the reverse, — unevenly ripened fruit, and unevenly ripened wood. Better not summer prune at all, and follow the lazy man's method of allowing the vine to take care of itself after pruning and tying, than to denude it of half its foliage and wood by the barbarous use of the sickle or knife late in the season.

Summer pruning must be a gentle checking early in the season, to lead the abundant sap which flows then, into other channels, developing laterals and leaves to shade the young fruit, not lopping off the tops at the most critical period, when all the foliage is needed to perfect the fruit. Summer pruning early in the season is beneficial; late in the season it ruins the crop and the vine.

That all these systems of training are only applicable to American vines, and the States east of the Rocky mountains, is self-evident. The pruning and training of the Vinifera will be treated on in Part IV of this volume.

CHAPTER XVI.

DISEASES OF THE VINE.

Fungous diseases of grapes and vines have become very prevalent and destructive throughout the United States, and are formidable indeed if left unchecked. Fortunately, however, remedies have been discovered which, when faithfully and skillfully applied, prove effective as preventives. The grape growers of the country are greatly indebted to the United States Department of Agriculture for assistance and advice in this direction. Its first secretary, Hon. Norman J. Colman, was the first to introduce and recommend the Bordeaux mixture, which had been tried in France by Millardet, Foëx and others. Under his successors, Secretaries Rusk and Morton, the work of study and experiments has been vigorously and intelligently prosecuted, to the great advantage of all interested in the culture of grapes and fruits of all kinds. The Bordeaux mixture in greatly modified forms, and other fungicides, are now so well established and understood that no one need fear fungous diseases who has energy enough to apply the remedies. The following are, in brief, the principal diseases of grapes and vines.

BLACK ROT (*Physalospora — Læstadia Bidwellii — Sacc. Viala and Rav.*).—This is, perhaps, the most

widely spread and destructive disease of grapes east of
the Rocky mountains, and for a time it threatened to
utterly destroy grape culture in some of the States.   It
commonly appears in warm, moist weather, as a brown
spot, like the sting of an insect, on the berry when one-
half to two-thirds grown.   It is, however, preceded by
brown spots on the leaves, which give the first warning
of its approach.   These brown spots on the fruit increase until they cover its surface, and spread rapidly
over all the grapes of the bunch, which become dry and
hard.   As it affects all the leaves, and even the young
shoots of the vine, the wood naturally becomes unhealthy.   It fails to ripen well and is consequently more
liable to injury from frost the ensuing winter, and to
attacks of disease the next summer, especially if the
fallen leaves and diseased grapes are left in the vineyard.
The spores live through the winter, and only await the
advent of warm weather to spring into life and multiply
indefinitely.   It is important, therefore, that all this
refuse be destroyed by fire, and an early spraying applied
to kill any spores that may remain.   It should be borne
in mind that all fungicides are more effective as preventives.   So destructive had black rot and downy mildew become in Missouri that my old friend and corre-
spondent, Hermann Jaeger, of Neosho, one of the most
persevering of pioneers in grape culture in his section,
had abandoned about all the Labruscas and their hybrids and confined his efforts to such ironclads as Norton's Virginia and Cynthiana, with a few of the Æstivalis and Rupestris sections.   Now, after thorough trials
since 1885, he finds that he can not only grow the varieties of American origin liable to the disease, but has
hopes of success with some of the Vinifera, with some
protection in winter.   He finds that with repeated spraying he can not alone obtain a good crop, but also keep
the foliage in a healthy condition, thus promoting the

ripening of the wood, and in consequence, the hardiness of the vine in winter. His experience will be more fully given in his own words in Part II of this work.

Prof. R. N. Price, of the Texas Agricultural and Mechanical College, has given the subject of black rot much attention. He propagated the fungus from spores, and published its life history in an illustrated bulletin, which is the most complete treatise on the subject I have yet seen. I regret that want of space forbids its reproduction entire, in this volume, but some of his experience will be given at the end of this chapter, as it relates to nearly all fungous diseases of the grape, and about the same remedies are applicable to all.

DOWNY MILDEW (*Peronospora viticola*).—This is also called "gray rot," as the young berries, when first attacked, show marbling or veins of gray. This soon changes to a uniform gray, entirely over the affected berry, which shrinks and drops. It attacks all the green parts of the vine, showing like a gray down on the underside of the leaves, and appearing as rusty blotches on the upper side. It usually appears in warm, sultry weather, after the berries are nearly grown, and as the fungus spreads very rapidly it is one of the most destructive if left unchecked. The spores are produced on the extremity of minute, threadlike stems, which protrude through the underside of the leaf. They are contained in small spherical sacs, which are blown about by the wind, and alighting upon the soft green surface of the leaves, soon burst and the liberated spores germinate, spreading the disease to all parts of the vine. As generation follows generation with great rapidity, the spores continue to spread through the entire vineyard until autumn, when the hardy winter spores are formed in small sacs with tough leathery coats which live through the winter, and renew the work of infection in the spring. The disease spreads very rapidly during cold, wet weather, although any weakness of the vines caused by overbearing, exhaustion of the soil, or other means, may induce its development or increase its injurious effects. The berries, when attacked by downy mildew, seldom attain more than half size. The surface, after the attack of the fungus, assumes a grayish color, which soon turns to brown, thus producing a brown or gray rot. The best preventive measures are to burn all infected dry leaves and rubbish in the fall, and to thoroughly spray the vines in spring with Bordeaux mixture.

POWDERY MILDEW (*Uncinula spitalis*). — Unlike downy mildew, this disease flourishes with special energy in dry, hot weather. It is not greatly destructive in the Eastern and Northern States, but more so on the Pacific coast. It draws its sustenance through filaments which pierce the outer membrane of the leaves and fruit, and presents the appearance of a dirty, powdery coating so well known to vineyardists, rendering the grapes unfit for market or for wine. The fungus is especially destructive in seasons of protracted drouth. In California, where it is quite prevalent, the usual preventive is powdered sulphur, dusted over and among the leaves, by means of a fine wire sieve, or a bellows made for the purpose. It is first applied when the young shoots are about a foot long, and before blooming. Should it appear at a later period a second application will be necessary. The disease often makes its appearance in June, during the period of bloom, affecting the embryo shoots and preventing their growth ; but more frequently, after the vines have escaped an earlier attack, it appears during protracted drouths, arresting the growth of the young shoots and the development of the berries, which crack, and attain only one-half their normal size. The disease not only impairs the growth and appearance of the grapes, but also prevents the fermentation of the must, if they are pressed for wine. The winter spores doubtless remain uninjured on the vines and fallen leaves, ready to spring into life the following summer.

It is doubtful whether spraying with Bordeaux mixture is a specific for powdery mildew. Experiments have been made with sulphur and Bordeaux mixture combined, but without success, as the sulphur was much weakened by the combination. Mr. Hermann Jaeger writes to me from Missouri that while the direct effect of spraying with copper mixture may not be specifically preventive of downy mildew, yet he finds that it promotes the general health and vigor of the vine, and thus assists it in resisting the attacks of fungus.

ANTHRACNOSE (*Glæosporium ampelophagum*).—This has never proved very destructive in California, though it appears to a greater or less extent every year, on a few of the vines. It is first seen during the latter part of June, in some cases affecting only a part of the vine, but more frequently infecting leaves, young shoots and fruit, and proving ultimately fatal. It is, in this State, also called Spanish measles, in reference to the light brown or reddish spots which first appear, and from which the disease spreads. The old Mission grape has been more largely infected than any other variety. The berries and branches are affected alike; the former become deformed and crack, and at length the affected part, or in some cases the entire vine, dries up and dies. The diseased parts should be promptly cut out and burned to prevent the spread of the spores. Applications of powdered sulphur and air-slaked lime in equal proportions are also recommended, as is also spraying with the copper solution mixtures. A remedial preparation called Fortite has recently been introduced from France, where the disease is much more prevalent and destructive than here. That the disease is of fungus origin there is no question, but the methods of success-fal treatment are not as well determined as are those for black rot and some other affections.

BITTER ROT (*Greeneria fuliginea*). — This disease takes its name from the bitter taste it imparts to grapes. It generally appears when the berries begin to ripen, as a brownish circle or spot, which enlarges until the entire berry turns brown, though for a time it retains its full size. Finally small, purplish pimples appear on the surface; the berry shrinks and falls.

WHITE ROT (*Coniothyrium diplodiella*).—This disease attacks the fruit and its pedicles, as well as the stem of the bunch, but not the leaves or branches. The pedicles become brown, the berries are at first very juicy; small gray or brownish pustules appear on the surface, and the berries dry up, assuming a grayish-white color, which distinctly marks the appearance of this disease from that of black rot.

ROUGEOT is not a fungous disease, but is the result of an interruption of the physiological processes in the plant. It causes a break in the equilibrium which should be maintained between absorption and transpiration. In this trouble the leaves turn red or yellow in spots or bands, and the vines are killed as a result of the death of the leaves. The first reported appearance of this disease on this side of the Atlantic was in 1890, when it was observed in the central region of New York. Its attack is marked by small, dark, irregular blotches between the veins of the leaves. These spots enlarge rapidly and darken to a dull purple or reddish brown, which become confluent, the leaf-veins alone remaining green or yellow. The contrast between the affected parts and the green leaf-veins gives the foliage a peculiar streaked appearance. In serious cases the leaves at length curl up and fall, leaving the vine bare. This denudation arrests at once the ripening of the fruit, and leaves it flat, insipid and sour. In severe cases the berries fall off, covering the ground beneath the vine with worthless fruit, to which a few fibers of the diseased pedicles still adhere. Even in mild attacks the berries shell off badly from the bunches, rendering them unfit for market, while the affected berries are of no value for wine.

The disease is most prevalent upon cold, heavy clay soils. Thorough underdraining of such soils will perhaps be found the best preventive. There is no apparent connection between the disease and sterility, for it appears equally on lands which have been heavily manured, and those without fertilizers. That the vine, in cases where its growth is materially checked by this disease, should be pruned very short, and possibly in extreme cases cut wholly back, would appear to be logical to every grape grower.

RIPE ROT (*Glœosporium fructigenum*).—It is only within the last five years that the disease has appeared to any seriously damaging extent, but its increase is such as to cause grave apprehensions. It commonly shows itself at first upon one or two berries in close, compact bunches, from which it spreads rapidly, especially in close, hot weather. In California it appears when the grapes are ripening, manifesting itself only by discoloration of the berries, and spreading to others. The quality is not affected for a time, as the grapes remain sweet and unchanged. In the Eastern and Northern States there appears to be a connection if not identity between this disease and the "bitter rot" of apples. In fact, the experts of the United States Department of Agriculture have agreed that it is one and the same disease. It certainly calls for the utmost vigilance on the part of grape growers. Early and persistent spraying with some of the mixtures recommended for black rot and downy mildew may also prove efficient against this.

THE VALUE OF SPRAYING.—There may even yet be

some skeptics who doubt the efficacy of spraying with fungicides for the purpose of combating, or rather of preventing, fungous diseases, but the experience of all who have used it early, carefully and persistently is wholly in its favor. The strongest proof of merit is its rapid and extensive spread since it was first made known to the public by Commissioner Norman J. Colman, of the United States Department of Agriculture. At first there may have been as many as fifty persons who adopted and tried it; now the number is not less than fifty thousand. No new method could make such progress if it did not possess genuine merit. It should be borne in mind, however, that spraying with any of the proved fungicides is preventive rather than remedial. The work must therefore begin in time, if it is to prove effective. Early applications are, besides, the most economical, as it requires less of the material to reach all parts of the vine when in a dormant or partly developed condition, than when all the foliage and fruit are fully grown. One of the earliest and most successful advocates and practical exponents of spraying is my friend, Hermann Jaeger, of Neosho, Missouri, who had given up, after long and patient trial, nearly all but the ironclad varieties, Norton's and Cynthiana, when he was appointed as agent of the United States Department of Agriculture to conduct the experimental work in Northwestern Missouri. His essay, read before the Missouri Horticultural Society in December, 1892, gives his experience so plainly that I cannot do better than to insert it in Part II of this work, with added details of his subsequent experience. He shows that greatly diluted applications have been fully as efficient as the stronger ones, and that the cost, aside from that for labor, is thus reduced to a mere trifle in comparison with the value of the vines and fruit thereby saved from destruction.

CHAPTER XVII.

INSECTS INJURIOUS TO THE GRAPE.

As the most destructive of all, because it works chiefly underground, and the mischief it does will only be perceived in its effects, I may consider the *Phylloxera vastatrix* or grapevine-root louse. Concerning the existence of this pest, we have for a long time been ignorant, until the efforts of our State Entomologist, Prof. C. V. Riley, and of other entomologists, especially Prof. Planchon, of France, have enlightened us upon the subject, and made us aware of the danger threatening our vineyards, but especially those of Europe and California, where the *vinifera* class had so far been cultivated almost exclusively. It threatens now to sweep out of existence that whole class, and it is a very noteworthy fact that from this country, from which the fell destroyer was imported into Europe, should also come the only effective remedy so far found, namely, the introduction of phylloxera-proof varieties of vines, which are found chiefly in the *æstivalis* and *cordifolia* (or *riparia*) classes. All other remedies, except inundation, seem to have failed, and Prof. Planchon, in a letter to me, expresses his firm belief that the only hope of saving that great source of wealth to the French nation, their vineyards, is in the introduction and general cultivation of our phylloxera-proof varieties of the grape, first as a stock to graft the *vinifera* upon, and secondly to cultivate our grapes for their fruit, if they can find varieties which will make such wines as the popular taste there demands. With this object in view millions upon millions of American cuttings and plants have already been imported into France, and the demand is still as active as ever. The Lenoir, or Jacques as they call it there, for a time promised to be all they wanted, as it was vigorous and made an exquisite red wine. But the dry rot appeared upon it; the Cunningham and Herbemont were imported largely, but it is feared they will not be quite hardy enough for Northern France. Their attention is now drawn towards the Taylor, as a very easy vine to propagate, and an excellent stock to graft upon, and if we once have varieties which have the phylloxera-proof roots of the Taylor, and which besides are abundant bearers, as we now seem to have in the Elvira and her sisters, we have found what is desired, and the supposition is but natural that they will become in time the wine grapes of the whole civilized world. It is indeed wonderful that, when this insect threatens to destroy the grapevines of the Old World, its remedy should be found here in our Missouri vineyards, and it may truly be called providential. It would require too much space to give the full natural history of the insect, and I refer those who wish to study it to the valuable Report[*] of Prof. Riley, of which I copy the most important part:

How the Phylloxera Affects the Vine.—Prof. Riley says: "The result which follows the puncture of the root louse is an abnormal swelling, differing in form according to the particular part and texture of the root. These swellings, which are generally commenced at the tips of the rootlets, eventually rot, and the lice forsake them and betake themselves to fresh ones. The decay affects the parts adjacent to the swellings, and on the more fibrous roots cuts off the supply of sap to all parts beyond. As these last decompose, the lice congregate

---

[*] Sixth Annual Report on the Noxious, Beneficial, and Other Insects of the State of Missouri, by C. V. Riley, State Entomologist. St. Louis, Mo., 1874.

on the larger ones, until at last the root system literally wastes away.

" During the first year of attack, there are scarcely any outward manifestations of disease, though the fibrous roots, if examined, will be found covered with nodosities, particularly in the latter part of the growing season. The disease is then in its incipient stage. The second year all these fibrous roots vanish, and the lice not only prevent the formation of new ones, but, as just stated, settle on the larger roots, which they injure by causing hypertrophy of the parts punctured, which also eventually become disorganized and rot. At this stage the outward symptoms of the disease first become manifest, in a sickly, yellowish appearance of the leaf and a reduced growth of cane. As the roots continue to decay, these symptoms become more acute, until by about the third year the vine dies. When the vine is about dying it is generally impossible to discover the cause of the death, the lice, which had been so numerous the first and second years of invasion, having left for fresh pasturage."

" The life-history of the Grape Phylloxera may be thus epitomized : It hibernates mostly as a young larva, torpidly attached to the roots of the vine, and so deepened in color as generally to be of a dull brassy-brown, and, therefore, with difficulty perceived, as the roots are often of the same color. With the renewal of vine growth in the spring, this larva moults, rapidly increases in size, and soon commences laying eggs. These eggs, in due time, give birth to young, which soon become virginal, egg-laying mothers, like the first ; and, like them, always remain wingless. Five or six generations of these parthenogenetic, egg-bearing, apterous mothers follow each other ; when—about the middle of July, in this latitude—some of the individuals begin to acquire wings. These are all females, and like the wingless mothers, they are parthenogenetic. Having issued from the ground, while in the

pupa state, they rise in the air and spread to new vineyards, where they deliver themselves of their issue in the
form of eggs or egg-like bodies—usually two or three in
number, and not exceeding eight—and then perish.
These eggs are of two sizes, the larger about 0.02 inch
long, and the smaller about three-fifths of that length.
In the course of a fortnight they produce the sexual individual, the larger ones giving birth to females, the smaller
to males.   These sexual individuals are born for no other
purpose than the reproduction of their kind, and are
without means of flight, or of taking food, or excreting.
They are quite active and couple readily ; one male being capable, no doubt, of serving several females, as Balbiani found to be the case with the European *quercus*.
The abdomen of the female, after impregnation, enlarges somewhat, and she is soon delivered of a solitary
egg, which differs from the ordinary eggs of the parthenogenetic mother only in becoming somewhat darker.
This impregnated egg gives birth to a young louse, which
becomes a virginal, egg-bearing, wingless mother, and
thus recommences the cycle of the species' evolution.
But one of the most important discoveries of Balbiani is
that, during the latter part of the season, many of the
wingless, hypogean mothers perform the very same func-
tion as the winged one ; *i. e.*, they lay a few eggs which
are of two sizes, and which produce males and females,
organized and constructed precisely as those born of the
winged females, and, like them, producing the solitary
impregnated egg.   Thus, the interesting fact is established that even the winged form is by no means essential to the perpetuation of the species ; but that, if all
such winged individuals were destroyed as fast as they
issue from the ground, the species could still go on mul-
tiplying in a vineyard from year to year.   We have,
therefore, the spectacle of an underground insect possessing the power of continued existence, even when confined

to its subterranean retreats. It spreads in the wingless state from vine to vine, and from vineyard to vineyard, when these are adjacent, either through passages in the ground itself, or over the surface. At the same time it is able, in the winged condition, to migrate to much more distant points. The winged females, as before stated, begin to appear in July, and continue to issue from the ground until vine growth ceases in the fall. Yet they are much more abundant in August than during any other month, and on certain days may be said to literally swarm. Every piece of root a few inches long, and having rootlets, taken from an infested vine at this season, will present a goodly proportion of pupæ ; and an ordinary quart preserve jar, filled with such roots and tightly closed, will furnish daily, for two or three weeks, a dozen or more of the winged females, which gather on the sides of the jar toward the light. We may get some idea, from this fact, of the immense numbers that disperse through the air to new fields, from a single acre of infected vines, in the course of the late summer and fall months.

"If to the above account we add that occasionally individuals abandon their normal underground habit, and form galls upon the leaves of certain varieties of grapevine, we have, in a general way, the whole natural history of the species."

He takes the ground that it is the cause of most of the diseases in the *Labrusca* class, and especially in the Catawba, as a vine with a diseased root can not produce healthy fruit, and these conclusions are certainly logical. He advises grafting on Phylloxera proof roots as a remedy, and to those wishing to save such varieties as the Catawba and Delaware, this is certainly the best course. But I think that they are already superseded by grapes of better quality, and my advice is to plant none but Phylloxera proof varieties. So far as I know, the follow-

ing varieties are especially subject to its ravages : Catawba, Delaware, Hartford, most of Rogers' Hybrids, Iona,
Isabella, Creveling, Diana, Maxatawney, Cassady, Rebecca, Croton. The following are not quite exempt, but are
so vigorous that they seem but little injured : Concord,
Martha, Gœthe, Wilder, Ives, Perkins, Telegraph, Mary
Ann. The whole *æstivalis* and *cordifolia* group appear
to be free from its ravages. It is strange, however, that
the gall-producing type of the insect will prefer the leaves
of the Taylor and Clinton, while the type which works
at the root does not affect them.

The other insect enemies, although very numerous, are
not so devastating as the Phylloxera.

The common Gray Cut-worm will often eat the tender
shoots of the young plantations, and draw them into the
ground below. It can be readily detected, so soon as its
ravages are seen, by stirring the ground about the vine,
when it will be found under some of the loose clods,
and easily killed.

The small worms, belonging to the leaf-folding class,
some of them white, some bluish-green, have already
been mentioned under " Summer-pruning." They
should be destroyed at that time ; closely watch them
when they make their webs among the young shoots, as
they will become very destructive if not checked in time.

Another leaf-folder comes about mid-summer, making
its web on the leaf, drawing it together, and then devour-
ing its own house. It is a small, whitish-gray, active
worm, which will drop to the ground as soon as disturbed.
I know of no other way but to catch and destroy it.

Several beetles will feed on the young buds before they
expand, one about the size and color of a hemp seed : another is of a steel-blue color; both are very active. They
can be caught in early morning, when they are yet torpid,
by spreading a newspaper under the vine and shaking it,
wl en they will drop upon the paper.

The Grape-vine Fidia, a small beetle, ashy-gray, sometimes comes in swarms, preying on the foliage, riddling it completely, and even attacking the young fruit. Hand-shaking, as above, in the morning, is also the best treatment for these, as well as for the Grape Curculio.

The Thrip, a small, three-cornered, whitish insect, has sometimes become very troublesome, as they eat the under side of the leaves of some varieties, especially of the *æstivalis* class, when the leaf will show rusty specks on the surface, and eventually drop. Carrying lighted torches through the vineyard at night, and beating the vines to disturb them, is one of the best remedies, as they will fly into the flames. They are a great annoyance and should be destroyed in time, before they get too numerous, as they will defoliate whole vineyards. It is strange that they have almost entirely disappeared in our Missouri vineyards, where they were so numerous formerly, and are now very annoying in the vineyards on Crooked Lake, New York, where I saw them in great abundance.

The Aphis, or Plant Louse, covers the young shoots of the vines occasionally, sucking their juice. The best remedy is taking off the shoot, and crushing them under foot.

The Grape-vine Sphinx is a large, green worm, with black dots. It is very voracious, but can easily be found and destroyed. The worms do a great deal of mischief, but fortunately are not very numerous. The best remedy against them, and all other caterpillars, is hand picking.

The Rocky Mountain Locust, or Grasshopper, as it is generally called, is one of the most destructive insects in those districts invaded by it. and ruined the crops of nearly two seasons in some sections in 1875. Fortunately its range is very limited, and it appears but rarely. But when once it gets into a vineyard, not a green leaf or shoot is left, and if this occurs as late as the first of

6

June, it stunts the vines for the next season. One of the best remedies is to dig a trench 2 to 3 feet wide, at the side of the vineyard from which they are expected, into which they will tumble, and they should then be crushed by dragging a log or roller along the ditch. If this is done repeatedly they may be kept out.

Wasps and bees are sometimes very troublesome when the fruit ripens, wounding the berries and sucking the juice. A great many can be caught by hanging up bottles with a little molasses, into which they will readily crawl and seal their fate. But while there are many injurious insects, we may also count some of them among our best friends, which will greatly assist in destroying the others, and which we should hold in grateful remembrance. Among these is the little Lady Bug, the small red or yellow and black beetle, which is always on the lookout and very active in destroying the Aphis and White Thrip. These should be fostered, and not destroyed, as is done by many ignorant persons. The Mantis, the Rear Horse, or Devil's Horse, as it is often called, but the correct name of which is Camel Cricket, is the friend of the vine grower. It destroys countless numbers of injurious insects, especially the native grasshoppers and katydids, which are so apt to cut off the bunches just before ripening. They and their eggs, which are often found on the vines glued together in a mass, like a rather square cocoon, should be carefully preserved, and even colonized. We place our common toad among our friends, as it is a great destroyer of noxious insects, and always on the hunt for bugs of all kinds. The toads and our common active little lizards should be treated with kindness by us, not killed, as they are by many unthinking people who have a mistaken idea that they are injurious and poisonous.

CHAPTER XVIII.

FROSTS—WINTER PROTECTION.

Our winters are rarely so severe as to injure or kill the hardiest varieties, such as Concord and Gœthe, although the winters of 1863, 1872, 1874, and 1878, may be cited as instances when even these and Norton's were injured. They often, however, harm the Herbemont, Cunningham, and Lenoir. These can be protected by bending the vines down in the fall, and covering them with earth thrown on with the plow. To prepare them for this, prune as soon as the wood is fully ripe, and after a rain, when the canes bend easily, go through, and while one man bends the canes down along the trellis, let the other throw a few spadefuls of earth upon them, to keep them down. Then follow with the plow, and they can be easily covered. But do not take them up in spring until danger of frost is over, for they will become more tender by being under ground all winter, and even a moderate frost will injure the buds. In taking up, run a fork under them and lift them out. They should not be covered too deep, a light protection is enough ; but to merely bend them down without covering, as some advise, is worse than leaving them on the trellis, as they are more easily injured here, where we do not often have snow to cover them. All hardy varieties should be cut loose in fall, as when the wind can sway them about they are not so apt to be injured. One of the surest preventives of injury by frost is, however, to plant none but the hardiest varieties. None of the *cordifolia* class, as far as I know, have ever suffered, and here again the Elvira stands pre-eminent, as not a bud was hurt, even during the hard winters of 1872–'74 and, '78.

But while we have methods to protect even the most tender in winter, by a little extra labor, I know of no generally effective means of protection against early frosts in fall and late frosts in spring. We should, therefore, avoid all locations subject to these, which are generally those near small streams, creeks, and rivulets, while locations on the large rivers, and on the high table lands, are generally free from them, and have, in fact, a season of a month earlier in spring, and a month later in fall, free from frosts. This is certainly very important to the grape-grower, and he should look to it closely before choosing his location. It is sad and disheartening to see the fair promise of early spring browned, wilted, and blighted by a single night's frost. But if it does occur, as it sometimes will, even in the best locations, do not become altogether discouraged. Every bud on the vine is, in fact, a triple one. The main fruit bud in the center will generally start first, and if this is destroyed, the two secondary buds will often push, and although they will not produce so many or as large bunches, will often yield a pretty fair crop.

But the vines are threatened with the same danger in fall in these unfavorable locations ; to have one's grapes and the still growing canes withered by an early frost in fall, when just ripening, and fit for nothing but vinegar, is a sad disappointment. Therefore look well to this, and do not select an unfavorable location, when there is an abundance of the best to be had.

CHAPTER XIX.

GIRDLING, THINNING, AND MISCELLANEOUS MATTERS.

The method of girdling appears to have been invented by Col. Buchatt, of Metz, in 1745. He claimed for it that it would also greatly improve the quality of the fruit, as well as hasten its maturity. It cannot be denied that it accomplishes the latter ; it also seems to increase the size of the berries, but I hardly think the fruit compares in flavor with that ripened in a natural way. But it may be of practical benefit to those who wish to grow the fruit for early market, as it will enable them to supply their customers a week earlier, and also make the fruit look better. I will, therefore, describe it briefly. It can be done either on the wood of last year's growth, or upon the bearing shoot itself ; but in any case only upon such as can be spared at next fall pruning. If you desire to affect the fruit of a whole cane, or arm, cut away a ring of bark by passing your knife all around it, and make another circle about half an inch above the first, taking out the ring of bark between them. It should be done immediately after the fruit is set. The bunches of fruit above the incision will become larger, and the fruit ripen and color finely about a week before the fruit on the other canes. If a single shoot only is to be affected, make the ring just above its base. Of course, neither cane nor shoot, thus girdled, can be used for bearing next season, and must be cut away. About the same result is obtained by twisting a wire tightly around the vine and thus arresting the flow of sap downwards, which then develops the fruit much faster.

Ripening can also be hastened by planting against the south side of a wall or board fence, where the reflection of the rays of the sun will create a greater degree of warmth.

But nothing is more absurd than the practice of some, who will take away the leaves from the fruit, to hasten maturity. The leaves are the lungs of the plant, the conductors and elaborators of sap, and nothing can be more injurious than to take them away at the very time when most needed. The natural consequence is the withering and wilting of the bunches, and should they ripen at all, they will be flat and deficient in sugar and flavor. The injurious " cutting in " of the young growth late in August, already referred to, is about of a piece with this folly, and will not only be detrimental to the fruit, but also to the ripening of the wood for next year. While all crowding of the young growth with the bearing canes should be avoided, to give free circulation of air, yet the leafy canopy of the young canes over the top of the trellis, will be in the highest degree beneficial to the ripening of the fruit. There is nothing more pleasing to the eye than a vineyard in September, with its wealth of dark-green foliage, and the rich clusters of the fruit beneath, coyly peeping from under their leafy covering. Good fruit will only ripen in partial shade, and such grapes will have a rich bloom and color, as well as a thin skin and a rich flavor, which those hanging in the scorching rays of the sun can never attain.

THINNING THE FRUIT.

It will sometimes be necessary to thin the fruit, in order to more thoroughly develop the remaining bunches. The best thinning is the reduction of bunches and bearing shoots, at the first summer-pruning, and which has already been mentioned. Let the vine dresser always remember that one fine bunch is worth more than two or three small, badly grown ones and, therefore, take away all the small, imperfect bunches and weak shoots. If the number of bunches on each fruit-bearing branch is reduced to two, it will do no injury, but make them so much more heavy and perfect. Thinning of the berries with a small pair of scissors, often resorted to with grapes grown under glass, is a very laborious process to follow in vineyard culture; though it will certainly make the remaining berries more perfect, it will hardly be generally adopted.

RENEWING OLD VINES.

Should a vineyard become old and feeble, it can be renewed by layering. To prepare for this, prune all the old wood from the vines, leaving but the thriftiest young cane, then dig a trench from the vine along the trellis, say 3 feet long and 10 inches deep, cut off the surface roots of the vine and bend it down into the trench, fastening with a hook, and let about three buds of the young cane come out above the ground, at the end of the trench. Then fill up with well pulverized soil. The vine will make roots at every joint, become vigorous and young again. Of course a season's crop will be lost, but the vine will amply repay for it the season following.

A FEW NECESSARY IMPLEMENTS.

PRUNING SHEARS.—These are very handy, as with them the work can be done quicker and easier than with

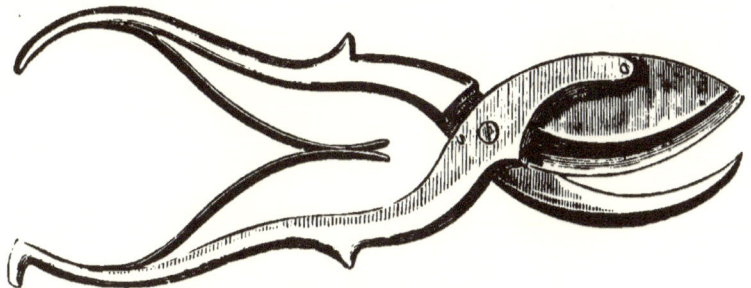

Fig. 12.—PRUNING SHEARS.

a knife, and but a slight pressure of the hand will cut a strong vine. Figure 12 gives the shape of one for heavy pruning. They are now made by several establish-

ments, and can be had at nearly all good hardware stores.
The springs should be of brass, as steel springs are apt to
break.   A much lighter and smaller kind, with but one
spring, is very convenient for gathering grapes, clipping
out unripe or imperfect berries, and also in making cuttings.   Shears will cut the stem easily and smoothly, without jarring the vine, and are much superior to a knife.
No one who has tried them will want to use a knife again.

PRUNING SAWS.—These are sometimes necessary to
cut out old, diseased stumps, although if a vine is well
managed this will seldom be necessary.   Figure 13 shows

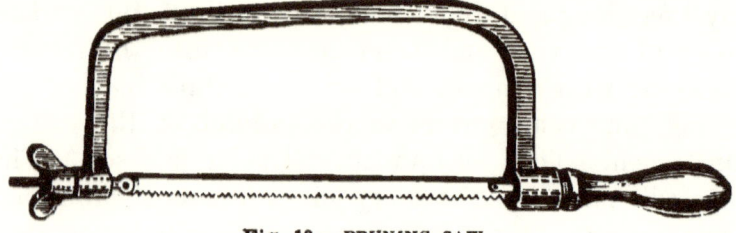

Fig. 13.—PRUNING SAW.

a kind very convenient for the purpose, as also for orchard
pruning.   The bow is of steel, the blade narrow, and so
connected with the wooden handle, that it can be turned
in any direction, and can be tightened by a screw and
nut above.

PART II.

EXPERIENCES OF OTHER GROWERS.

INTRODUCTORY.

The following is the result of correspondence with prominent grape growers of other States—men of high standing and large experience in viticulture. It brings down the record to more than ten years later than that of the first edition of this work. Many of my co-laborers in the early days of viticulture have passed away—men who have been an honor to the craft, such as Longworth, Buchanan, Bateham, Wilder, Barry, Muench, Eikel, Dresel and Burr.

To all who have aided by their contributions, I tender my hearty thanks—I shall ever hold them in grateful remembrance.

GEORGE HUSMANN.

CHAPTER XX.

GRAPE GROWING IN CENTRAL OHIO.

GEORGE W. CAMPBELL.

What I have to put on record in regard to this topic will be founded mainly upon my own experience, in this, a locality which is not specially adapted to grape growing. Frosts late in the spring often injure and sometimes destroy the grape crop, about the time of blooming, while early autumn frosts render the cultivation of late ripening sorts unprofitable. I have not been able to ripen the Catawba in full, open exposure in thirty years, so my experience, it will be seen, has not been with late ripening sorts.

A few words as to the behavior and character sustained during the past twelve years by those mentioned in your former edition, may not be without value to those wishing to plant in localities similar to mine.

The LADY grape has fairly sustained its character, is hardy, healthy, productive, and still among the best early ripening white Concord seedlings. It ripens here from the middle to the last of August, about ten days earlier than Concord. In quality is good, color a light greenish yellow, skin thin, pulp tender, seeds few and small, flavor rich, sweet and slightly vinous. Berries a shade larger than Concord, clusters smaller. Desirable for near-by markets.

MARTHA has measurably given place to newer and better varieties.

WORDEN has steadily increased in favor as a popular grape. In many places it is regarded as superior to Concord in size and quality, and equal in health and productiveness. In habit of growth and appearance it strongly resembles Concord, but it ripens from ten to fourteen days earlier. Its greatest fault is its thin and tender skin, which breaks easily and makes it a poor shipping grape.

MOORE'S EARLY has grown in public favor as a good, early ripening black grape of the Concord type. The vine is hardy, healthy and vigorous, a good and regular bearer, and sufficiently productive. It ripens two weeks earlier than the Concord. It is largely planted in the Northern and Middle States.

CONCORD still holds the position of being the most popular and most extensively planted variety.

BRIGHTON has deservedly maintained a fair degree of popularity. Under favorable circumstances its growth is very vigorous and its foliage healthy, clusters large and quality very fine. It requires winter protection here, being not quite hardy. The blossoms are somewhat imperfect, and the clusters are likely to be loose and uneven if cool, rainy weather prevails at the time of blooming. It is medium as to time of ripening.

PURITY, I regret to say, has not fulfilled its early promise. I still grow it to some extent, but its small clusters and the great difficulty in propagating it render it unprofitable. Its quality is very fine and it is among the earliest to ripen.

DELAWARE still holds its place among the best and finest flavored of all our American grapes. Mildew of the foliage and a tendency to overbear prevent its success in some localities. The former is being prevented by spraying with Bordeaux mixture and other fungicides, and the area of its successful cultivation is thus being extended. Its high character will probably always make the Delaware a favorite for the amateur as well as profitable for market and wines.

ELVIRA does not seem to have fulfilled the expectations of its introducers. It is not good enough for the table and it has not attained sufficient popularity as a wine grape to render its cultivation desirable or profitable.

NIAGARA was introduced with extraordinary claims and under close restrictions and at very high prices, but it has not sustained the high character claimed for it by its introducers, though it retains considerable popularity and is profitably grown in some localities. The vine is very vigorous and productive, clusters and berries large and handsome, and quality, when fully ripened, fairly good—quite acceptable as a market variety. It is not uniformly hardy in this section without winter protection or in most places north of 40° of latitude, and it has seemed more inclined to rot than most other kinds. It is reported as profitable in some parts of the South.

POCKLINGTON, which was introduced about the same time as Niagara, has attained considerable popularity and is being quite largely planted. It is a good, showy, white, medium late, market grape. The vine is among the hardiest and most productive of the so-called white Concord seedlings. Its clusters and berries are among the largest, and when well grown and well ripened, are quite acceptable in quality. By reason of its hardiness, it can be planted over a much larger territory than the Niagara.

PRENTISS proved, upon extensive trial, to be a failure in most places, and is now little planted or called for. A single vine on a south wall sometimes gives me a few handsome clusters of fine grapes, but it is generally unproductive.

LADY WASHINGTON has never achieved general popularity and is little grown, except by amateurs. Judging from my own experience, it is quite unreliable.

JEFFERSON has many good qualities, but is not quite hardy in severe winters and is too late in spring, for most localities. It is a good grower, with healthy foliage, blossoms perfect, clusters large and handsome, often double shouldered, very fine in quality, pure flavored, resembling Iona in its best condition. It sets more fruit than it can mature, and to produce best results a portion must be removed. By this means, a vine on a stone wall with an eastern exposure gives me an annual crop of fine grapes. It has been, with me, more reliable than Iona, either on the wall or in open exposure.

Among the more important later introductions tested here since the publication of your first edition are the following:

EMPIRE STATE, which was originated by J. H. Ricketts of Newburgh, N. Y., and highly commended in its introduction, has not proved generally successful. It is a white grape, handsome and of good quality when well ripened. It has a tendency to overbear, or the inability to carry a fair crop to maturity. It is a good grower, with an abundant and healthy foliage, large clusters, berries medium, seeds few and small, with a flavor suggestive of the Muscats or Frontignans. Its originator claims it to be a cross between Hartford and Clinton, but I am inclined to the opinion that it is a cross or hybrid, with too much of the foreign element in its composition.

ULSTER (Ulster Prolific), originated by the late A. J. Caywood, has many good qualities and will probably attain a fair position among desirable varieties for general use. The vine appears hardy and productive, of good foliage, and is a moderate grower. The berries are medium to large, with color like Catawba and a somewhat similar flavor; medium early in ripening, and a good keeper after being gathered.

NECTAR, another of Mr. Caywood's grapes, which is said to be a seedling of Delaware and which was at first called Black Delaware, seems a promising variety. The vine is healthy, hardy and productive; a vigorous grower; berries and clusters medium large and well formed; flavor pure, sprightly, sweet and good. If it does as well elsewhere as here, it will prove a valuable grape for general use.

WITT, named for its originator, the late Michael Witt of Columbus, Ohio, is among the best of the white Concord seedlings. It has proven fully as hardy and healthy as the Concord, not quite as vigorous in growth, but quite productive. Berries large, oval; skin rather thin; seeds few and small; clusters medium to large; pulp tender; flavor rich, sweet, sprightly; quality good to very good. Ripens early—a little later than Lady. It is difficult to propagate and is of slow growth until established.

COLERAIN is another white Concord seedling, originating at Colerain, Ohio. The vine is healthy and vigorous, fairly productive; clusters of medium size, early and of fine quality.

DUCHESS has not proved generally useful, though it is prized in places where it can be successfully grown. Here it is not hardy and is especially liable to mildew and rot.

GREEN MOUNTAIN, from Vermont, is a recent introduction, promising to be valuable as one of the earliest ripening grapes of fine quality. Vine is moderately vigorous and hardy. Cluster and berry medium, color light green, quality fine. A grape known in some sections as Winchell is said to be the same variety.

MOORE'S DIAMOND, originated by Jacob Moore of Brighton, N. Y., highly commended generally, with me has been too unproductive for profitable planting. It seems as hardy as the Rogers' Hybrids or the Niagara, with good foliage.

WOODRUFF RED is a large and attractive grape of the Labrusca type and is said to be a Concord seedling. It

originated at Ann Arbor, Mich., and has attained popularity as a market grape. The vine is vigorous, hardy,
healthy and very productive. Though not of high quality, it is generally acceptable and may fairly claim a
place among standard varieties.

EATON, probably another Concord, or perhaps an Isabella seedling, a very large and showy black grape, much
like the old Union Village, is now under trial. I do not
think it is a new variety, for I had it, or its double, in
my garden for some twenty years, and never regarded it
worthy of introduction. The vine and foliage are like
an exaggerated Concord, and the fruit also. In quality
it is not equal to Concord, and it is later. It is fairly
productive and may prove a profitable market grape.

VERGENNES has been favorably received and is a
handsome red grape of good quality, ripening a little
after Concord and keeping well after gathering.

MOYER, which originated in Canada, is a small red
grape, resembling Delaware, but with healthier foliage.
Moderately productive. In quality it is good, not equal
to Delaware.

JEWEL is a small black grape, originated by John
Burr of Kansas. It has too many imperfect clusters to
be valuable.

EARLY OHIO is a black grape of recent introduction.
As I have seen it, it appears to be inferior in quality,
and probably no earlier than the Champion.

Within the past few years I have received, through
the courtesy of Prof. T. V. Munson of Texas, some very
interesting specimens of the results he has already
achieved by growing seedlings from a great variety of
grapes, crossed both naturally and artificially. I have
found the grapes he has sent me, as a rule, of great excellence and beauty. I have grown but few of them
and fruited but one long enough to say anything posi-
tive. This is one he has named Brilliant. The vine is

a strong grower; foliage large and healthy, not subject to mildew; hardy here when exposed to 10° below zero. Cluster and berry of medium size, compact, handsome, of quite dark, brilliant red color; quality nearly equaling Delaware. I regard it as a grape of great promise.

Of my own comparatively small efforts, I wish to say very little. Though I have been, for more than thirty years, growing crosses between our native and foreign grapes, re-crossing and combining, wherever the indications pointed to the results for which I was striving, and though my disappointments have been many, the pursuit has been interesting, and I believe I have learned something as to the probabilities, as well as possibilities, of success through the agencies which nature yields only to him who carefully studies, and works in harmony with her laws. My later efforts have been directed toward the production of a grape that shall have all the good points of the Concord, or Worden, combined with better keeping and shipping qualities. This would require a more tenacious skin, and a little more firmness of flesh, forming a berry not easily broken by ordinary handling. Earlier ripening, especially if accompanied by better keeping qualities, would be for many sections most desirable. Vigor of growth, abundant productiveness, hardiness against severe winters, health of foliage, resisting of mildew under all ordinary circumstances— would also be indispensable. If the clusters and berries could be larger and more perfectly formed, and the quality higher and better, the combination would be still nearer to the "perfect grape." I am now willing to say that, after five years bearing, I believe I have accomplished very nearly, if not quite, the hoped-for result, and that I may reasonably expect to offer a grape of the Labrusca type, with the sanction of my own name and approval, which will be of acknowledged worth and value, wherever

7

the vine and its noble fruit are prized by the horticultur-
ists of our Union.

A word as to the value of the discoveries, by scientific
men, of remedies against the encroachments of fungous
diseases and insect enemies, which have in so many places
injured or destroyed our grapes and other cultivated
fruits. That the timely and persistent application of
the Bordeaux mixture, "*Eau Celeste*," and kindred
remedies now easily attainable, will effectively prevent
the attacks of the greatest enemies the grape grower has
to contend with, there can be no doubt. And I believe
that through their use, many of the finer varieties can
be perfectly and successfully grown in many sections
where it has been heretofore impossible.

I do not think that vines in this section are as liable
to mildew of foliage and rotting, as in many other
places ; for I have always been able, by early applications
of sulphur and quicklime mixed in about equal parts,
and blown upon the foliage with an ordinary sulphuring
bellows, to prevent any serious injury from either. And
I have found this remedy, used as a preventive, very
nearly as effective as the later and more popular sulphate
of copper mixtures.

CHAPTER XXI.

THE GRAPE-GROWING DISTRICT OF CENTRAL NEW YORK.

D. BAUDER, SECRETARY AND TREASURER PLEASANT VALLEY WINE COMPANY.

This comprises what is locally known as the Lake Keuka district, with about ten thousand acres; Canandaigua lake, including Naples, five thousand acres; and Seneca lake, five thousand acres. The average yield is estimated at one ton of grapes per acre. The disposition for the crop of 1893 was in the aggregate about as follows: Fourteen thousand tons shipped for table use; two thousand tons to wine makers in other places; and four thousand tons made into wine by local wine makers. Two hundred thousand gallons of this wine were made into champagne, producing about one million bottles. The largest makers were the Pleasant Valley Wine Company, next the Urbana Wine Company, and a few others of less importance. The champagne is made by the long or French process.

The varieties grown and in quantity in the order named are Concord, Catawba, Delaware, Isabella, Clinton, Ives, Diana, Elvira, Iona, Eumelan, Niagara, Norton, Moore's Diamond, and many others in small quantities. A large percentage of the finer kinds, such as Delaware, Iona, Elvira, Eumelan and Isabella, form the basis for the champagne cuveé; Concord and Catawba are for table, and the balance for still wines.

Prior to 1889 there had been but two seasons that the crop was materially impaired by any disease or insect. The season of 1889, being very wet, especially in June, developed mildew or brown rot quite generally, and in some places to an alarming extent, with a sprinkling of black rot; and later came powdery mildew. Ordinary mildew, brown and black rot are too well understood to need any comment or description. Powdery mildew does not entirely destroy either foliage or fruit, but impairs growth and ripening. Henry O. Fairchild, a prominent grower, made the first experiment with what is known as the Bordeaux mixture, for the above-mentioned disease, and met with gratifying success. Other growers soon followed and last year spraying with this mixture became almost universal, and the result was an average full crop.

This mixture is applied in the form of a spray made by a peculiarly constructed nozzle under pressure. Large and comparatively level vineyards use horse power, others hand pump—"knapsack sprayer." The first spraying is done when the shoots are from six to eight inches long, again immediately after blossoming, and later as deemed necessary. It should be done carefully and all parts of the vine covered. The mixture forms a thin covering, on which the spores make no impression and die. The mixture consists of eight pounds of sulphate of copper, six pounds of unslaked lime and forty-five to fifty gallons of water. Many who cultivate table grapes, for the late spraying substitute two quarts of aqua ammonia in place of the lime, as this solution does not stain the fruit. There is also a slight sprinkling of anthracnose, usually found at or near the mouth of gullies, which are numerous on the shores of all Central New York lakes, and where the surface is quite wet. Up to this time its ravages have been slight; the Bordeaux mixture seems to check it materially.

Of insects we have but few; while we have phylloxera, yet the severe winters keep it in check, and no perceptible damage has been noticeable. The thrip, a small white fly, did some damage to the foliage of Delawares and Isabellas, and less upon the Catawba; it has almost disappeared since the vines have been sprayed. The steel beetle is the worst insect we have ; it attacks the buds early in the spring, by boring a small hole, and eats out the heart. This little insect does its greatest damage in vineyards adjoining woods or uncultivated fields. The only remedy that has proved effective is daubing the buds with a solution of Paris green thickened somewhat with flour ; this covers the bud with a thin, varnish-like substance, and the little fellow gets sick before he can do much damage.

The estimate of one ton per acre embraces good, bad and indifferent vineyards. A well-cultivated vineyard in a good location will yield from three to five tons of Concords, two to three tons of Catawbas, one and a half to two tons of Delawares. and so on.

CHAPTER XXII.

GRAPE GROWING IN THE HUDSON RIVER VALLEY.

WILLIAM D. BARNS.

The early settlers of this region found the grape growing wild, and transplanted some of the better kinds to their gardens, where they ministered to their wants. No special progress was noted until 1816, when William Prince, of Long Island, brought the Isabella grape from the South and propagated it, soon after which it became rapidly disseminated in this region. A few years later the Catawba was introduced. In 1823 the first attempt was made to record the merits of native grapes for cultivation. In 1846 J. J. Thomas, in his "Fruit Culturist," mentioned only six "American hardy varieties." Excepting the Isabella and Catawba, none of them are grown for market now. Their enormous crops and excellent quality made them popular, and ere long nearly every residence had its grapevine. In 1853 the Concord was brought to public notice, and almost immediately found favor. Other varieties were produced from chance seedlings and by hybridization, until now specimens of probably three hundred varieties may be found in cultivation in this valley. The number considered profitable to grow for market is comparatively small and at the present time does not exceed twenty.

The introduction of the Concord in 1853 gave a great impetus to grape growing. Its beauty, hardiness, vigor, productiveness and quality commended it to the grape growers of this region; it soon took a leading place among vineyardists, and is now produced in larger quantities than all the other varieties combined. The Delaware, from its superior quality, and the high price it commanded, was a favorite with many, and is still largely grown for market. The Diana, in spite of its excellent keeping quality and beautiful appearance, because of its lateness in ripening has been discarded.

As the Rebecca could not be profitably grown on the west side of the river, cultivators were anxious to find a hardy white grape for market. The Martha was the first to be introduced that seemed to fill the bill. This variety is still grown to a considerable extent, although the Niagara and Pocklington, from their superior appearance, are more prized and have been much more largely grown in late years. Moore's Diamond, being earlier than either, and quite as attractive in appearance as well as of better quality, finds much favor. But since its introduction the market demands seem to be more for dark colored than light grapes. The Duchess is a showy grape of very superior quality, but lacks hardiness, and its cultivation for market has been nearly abandoned.

At present Concord, Champion, Cottage, Brighton, Bacchus, Delaware, Elvira, Empire State, Hartford, Moore's Early, Martha, Niagara, Pocklington, Duchess, Worden, Wyoming, Red and Ulster comprise nearly all the varieties that are grown for market.

TRAINING THE VINE.

When grape growing was commenced in this region, there was no established method of training the vine. The single or half dozen vines that had been grown for family use were trained to the side of a building or over a large arbor. For field culture the need of a different system was imperative. Some tried the European plan of short pruning and training to a single stake. The difference in the habit of the native and foreign vine made this method impracticable. Most growers used numerous stakes set in the row of vines. When the nature and requirements of the vine were carefully studied and this method of training skillfully done, it produced good results. Fuller's "Grape Culturist" in 1864 called attention to his modification of the European plan, which still carries his name. This, however, was followed in but few vineyards, as the Kniffin system, which had been introduced ten years before, was given the preference.

THE KNIFFIN SYSTEM was originated and practiced by one of the pioneers of grape growing in the Hudson River valley. William Kniffin of Clintondale, after much consideration, adopted the system of training the vine to two wires suspended and stretched, the one about three and a half, the other about six feet from the ground. A single main stalk is grown from the ground to the upper wire. All buds or branches are broken from this except four, the growth from which is trained to grow along the wires. Usually two are left just below each wire, and as each shoot grows it is loosely fastened to the wire, one in each direction from the main stalk, forming four arms. The next year each of these arms is to be cut back to from four to eight buds, according to the vigor of the vine. These shortened arms are to be firmly tied to the wire, and shoots springing from each bud encouraged to hang down with their clusters of growing grapes.

This system of training the vine is believed to be the most economical, and one of the most successful known. It is almost universally used in the Hudson River valley. Its methods and merits are being studied, and it is being adopted in other sections of the State.

MODIFICATIONS OF THE KNIFFIN SYSTEM.—One of these is—*The Trunk System*, where two stalks are grown from root, and two arms trained from the one to the lower, and from the other to the upper wire.

The Umbrella Training,—where the trunk is tied to each wire, and two arms with nine to fifteen buds each are left at the upper wire, and none suffered to grow at the lower one ; these long arms are, near their base, fastened to the upper wire and then bent down and the top fastened to the lower wire. This method finds considerable favor.

The Overhead or Arbor Kniffin is another popular modification of this system. The overhead arbor is formed by spiking cross-bars three feet in length at right angles to the row, to posts set in the row of vines, about six feet from the ground. Three wires are stretched the length of the row, and fastened equidistant on these cross-bars. The vine is trained without branches to the center wire, and six arms are trained, one in each direction on each wire. This method allows working both ways with a horse, and the fruit hangs below the foliage, and when ripening, becomes more perfectly covered with bloom, it is claimed, than when grown by any other system of training.

The Cross-Wire System has small posts set by each vine ; a single wire runs from post to post in each direction six and a half feet from the ground. The trunk of the vine is tied to the post, and four arms are trained, one along each wire. Lighter posts are required by this system than any other, but the posts at the ends of the rows have to be braced or anchored. It admits working each way with a horse. This system is of recent introduction, and possesses considerable merit.

DISEASES AND INSECTS.

The remarkable health, vigor and productiveness of the vine led cultivators to believe that the various diseases which had made grape growing unprofitable in so many other localities would find no place here. Even when reports of the ravages of black rot in New Jersey reached us, cultivators of large experience, like the late A. J. Caywood, believed that our favorable surroundings would prevent the disease from causing serious injury here.

Others believed every precaution to prevent its introduction and spread should be taken, and kept themselves fully informed of the investigations and experiments made by the direction of the Commissioner of Agriculture. Before the black rot made its appearance here, several persons had experimented with the Bordeaux mixture as a preventive of mildew, and reported results to the United States Department of Agriculture.

In the year 1887 black rot appeared to considerable extent in some vineyards in the town of Gardner, Ulster Co. The next year the crop of these vineyards was nearly destroyed. In 1889 the disease made its appearance in nearly every part of the valley of the Hudson. With the inadequate facilities then possessed for spraying, many vineyards had small blocks of vines sprayed or sprinkled with the Bordeaux mixture. The results were uniformly encouraging.

During the winter of 1889 the subject of black rot and its prevention by spraying was discussed by the press, in fruit growers' associations, and elsewhere. All who had experimented the previous year urged all grape growers to procure suitable outfits and spray thoroughly the coming year. The few who did were richly paid, as they saved nearly their entire crop, while those who did not, lost from ten to ninety per cent.

The experience of 1890 fully demonstrated the value of the practice as a preventive of both black rot and mildew. One large grower claimed the operation saved him one hundred tons of grapes. Instances were common where adjoining vineyards showed nearly complete destruction by black rot in the unsprayed, and a perfect crop where the vines had been sprayed. The foliage of Delaware vines, where sprayed, was as healthy and clean till frost came, as that of Concords.

The fact that applications of copper salts will prevent other forms of fungus than black rot, makes the growing to perfection of many delicate hybrid grapes possible. During a season of frequent heavy rains the successful treatment of a vineyard is expensive, and in some cases almost impossible.

Anthracnose has made its appearance in many vineyards, but while affecting the vitality of the vine more seriously than does black rot, it does not spread so rapidly. It yields to an application of a saturated solution of sulphate of iron to the trunk and arms of the vine before the buds swell in the spring.

But few vineyards are damaged by phylloxera. In some sections the steel beetle is destructive by eating into and destroying the opening bud. Spraying with Paris green is done for the destruction of this pest. The rose bug, by eating the blossom and embryo grape, is occasionally very destructive. Hand picking, and jarring the insect into a basin of kerosene, in the cool of the

morning, are the rather unsatisfactory methods adopted
for its destruction.

Occasionally the grape-leaf hopper, more commonly
known as thrips, appears in such numbers as to defoliate
a vineyard and inflict great injury. When the wind
blows across the rows of vines, on a hot day, millions of
these may be entrapped by tacking a large sheet of
heavy paper, smeared with tar, to a light frame carried
on the leeward side of the row, and suddenly jarring
the vine. The insects rise in a cloud and are carried by
the wind against the soft tar.

These named comprise the fungous diseases and
insect pests that are most prevalent in this region.
On the whole, the health and productiveness of the
vine are probably equal to that in any other grape-
growing section.

SEASON AND METHOD OF MARKETING.

From the location and environment of this region, the
crop of grapes ripens earlier in it than in any other section of the State. The market requires a good table
grape. Hitherto the earlier in the season it could be
furnished the higher the price realized. For nearly
twenty years the Champion has been the earliest variety
that was marketable. Though prolific and handsome,
the quality is poor, and growers have earnestly sought a
kind possessing its merits and of better quality. Moore's
Early comes nearest to taking its place. Unfortunately,
this variety does not seem adapted to all locations, and
in some places is a shy bearer.

The high price paid for early grapes has tempted
many growers to ship grapes before they were fully ripe.
This always has a depressing effect on the market.
Now, profiting by experience, most shippers are careful
as to the quality as well as the appearance of their fruit
when placed in the market.

New York receives the bulk of the crop grown in this region. Large shipments are made to Philadelphia, Boston, Buffalo, Baltimore, Washington and intermediate places. Early in the history of this industry, the crates made for carrying strawberries and raspberries were used for shipping grapes. New York being a great distributing point, buyers for shipping to other places were seriously incommoded by the necessity of returning the crates. To obviate this difficulty, baskets holding five or ten pounds of grapes were introduced, and soon came into quite general use. But as the supply of fruit increased, and prices became lower, the cost of carting from boat or car to the stores was felt to be a serious handicap to the business. Then a cheap crate—non-returnable—found favor. At this time crates containing eight light tills, and holding forty pounds of grapes when filled, are generally used.

GIRDLING THE VINE.

According to Prof. L. H. Bailey, "girdling, or ringing various fruit trees was certainly practiced by the Romans, and the Agricultural Society of France awarded a premium to Buchatt about a century and a half ago, for a method of girdling the grapevine. * * * The first valuable experiments made with ringing the grapevine in America was begun in 1877 at the Massachusetts Agricultural College, and the practice has been employed more or less continuously since that time. * * * Girdling usually hastens maturity and increases size of the fruit; it is supposed to lessen the quality of the fruit; its effect upon the vine has not been clearly determined." Mr. John Burroughs, who resides in this grape region, says: "My opinion of the practice of girdling grapevines is, that on the whole it is poor business." * * * "If all take to girdling, where is the advantage? It is like the crowd all getting up on chairs at the show."

Girdling, to hasten the ripening of grapes for market, was commenced in the neighborhood of Highland about thirteen years ago. The operation consists in removing a ring of bark nearly an inch broad from the arm or branch of the last year's wood. The practice has continued since, and been adopted by many persons. Great discretion and care are requisite to make the operation a success. The quality of some varieties is ruined by it. Heavily loaded vines, if girdled, never ripen their fruit. Feeble growing vines are seriously injured by the operation. Grapes of delicate flavor seem to suffer most in loss of quality when the vine.is operated on. When judiciously done it has doubtless increased the net returns of the grower. But it is not probable or desirable that the practice should be universally adopted.

WINE MAKING.

The price realized for table grapes until recently kept the best quality out of the wine makers' hands, except in limited quantities.

The cause of viticulture has been materially favored by the labors of the late A. J. Caywood of Marlboro, Dr. W. A. M. Culbert of Newburg, and James H. Ricketts, formerly of Newburg and now of Washington, D. C. In this region especially has their influence been felt, while the valuable varieties originated by them are known all over the United States.

CHAPTER XXIII.

VITICULTURE IN SOUTHWEST MISSOURI.

HERMANN JAEGER, NEOSHO, MO.

When locating in Southwest Missouri, the first wild grapes to attract my attention were those of the *Lincecumii* type of *Vitis æstivalis,* popularly known as "Summer" grapes here, and "Post Oak" grapes in Texas. Many of these I selected and cultivated. Some had produced heavy loads of fruit in their wild state, blooming near staminate vines of their species, while under cultivation they proved shy bearers. Others produced well in the vineyard, and of these I still cultivate some, like Neosho, Racine, Nos. 32, 52, 13 and 43.

Nos. 13 and 43 are as large as Ives and Concord respectively, and while no better than these in quality, I valued them as extremely hardy and prolific late grapes, remaining sound where the Concord crop was entirely ruined by black rot.

Vitis rupestris is another native of the Southwest that attracted my attention, on account of the purity of its grapes and their freedom from rot and mildew. Some of these I sent to France to be tried as stocks able to resist phylloxera. Their adaptation to the thinnest, dryest and stoniest soils; their hardiness, superior to all other vines, and their easy propagation, made them very popular for grafting stocks. Even for the creation of Franco-American hybrids our French co-laborers prefer the *rupestris* to other native species, because it is free from any of the peculiar American flavors so objectionable to those who formed their taste on European grapes.

While searching for *rupestris* vines to export, I selected some with large fruit to cultivate. Even these are only similar to a currant in size of bunch and grape, and therefore can not become popular. Yet repeatedly I was glad to have these vines, covered with small bunches capable of yielding a good claret, when nearly all other grapes were destroyed by rot and mildew. Thanks to spraying with copper solutions, both black rot and mildew are now under our control, and we can do better than grow *rupestris* grapes. To create new varieties of extreme hardiness and to purify the flavor of our varieties, the infusion of *rupestris* blood will remain of prime importance.

The following I consider my best seedlings and hybrids:

Jaeger's No. 70 is a seedling of my *lincecumii* No. 43, crossed with a male vine of *Vitis rupestris*. Most hardy and productive ; black, bunch and berry as large as Ives but less compact ; it colors early and ripens ten to twelve days before Norton. When fully ripe it has some of the peculiar *lincecumii* flavor, which remains in its wine, a very dark, rich claret, much admired here for its "fruity" aroma.

Jaeger's No. 72 is of the same parentage as 70. Foliage and wood retain more of the *lincecumii* character than 70 (which resembles *rupestris* more). Grape black, with pale bloom, and of Concord size. Bunch very compact, of medium size. Ripens just before or with Norton, and, like 70, hangs long to vine. Flavor pure like *rupestris*, sweet, a fine table grape, yielding a claret of great purity and good color.

Jaeger's No. 100. A seedling of Elvira, as large as Concord in bunch and berry. Color yellow to grayish pink when very ripe. Quality and flavor similar to Catawba ; ripens with Delaware. Vine of *labrusca* character ; very hardy and productive. Uses : table and white wine. Liable to crack when ripe, like Elvira.

This No. 100 I crossed with a male *rupestris*, and also with a male vine of *rupestris* × *cinerea*. The first cross gives early and the second late grapes of extreme hardiness, fine quality and pure taste. A number of these fruited, some twice. It is too soon to select the best.

Among the first hybrids I produced over fifteen years ago are Nos. 50 and 56. They are crosses between a large Summer or Post Oak grape and the delicious, but very tender Herbemont. In quality, character of fruit and vine, they have a close family resemblance with various similar crosses evolved by Prof. T. V. Munson of Denison, Texas.

Besides being very liable to rot and mildew, I found Nos. 50 and 56 entirely too tender to stand our extreme climate, and therefore never propagated or even publicly mentioned them.

Of late years I find that spraying not only keeps them free from rot and mildew, but that likewise (preserving their foliage healthy till frost) it helps to ripen their wood a great deal better. Thus these vines, which used to suffer in our mildest winters, last January stood unprotected and unharmed a temperature of 22° below zero. Therefore I now consider Nos. 50 and 56 most valuable grapes, especially so because they mature later than Norton, are fine keepers, and may easily be made to prolong our grape season from six to eight weeks.

No. 50 is a very compact, medium-sized bunch with medium-sized grapes; black, with light bloom; as sweet and pure and sprightly as Herbemont.

No. 56 is nearly of Concord size in bunch and berry. Light Catawba color with white bloom. A sweet, pure, beautiful and delicious grape, though not having all the Herbemont sprightliness of No. 50. Both will no doubt make fine white wine. These, as well as Mr. Munson's new grapes of similar origin and hardiness, I now consider the most exquisite late varieties we can grow in the Middle and Southern States.

TREATMENT FOR MILDEW AND ROT.

An address to the Missouri State Horticultural Society.

BY HERMANN JAEGER.

Black rot and *Peronospora,* or downy mildew, have been the two most formidable foes of American grape-vines. The ravages of these microscopic mushrooms discouraged and disheartened nearly all our grape growers. The few men that kept their vineyards, came to the conclusion that profit from grape growing could not be expected, except, perhaps, with very few varieties resisting rot and mildew better than most others.

Nothing, therefore, could have pleased us better than the fact established after three years' experimenting with copper remedies, under the direction of our National Department of Agriculture;—the fact, I say, that not only mildew (as had already been proved in France), but likewise the still more fatal pest of black rot, are under our control, and can both be entirely prevented by correct spraying with Bordeaux mixture or other copper solutions. This was in 1890. Our experience in 1891 fully verified this claim. The season of 1892, with an extremely wet spring and early summer, proved that by spraying we can succeed in most unfavorable years, not only with Norton, Ives and Perkins, but with Rogers' Hybrids, Delaware, Triumph, and the long list of varieties that, even in fair seasons, used to be a mere source of disappointment.

Last summer it required from five to eight sprayings to keep our vines free from rot and mildew, while three to five applications are quite sufficient in ordinary seasons. A neighbor of ours who postponed his spraying, because the incessant rains would be sure to wash off the solution, made almost as complete a failure as another neighbor who argued spraying was useless until dry weather had set in, because "the rain would wash away

8

all rot and mildew from the fruit." Just such mistakes as these are to blame for all failures in spraying grape-vines, for wherever fruit and foliage are covered with a copper solution, the germination of the spores or seeds of the fungi causing rot and mildew is impossible. But just as impossible it is for any spray to be of the least benefit, if applied after this germination has taken place. When by naked eye we can discover the least trace of mildew or rot, it proves that we should have commenced spraying at least ten days before.

Bordeaux mixture and the ammoniacal solution of carbonate of copper, are now almost exclusively used. For the last two years I have treated about eight acres of vines with one, and eight acres with the other solu-tion, and both with equally good success. I use a Eureka knapsack sprayer with Vermorel nozzle. In va-rious parts of my vineyards I dig holes to collect rain water, and at these holes fill the knapsack, adding the needed proportion of ammonia solution or concentrated Bordeaux mixture. Thus water carrying is reduced to a minimum. A Bordeaux mixture of one and one-half pounds of bluestone to twenty-two gallons of water is just as effective as the stronger solution formerly used. This summer I allowed the Bordeaux mixture to settle, using only the clear liquid for spraying. This avoids clogging of the nozzle, makes spraying easier, and keeps the fruit clean, without impairing the effectiveness of the spray. To the sediment water may be added again, and the bluish whitewash used for sprinkling strawber-ries, melons, potatoes, tomatoes, etc.

Finally, I claim one more benefit for spraying; it greatly improves the hardiness of our vines. Ability to resist low temperature mostly depends on the perfect ripening of the wood. The fruit, canes and buds can only ripen while the foliage is sound. Well-sprayed vines keep their leaves perfect till killed by a hard frost, and thus reach the highest possible degree of hardiness. On the 19th of last January the thermometer at the United States fish hatchery at Neosho, fell to 22° below zero. This was sufficient to kill nearly all the fruit buds on unsprayed Norton or Cynthiana vines, while all those that had been well sprayed the summer before, brought a fine crop. I mention the Norton because it is perhaps less affected by mildew than any other vine. Varieties subject to mildew show still more clearly the benefit of spraying. European hybrids like Triumph, Campbell, Brilliant, Goethe, Carman, and many others, produced fine crops after standing last winter unprotected. Still more agreeably was I surprised to get grapes from my Nos. 50 and 56, two varieties produced about fifteen years ago by crossing the delicious, but very tender Herbemont, with one of our large wild Summer grapes (*Vitis æstivalis*, type *lincecumii*), usually called Post Oak grapes in Texas.

Nos. 50 and 56 are fine grapes and our very latest varieties, but proved too tender to be valuable, and therefore were never propagated. Now I consider them about as promising as any grapes we have, and I dare say that in quality and appearance they closely resemble the varieties Prof. T. V. Munson has originated by similar crosses.

Among that splendid list of twenty-nine new grapes, by far the finest collection ever offered in America, now being introduced by T. V. Munson of Denison, Texas, eight of the most exquisite varieties are crosses of Herbemont on wild Post Oak or Summer grapes of Texas and Southwest Missouri. Mr. Munson, with his characteristic conscientiousness, recommends these for the South only. I am glad to be able to state that four of them were tried here and have stood 22° below zero, as well as Nos. 50 and 56. It seems safe therefore, to conclude that with good spraying these Southern grapes will prove hardy enough for the latitude of Central Missouri. Mr.

Munson's other grand acquisitions will succeed far north
of Missouri. His "America," for example, is a seedling
of Jaeger's No. 70, containing the blood of our large
native summer grape crossed with *Vitis rupestris*, and
consequently surpasses in hardiness any American vine
heretofore cultivated. Mr. Munson's great work insures
an immense improvement in the quality of our grapes,
and spraying with copper solutions has made their yield
so much more certain, that we can confidently look for-
ward to a great revival of American viticulture.

CHAPTER XXIV.

VIEWS OF A VETERAN.

SAMUEL MILLER, BLUFFTON, MO.

The following are among the newer varieties of grapes
which appear to be promising in this section :

EMPIRE STATE (white).—A strong grower, bears well,
perfectly hardy. Bunch large, long; berry above medium, round, sweet, and of excellent quality.

MOORE'S DIAMOND (white).—Vine strong, hardy,
healthy and productive; bunch and berry large; when
ripe almost translucent; best quality of any white grape
we have

MILLER'S GOLDEN BEAUTY (white).—Vine all right;
bunch and berry above medium; quality good; very
handsome.

The above varieties are all the white ones I care to
grow; they fill the bill.

WOODRUFF'S RED (red) is a good grower; bunches
quite large; berries of the largest size. Very showy
and good

VERGENNES (red) has fruited just enough here to show that it is a valuable one. Bunch and berry medium.

BRIGHTON (red). A large bunch and berry, above medium. Superior quality, but the vine is not fully hardy.

THE EATON (black) has been highly spoken of as to size of bunch and berry, but the quality is said to be poor.

GARBER (black).—Hardy and productive. Bunch and berry a little below medium, of good quality, and will undoubtedly make an excellent dark-red wine. Among the earliest.

MINGO (black).—A small bunch and berry, but ripens before any other. Makes a heavy, very dark wine ; can write with the juice and it would be taken for ink.

HERO (black).—A sport of the Concord, nearly double the size and of fair quality.

There are others on trial, but as they have not fruited here I cannot say how they will do.

CHAPTER XXV.

GRAPE CULTURE IN MISSISSIPPI.

S. M. TRACY, MISSISSIPPI EXPERIMENT STATION, STARKVILLE.

Grape culture in Mississippi has been developed almost wholly within the last ten years, and is now increasing more rapidly there than is any other one branch of fruit growing. In the northeastern part of the State, from Booneville to Corinth, are many large vineyards, and in the region about Starkville, in the central part of the State, are several covering from ten to fifty acres each, while from along the Gulf coast large quantities of grapes and small amounts of wine are shipped annually. The long growing season in this State enables the vines to make fully double the amount of wood which they can make in the Northern States, or even in Missouri, and the winters are so mild that the wood is never injured by cold. The black rot, the downy mildew and the powdery mildew are almost unknown, though the "ripe grape rot" (*Melanconium fuligineum*) is often injurious to the late-ripening shipping varieties, though it does not attack the early-ripening market sorts, nor those of the *rupestris* and *lincecumii* types recently introduced by Munson. In the central part of the State, Champion and other early sorts are ready for market from July 5 to 10, while from the Coast region they may be shipped from a week to ten days earlier.

Among the more popular varieties for market are Champion, Delaware, Herbemont, Ives, Moore's Early, Niagara and Perkins. For table use Brilliant, Delaware, Gold Coin, Green Mountain, Hermann Jaeger, Moyer, Mrs. Nellie Munson and Rommell are among the more popular sorts. Wine making is a rapidly growing industry along the Gulf coast, where the Scuppernong varieties grow to perfection. At Biloxi, Bay St. Louis, and other points, several French colonies have been located and are planting the Scuppernong quite largely, and are said to be making wine of excellent quality.

The horizontal trellis has given us better satisfaction than has any other which we have ever seen, and is the one which we recommend for general use. In making it, the posts are set as for the vertical trellis, the tops are sawed off square at five feet from the ground, and a crosspiece of 2x4, two feet long, is laid on the top of each, and nailed at right angles to the direction of the row. Three No. 12 wires are stapled to these crosspieces, one directly over the post, and the others one inch from the ends of the crosspieces. The cost of material is the same as for the vertical trellis, with the addition of the crosspieces, which cost one cent each. Our reasons for preferring the horizontal trellis are, that it makes pruning much more simple and easy, that it keeps the lower part of the vine free from sprouts and branches which would interfere with cultivation, that it affords much greater protection to the growing and ripening fruit, that it holds the fruit where it can be easily reached in spraying, and that it gives partial immunity from the attacks of fungous diseases. It is a well-known fact that very few fungi can germinate excepting in the presence of moisture. With the horizontal trellis, nearly all of the fruit is found hanging below the wires, where it is protected from rain and dew by the leaves, which are almost wholly above the wires, and so the spread of disease is, to a large extent, held in check. The overshadowing leaves also protect the fruit from sun scald, from which many of the thin-skinned varieties suffer severely. Whatever style of trellis may be used, it should always run north and south, so that the fruit may be protected from the sun during the hottest hours of the day.

CHAPTER XXVI.

GRAPE CULTURE IN NEW MEXICO.

N. SPATCIER, LAS CRUCES, N. M.

An active experience in the vineyard for the past seven years has thoroughly convinced me of the paramount value of the Mission grape. It is hardy, requires less labor and attention, and is productive. Brought here by Jesuit missionaries 400 years ago (whence its name), I believe that a cutting from it to-day will produce as rank and healthy a growth as in its earliest days.

In the early days of my experience, owing to impositions and accidents in refilling vacant places in my vineyard and in enlarging it, I found vines of numerous sorts, such as Muscat of Alexandria, Rose of Peru, and others, mixed with my Missions. What at first seemed a matter of regret was later one of congratulation, for wherever the vines were mixed, there the fruit was better, with larger clusters and berries, and a larger aggregate of crop. I attribute this to the cross fertilization, the workings of which were effectively aided by my Italian honey bees, of which I keep twenty-five colonies. I would not, for $500 per annum, deprive my orchards and vineyards of the coöperation of my bees.

I practice close pruning, never leaving more than one or two buds on a spur, although three may be left if it is desired to build up a young vine. Leaving more will increase the crop for the season, but is apt to impair permanently the vitality and productiveness of the vine.

The wine-making industry is yet in its infancy here. With a proper selection of grapes, we can have the best of wine. Among these is the native early Muscatelle, which makes one of the finest and most aromatic of wines, and is especially useful for blending with other wines to add to their bouquet. The Black Burgundy grape is also an excellent kind for mixing with the Mission grape and for adding color to lighter wines from other grapes.

CHAPTER XXVII.

VITICULTURE IN SOUTHERN TEXAS.

F. M. HALBEDL, SAN ANTONIO.

Texas is just beginning to comprehend the importance and vast possibilities of viticulture within her borders. Seven years ago I contemplated a visit to California with a view to locating there, but changed my mind and traveled instead through Texas, gathering information and examining the soil. I found what I wanted along the Southern Pacific railroad, near Harwood, nine miles east of Luling, in Gonzales county. I bought land at $10 an acre and planted a vineyard and an orchard. The first year I set out 10,000 cuttings, nearly all of which took root and made luxuriant growth; since that I kept on enlarging it from year to year. The soil is partly light, partly dark, sandy loam, covered with Post oak, Black-Jack and hickory timber, and having a clay subsoil at moderate depths varying from eighteen inches to three feet.

My original intention was to raise grapes for wine, and I therefore planted chiefly Herbemont, Black Spanish, Black Eagle, Black July and Concord, all of which do well in Texas. But I soon discovered it to be more profitable to raise table grapes, and therefore imported from Newcastle, Cal., the leading California varieties for a trial. Of these I determined upon five as having given the best results during three successive years. They are the Fontainebleau, which begins to ripen about the 24th of June, and forms perfect bunches and berries free from disease; the Flaming Tokay, which makes immense bunches, and berries as large as my El Paso plums; Malaga, Black Prince and Black Morocco. I sent specimens of my Malaga to my brother-in-law, who at that time owned a fruit ranch near Newcastle, California, and he pronounced them superior to his own in compactness and flavor. I propose to raise the above-named varieties exclusively, feeling full assurance of success. I have, so far, supplied the market of San Antonio with my grapes, realizing twelve and a half cents per pound, but am confident of obtaining better prices in Northern markets when I begin to ship by the carload. The shipping season extends from June 24 to August 7, when there is no California grape in sight, while the El Paso grapes from the Rio Grande region are just beginning to come in, giving us, therefore, the best opportunities to monopolize the market. The yield of some varieties is enormous. For example, the Black Spanish (Lenoir) yielded, without irrigation, during the last two (dry) years, from 20 to 50 large bunches per vine (vines 12 feet apart and trained on three wires); next comes Herbemont, also a prolific bearer and safer than the first, being immure from all disease, while the first, in wet years, shows signs of black rot. Wet years, though, are a rarity. Of late, there have been many vineyards started in my vicinity for wine-making purposes, also around Luling and other places. In fact, throughout Central and Southwestern Texas down to Corpus Christi on the Gulf, both soil and climate are eminently adapted to viticulture, requiring no irrigation, as the rainfall during winter and part of spring is sufficient and the clay holds moisture long enough to insure the crop.

I have also made wine, which I sell at one dollar a gallon, but intend to abandon that branch except for home use. My wines are made from the pure grape juice, without the addition of sugar, water or anything else, and are almost too alcoholic for my taste. Our grapes contain much more sugar than the California grapes now sold here, which taste watery.

CHAPTER XXVIII.

ON THE RIO GRANDE.

CHARLES W. WILSON, LAREDO.

The grape industry in this section is in a comparatively early stage of development as yet, although sufficient progress has been made to establish its adaptability
to the soil, climate and seasons, and in the early ripening of the grape to give it precedence o any other
section of the United States.

The varieties mostly grown are the Muscat of Alexandria, Tokay, Black Morocco, Rose of Peru, Black Hamburg and Zinfindal. These are enumerated in the order
of the number of acres devoted to each, although the
Black Morocco is gaining in popularity as a profitable
shipping grape on account of its heavy yield. The
above-named grapes ripen in succession, from July 1 to
December 1. The Muscat is ready for market usually
about the middle of June, and some other varieties mature as early as the latter part of May.

The vines show a prodigious growth, but irrigation is
necessary to their culture, as the summers are long and
dry. The water is raised from the Rio Grande river by
steam pumps. On account of the cheapness of coal and
wood, this proves to be an economical method of handling the water. No particular diseases of the vine have
been made manifest thus far. A small fly has attacked
isolated vines in places, causing the leaf to turn brown
and present a mottled appearance. The area of vineyards at this time about Laredo is about 175 acres, and
many more acres will be planted.

The Thompson's Seedless grape has recently been introduced, but has not reached bearing age yet. Much

hope is expressed that it will prove excellently adapted
to this locality. Altogether the culture of grapes promises to occupy an extensive and profitable field in Southern Texas.

CHAPTER XXIX.

T. V. MUNSON'S NEW VARIETIES.

DENISON, TEXAS, Feb. 21, 1894.

PROF. GEO. HUSMANN.

MY DEAR SIR: In accordance with your request, I
select from among my published and tested varieties of
grapes the following, which have received the commenda-
tion from critical disinterested parties in greater degree,
perhaps, than others in my numerous collection, and give
short, accurate descriptions of them, as requested by
you. They ripen in the succession here named, the first,
Brilliant, ripening here early in July, the last in
September.

Yours truly,

T. V. MUNSON.

VARIETIES. (Flowers all perfect.)

BRILLIANT.—A seedling of Lindley pollinated with
Delaware, originated in 1883. Season of leafing out,
medium; leaf large; sheds foliage early. Flowers at
Denison, Texas, first week in May. Growth good;
healthy; attacked by downy mildew about the same as
Delaware; anthracnose none; black rot little more than
Delaware. Appears to endure cold equally with Dela-
ware, and drouth as well as Rogers' Hybrids. Inclined
to overbear; needs short pruning; cuttings root well.
Size of cluster medium to large, cylindrical, often shoul-

dered, fairly compact. Berry persistent, large, spherical; bright currant red at first, in ripening, becoming bronzy red at full maturity, with covering of white bloom. Skin thin, tough, pleasant to the taste; pulp juicy, tender; flavor very agreeable, sprightly and pure; very sweet; seeds one to three, medium. It has received high praise at the hands of critical testers at the Georgia Experiment Station, also in New Jersey, New York, Ohio, Michigan, Kentucky, Missouri, Texas, etc.

ROMMELL.—Parentage, Elvira pollinated by Triumph, originated in 1885. Season of leafing, flowering, ripening and shedding leaves a few days later than Brilliant. Leaf of medium size, coarse, sharp teeth, not lobed, of good substance. Resists mildew and rot well; growth good; short jointed; as hardy in cold and drouth as the best of Rogers'; overbears unless pruned short; cuttings root with ease. Cluster medium, cylindrical, often with shoulder half as large as main cluster; compact; very heavy, proportional to bulk. Berry persistent, round or slightly oblate, large if well grown; yellowish green when ripe, without bloom; skin very thin though tough, much less inclined to crack than Elvira and its seedlings; pulp very tender and exceedingly juicy and sprightly, with fine, pure flavor; ranking as best when well grown. Seed few, small, separating readily. It is a splendid near-by market grape, but will not endure long carriage so well as Brilliant. Very promising for a delicate, white, light table wine.

AMERICA.—A seedling of H. Jaeger's No. 70 (now named T. V. Munson), which is Mr. Jaeger's best hybrid of *V. lincecumii* with *V. rupestris*, both natives of Southwest Missouri. Produced in 1885. Leafs out and flowers late, and holds foliage late; ripens fruit about with Concord; growth vigorous; neither mildew nor rot yet observed on leaf or fruit. Endures severe and sudden cold with impunity, and heat and drouth well;

fully resistant to phylloxera; prolific; joints of medium length; cuttings grow with great ease. Cluster medium to large, conical, compact enough, but not crowded; berry persistent, round, medium to large, jet black; skin thin, delicate, yet not inclined to crack; pulp tender, juicy, pure, with characteristic flavor, and exceeding rich in violet coloring matter; rich in wine properties. Hangs on well, and finally dries into a fair black raisin. Seeds three to five, small, slender. For a very dark red wine, this grape appears to have great possibilities.

R. W. Munson.—Hybrid; mother a very large-berried *V. lincecumii*, of Grayson County, Texas. Pollinated with Triumph, originated in 1887. Leafs out, flowers, ripens fruit and sheds leaves late, shortly after Concord; growth strong, very vigorous, and drouth resisting; little attacked by mildew or rot. Bunch endures sudden changes of temperature better than Concord, but vine will not endure such hard winters, yet it appears hardier than Rogers' Hybrids; well suited to the variable Southwestern climate; cuttings root quite well. Cluster medium to large, cylindrical, shouldered, properly compact; berry persistent, large, coal black with little or no bloom; skin thin, tough; pulp tender, juicy, with very agreeable pure flavor, pronounced by many persons, in a critical test, not knowing the name or origin of variety, far better than Concord; juice red; seeds few, small. A variety well worthy of extensive trial.

Beacon.—Parentage *V. lincecumii*, Northern Texas, having large cluster and berry, pollinated with Concord. Produced in 1887. Growth strong; very healthy, enduring drouth and cold very well, and resistant in a large degree to all maladies; cuttings root well. Leafs out late, holds foliage very late; leaf large, of fine substance; flowers a few days later than Concord and ripens with it, but will hang on much longer. Clusters very large, cylindrical, often having a short shoulder. Berry persistent, rather larger than Concord; black, with less bloom; skin rather thin, tough, underlaid with abundant dark-red juice; pulp more tender than in Concord, freeing the two to four medium seeds easily; quality purer and finer than Concord, yet having a degree of its flavor, without the earthy taste of that variety, and having a faint Concord odor, which is quite agreeable. Altogether, the appearance and quality are superior to Concord, and its carrying and keeping qualities much better. It promises to succeed over a wide extent of country, and to be one of "the grapes for the million." It might be said truly of this, that it is Concord improved in both vine and fruit, with far better adaptation to the South

DELICIOUS.—Parentage, the same mother as Beacon, pollinated with Herbemont. Produced in 1887. Growth very vigorous and healthy, well adapted to a hot, dry country, yet endures cold much better than Herbemont. More resistant to black rot than Herbemont, otherwise very healthy; cuttings root fairly well, about equally with Herbemont. Leafs out late and retains foliage very late, but matures its wood well; leaf of medium size, deeply three to five lobed, giving a very characteristic appearance; joints short; very prolific. Cluster medium to large, conical, compact but not crowding; berry persistent, medium; the largest Post Oak × Herbemont yet produced by me; black; skin thin and tough; pulp melting almost equally with Herbemont, with a delicious, refreshing, vinous flavor, about best. Seeds small, one to three. Promising for table, market, and especially for a light colored red wine of much body. Name was suggested by Mr. H. Jaeger, in describing the quality as "delicious."

CARMAN.—Parentage *V. lincecumii* (Post Oak grape No. 1 of my finding in Grayson County, Texas), polli-

nated with Triumph. Produced in 1885. Growth very
vigorous and healthy, enduring drouth and cold to a
high degree, and resisting maladies almost perfectly; cuttings root readily; joints of medium length; leaves of
good size and substance, sometimes shallow three-lobed,
with serrate margin. Leafs out and flowers late, after
Concord; holds foliage late; ripens wood perfectly;
fruit ripens about a week after Concord, and hangs on a
long time, improving in quality; very prolific. Cluster
large to very large, conical, compact, with one, two or
three lobes; very handsome, with strong, long peduncle;
berry medium or above, persistent to a remarkable degree; black, little bloom; skin thin but quite tough;
of agreeable flavor, having little or no coloring beneath;
pulp meaty but not tough, moderately juicy, separating
readily from the small, two to three seeds; quality very
pure, agreeable and sweet; really rich, and were the
pulp a little more melting, would rate as about best.
Dr. W. H. Morse, consulting chemist, who makes a
specialty of testing, having received a sample of the Carman from a person testing the variety in New Jersey, in
1893, voluntarily wrote me as follows concerning it:
"Last fall I was given the privilege of examining specimens of the Carman grape. I did not know till I found
your advertisement in the *Rural New-Yorker* of this
week that you have the vines for sale. I am not a con-
noisseur, but the striking resemblance of the Carman to
the Saumur grapes, and the excellence of the Saumur
wines, make for them the highest praise. The Carman
is a grape of great possibilities. I know nothing of its
vigor or prolific character; my reference is to the quality of the fruit, especially that quality as estimated for
its wine production. The fruit resembles very closely
that of the variety from which the best wines of Saumur,
France, are manufactured; and its wine should contain
in nearly the same proportion the substances character-

istic of the clear, sparkling Saumur wine, which is notable for having champagne qualities. It is high praise to give a grape, that it has champagne possibilities. The value of the Carman is high-gauged."

W. B. MUNSON.—Parentage *V. lincecumii,* of Grayson County, Texas, No. 3, pollinated with Triumph. Produced in 1887. Growth vigorous, healthy, well adapted to a hot, dry climate. Prolific; cuttings root readily; leafs out and sheds late; flowers a week later than Concord; leaves medium to large, handsome and substantial; cluster large, cylindrical, sometimes shouldered; berry medium, black, persistent; skin thin, tough; red juice beneath; pulp juicy, melting, sprightly, of very fine quality, separating easily from the one to three small seeds. In a critical comparison, by many persons, was pronounced the best black grape in my collection.

MUENCH.—Parentage Jaeger's Neosho (a Missouri Post Oak grape), pollinated with Herbemont. Very late in leafing out, flowering, ripening and shedding leaves. Produced in 1887. Growth very vigorous and healthy; well adapted to the South, and endures cold better than Herbemont; cuttings root about equally well with Herbemont; rather short jointed; leaves larger than those of Herbemont, resembling them somewhat, and of good substance; cluster large, handsome, cylindrical, or shouldered; berry dark purple, round, little below medium; persistent; skin thin, delicate, tough; pulp melting, juicy, very rich and sprightly; juice white; promising for a white wine of excellent body; seeds few, small. It will probably be preferred to Herbemont when better known, and will succeed farther north.

GOLD COIN.—Parentage Cynthiana (Norton), pollinated by Martha. Produced in 1883. Late in leafing, flowering and ripening; ripens wood well, and sheds

9

foliage late. Quite resistant to all maladies; season as late or later than Catawba; productive; cuttings rather difficult to root; cluster medium, cylindrical, or ovoid, often with a simple shoulder; fairly compact; berry medium to large, persistent, round, yellow when fully ripe; skin thin, tough; pulp rather tough, about same as Concord; juicy, mild, pleasant, very sweet, a trace of Labrusca odor and flavor; hardly sprightly enough for a fastidious taste, yet liked well by most persons. It takes well in market, owing to its rich, yellowish color; seeds rather small and few. It carries well, and is a very certain cropper. It is thought that it will produce a really good white wine of good keeping qualities.

FERN MUNSON.—Parentage Post Oak No. 1 × Triumph, produced in 1885, from same lot of seed as the Carman. Very vigorous and healthy. Very late in leafing out, flowering, ripening and shedding foliage; leaf large and excellent; cuttings root fairly; cluster large, conical, not very compact; berry large, round, very persistent; black, with some bloom; skin thin, fairly tough, with pale red juice beneath; pulp very juicy, tender, and sprightly; best quality; seeds few and small. Ripens in Northern Texas in first part of September, and hangs on with improving quality into October. A grape of much promise for late market and wine. Sold in market in Denison at same price as the Mission grape, when that variety was abundant.

LAUSSEL.—Parentage Post Oak No. 2, of Grayson county, Texas, × Gold Coin, 1886. Vine of great vigor and perfect health, enduring great extremes of heat and cold. Very late in leafing out, flowering and shedding foliage. Leaf large and fine; fruit ripens in September and holds on to late in October; cluster ovoid, often shouldered, very compact, and heavy for its size; berry medium to large, round, very persistent; skin thin, but very tenacious, rarely cracking, causing the berries to compress one another; dark purple or nearly black when fully ripe, with pale red juice; pulp juicy, tender, and possessed of a rare, peculiar, pleasant flavor; sprightly, high quality; seeds small, two to four. The vine is long jointed and requires long pruning, to get a full crop; it will easily carry all it can be made to set. Promising for late market and a fine characteristic wine.

There are a number more of my varieties that will take high rank among these, but these give a fine succession and variety in quality, all good.

CHAPTER XXX.

THE CHAUTAUQUA GRAPE BELT.

GEO. A. MARTIN, CHAUTAUQUA CO., N. Y.

A glance at a meteorological map of the State of New York, on which the amount of precipitation is indicated by depth of shading, will reveal a very light streak along the southern shore of Lake Erie. That strip, extending from a little west of Buffalo nearly to Erie, is the Chautauqua grape belt. Its southeastern boundary is fixed by the so-called "Chautauqua ridge," a hilly range five to seven miles from the lake, with an average altitude of over seven hundred feet above the level of the lake, and about thirteen hundred above the ocean. Lake Erie is the shallowest of all the Great Lakes. Its depth is only from five to eight fathoms, save around Long Point, which juts out like a wing-dam from the northern shore, and the channel thus restricted has scoured out the bottom to a depth of twelve fathoms. This shallow body of water becomes warmed to tepidity in the glowing summer days, and gives out its heat slowly during the autumn and early winter months, then freezes over more or less completely.

The narrow belt of territory, green-walled on one side by the Chautauqua ridge, and flanked on the other by this immense reservoir, has a climate quite unlike that of the region immediately south of it, or of the State at large. In spring the chilly airs from the lake usually retard the swelling buds until the season is well established, and in autumn the breezes, coming across the waters now warmed by summer heats, protect the belt from killing frosts. Another climatic peculiarity of the region resulting from the proximity of the lake, is the limited precipitation of rain and dew. The soil is clay, or glacial drift on clay subsoil. The underlying rock is soft argillaceous shale.

It will be readily seen that this region is peculiarly well fitted, by soil and climate, for successful grape culture. Experience has proved it to be so, and flourishing vineyards are found throughout its entire length and breadth. Grapes were cultivated here more than thirty years ago, but it is within the last half of that period that the business has expanded to any great commercial importance. There are now about twenty-six thousand acres of the region planted to vineyards, and the annual crop is worth over a million dollars.

The Concord is universally cultivated as the standard sort, far more acreage being devoted to it than to all others together, which are spoken of in a general way as "varieties." All the other American grapes which have been tried here succeed equally well, but the Concord is so eminently successful as a leading market grape that it is largely the favorite. Furthermore, it is beyond question that the Concords grown in the Chautauqua grape belt possess a finer and richer flavor than those from other regions. Moore's Early is cultivated to some extent, and Champion still less. Worden is increasing in favor. Catawba, Wyoming Red, Pocklington, Niagara, Agawam, Delaware, Martha, and some others, are grown. Of new varieties the Moyer, Coleraine, Eaton and Diamond are found in the vineyards of progressive growers. Diamond has proved quite satisfactory in flavor, productiveness and shipping qualities, but its liability to attacks of anthracnose renders faithful spraying necessary to its successful cultivation.

In the early years of grape culture in this region, it was the usual practice to set the roots at a distance of eight feet, or even less, each way. But in the more recently planted vineyards, Concord and other strong-growing vines are placed nine feet apart both ways. It is regarded as desirable to have the rows extend northerly and southerly, with a view to more uniform exposure to sunshine. The so-called arm and renewal system of pruning and training is almost invariably employed in the Chautauqua grape belt. Posts of chestnut or oak, seven or eight feet long, are set, one to every third vine in the row. The spade and post-hole augur are little used in modern practice. The posts are sharpened at one end, and holes made by the aid of an iron bar, terminating in a long slim cone of iron or steel, which is cast on the bar and finished in a lathe. Into the hole made by this bar the sharpened end of the post is driven by a cast-iron maul weighing from fourteen to seventeen pounds. A recent successful method is to drive at least every alternate post the first year after the roots are planted, and string only the lower wire. Then all of the first year's growth having been removed, except one strong cane, this is cut back to the wire and tied firmly. As the shoots start they are all rubbed off except the two uppermost, which, in the course of the season, grow along and cling to the wire, forming arms for the future. The ensuing spring the trellis is completed by supplying the remaining posts and wires. A more common practice is to cut the young vines back to two or three buds, at the end of the first year's growth, allowing the canes of the second year to trail on the ground, an obstruction to the work of cultivation, driving posts and stringing wire. The most usual form of trellis consists of two No. 9 plain steel wires stapled to the posts. Three wires possess many advantages, but have not come into general use. Of course it is found necessary to keep the vineyards thoroughly cultivated and free from weeds and grass. Underdraining is also indispensable to the highest success, except on those soils composed of gravel drift. Spraying with fungicides has never come into very general practice in the Chautauqua grape belt. The principal reason for this is that the vineyards in that favored region have been almost wholly exempt from mildew, black rot and other fungous diseases. The Concord vines especially have, in this region, always remained perfectly healthy without spraying or other protection. There is a prevalent idea that this comparative immunity is due to the pure fresh breezes from Lake Erie. But it doubtless results mainly from the restricted precipitation of rain and dew through the growing season. Still, this exceptional good fortune can hardly be expected to continue forever, especially as some new and otherwise desirable varieties are not entirely healthy in foliage and fruit, if left without protective treatment. Wide-awake, progressive vineyardists are providing themselves with spraying outfits, and learning to apply preventive treatment for fungus and insect enemies.

The grape harvest begins in September. The grapes are picked in crates two feet long, twelve inches wide and six inches deep. When filled these are hauled to the packing house, where they stand twenty-four hours or more, before the grapes are packed in veneer baskets.

For the general crop nine-pound baskets are used, the "pony" baskets of four or five pounds being in little demand, except for the early or extra sorts. The packing house is a feature of every grape farm, some being very large and handsome. The work of picking and packing furnishes employment to large numbers of men, women and boys, many of whom come from a distance. The grape harvest is a season of great activity and care, mingled with not a little social pleasure. Women and girls come singly, in groups, or even in car-loads, mostly in pursuance of previous engagements. Between this welcome element and the resident population social ties are readily formed; balls and other gatherings are common, and many an acquaintance is begun which afterwards ends in marriage. The great bulk of the Chautauqua crop is marketed as table grapes, the amount made into wine being a very small proportion. But the preparation of unfermented grape juice is increasing, and promises to attain commercial importance.

Many efforts have been put forth to secure effective coöperation among the Chautauqua grape growers. Several years ago the Chautauqua and Northeast Grape Union, embracing the entire belt, was organized. For several years it rendered valuable aid in marketing the grapes. But it failed to receive hearty and general support, and after the close of the season of 1894 it was disbanded. Several smaller organizations have since been formed, either by voluntary association or legal incorporation.

The output of table grapes from the Chautauqua belt is from 40,000 to 50,000 tons yearly. The railroad shipments of 1891 were 3100 carloads of twelve and a half tons each; those of 1894 were 3600 carloads; of 1895, notwithstanding the destructive freeze of May, they were 3200 carloads. The net receipts to growers were $1,159,200 in 1894, and $1,209,600 in 1895, the increased price more than compensating for the reduced amount of the crop.

The freeze of May 13, 1895, was wholly exceptional, nothing like it having occurred in thirty-six years. The local meteorological conditions were overcome by influences which extended over a large area, both east and west. Yet severe as was the freeze, and although the grapevines were just putting out their fruit buds, they escaped with less damage than many other fruits, forest trees, or even meadows. Dwarf pear trees were, in some cases, frozen dead within fifty feet of Concord grapevines, which survived and bore nearly a full crop of fruit.

PART III.

AMERICAN WINE MAKING.

CHAPTER XXXI.

It can hardly be expected, in a book which only aims to be the guide of the average cultivator, and to render grape growing and wine making easy for the masses, that I should enter into the secrets of the wine dealer and chemist, giving elaborate descriptions of the manufacture of sparkling wines, and the artificial compounds of the so-called sweet wines, *vins de liqueur*, etc. My chief aim is to demonstrate in a simple and plain manner, the rules which are necessary to success. Wine making is a very simple art, which every one with sound common sense may acquire, yet it can not be followed successfully without a strict observance of these rules. I shall be as concise as possible, and hope that this little volume may enable every one, who wishes to do so, to make healthful and palatable wine for his own use, and at the same time to assist the owner of ten or twenty acres of vineyard to convert the products of it into a salable article of commerce.

THE CELLAR.

Before making wine, room should be provided to keep it. If you want to make only a small quantity for your own use, and have a common house-cellar, it will answer the purpose, although not likely to be cool enough in summer. The main consideration is to always have the wine thoroughly fermented and finished during

(139)

the first winter.   If this is the case, it will keep even in a
temperature of 65°, though 45° would be better.   But if
one wishes to take up wine making as a business, and
manufacture several thousand gallons, a special building
for the purpose is necessary.

A steep hillside, sloping towards the north, is the
most suitable locality, and the most economical and
most convenient building is one of three stories.   The
lower one, for keeping the wine when finished, should be
completely underground, the second story, intended for
the fermenting cellar, partially so, at least, and the third,
intended for the press house, can be entirely above ground,
so that the grapes can be conveniently carried into it.
The lower story should be well walled and, if possible,
arched with stone, though this is not indispensable.   If
arched, it should be about 18 feet wide by 12 feet high
from the floor to the middle of the arch, so that there is
room for casks 5 feet long in two rows, one on each side,
space enough between the casks and the wall to pass behind them, and a passage of 5 to 6 feet in the center, to
allow space for drawing off wine, moving casks, etc.
The length can be suited to the wants of the builder ; the
entrance should, if possible, be even with the ground,
and if built into the hillside, it can easily be made so,
and the back part of the cellar slightly elevated, so that
it will drain towards the door.   It is best to have a room
in front, so as to keep out the cold air ; this can be
used for storing empty casks, cellar utensils, etc.   The
cellar should be well ventilated on the sides by air flues
built in the wall, and constructed somewhat like chim-
neys, commencing at the bottom and terminating above
the arch.   These are to be closed by a grate and trap
door, so that they can be opened at will, to admit air and
light.   The cellar is to be closed by strong double doors.
Place on each side two rows of beams, lengthwise, as
layers for the casks, one to be about 2 feet from the wall,

the other $4^1/_2$ feet. It will be best if the floor is paved with brick or flags.

The second story of the building is intended for the fermenting cellar, and may be made either of stone, which is certainly the most durable, or of wood, if cheaper and more convenient ; it need not be arched. It should be, at least, 9 feet high, and partly under ground, with its entrance from the rear, as this will be more convenient. There ought to be holes through the arch of the lower cellar, large enough to admit the passage of a hose, by which the wine can be racked from the casks in the upper cellar into the casks below. This room need not be arched, but should be so constructed that it is free from frost, and can be heated by a stove, if necessary, to regulate the temperature while the must is fermenting. Place layers, or beams, to receive the casks, on both sides, as in the lower cellar.

The third story is above the ground, and is calculated for the press room, with the entrance from the back, and is intended to contain the wine press, grape mill, and fermenting vats, together with all the necessary implements for wine making. The whole is to be covered with a good roof, and there should be a large cistern, to receive all the water from it, and as convenient to the press room as possible, so that the water can be drawn into the room by a force pump. If the press room is so arranged as to be heated by a stove, it will be found convenient in winter as a shop in which to prepare cuttings, etc.

To sum up, there should be : 1st. A cellar to keep the fermented wine altogether below ground, so that it will remain at as even a temperature as possible. 2nd. A fermenting cellar, or good, air tight room, which need not necessarily be below ground, if it can be kept free from frost until about December 15th, to put the must through a rapid and thorough fermentation. 3d. A press room for receiving and washing the grapes, and, when necessary, passing them through a light fermentation before pressing, with sufficient room for all the implements. 4th. Plenty of good cistern water for all purposes. All the stories, for greater convenience in working, to be connected by hose.

As observed before, any one can make and keep a small quantity of wine for home use, even without a regular wine cellar. One of the most successful wine makers I ever knew, and who afterwards made it by tens of thousands of gallons, stored his first crop in a hole in the ground, 8 feet deep, and planked inside, with a board roof ; in this he placed his casks, and covered the whole with earth. But for the cultivator who would make grape growing and wine making his business, a separate wine cellar will become absolutely necessary, and should be built as soon as possible. The expense will be according to the dimensions ; a building 30 by 18 feet would cost here now about $1,500, and have a capacity of 5,000 gallons in the lower cellar, provided casks of not less than 500 gallons are used.

CELLAR FURNITURE.

We now come to the utensils necessary for wine making. You need :

1st. A PRESS.—The most convenient one for a medium-sized establishment, to press say not over 5,000 gallons per annum, I have found to be one made at Belleville, Ill. It is compact, takes little space, and it has a false bottom, which can be easily taken off and cleaned. The hopper is in the shape of a double-grooved ring, so that the juice can flow off towards the middle, the outside, and the bottom ; it does the work quickly and well. A strong iron screw is in the middle, and is worked by a lever on top. It costs about $35 to $40. It is durable, easily cleaned, and takes little space. A small quantity of grapes can, of course, be pressed with any kind of a cider press. One will press about a barrel at a time, and twenty barrels can be worked off in a day.

2nd. THE MILL.—For mashing grapes, a simple pair of wooden rollers, connected by cog wheels, and running against each other, so arranged that they can be set by screws to any desired distance apart, will do the work better than anything else, and a boy of ten years can turn them. The rollers are in a frame which can be set over the vat ; a hopper on top to receive the grapes, completes the arrangement. The rollers can be either plain or grooved, as desired, and the whole will cost from $12 to $15. Small quantities may be mashed with a wooden pestle in a tub. The rollers should be so set as to break the skins of the berries, but not to crush the seeds or stems.

3d. FERMENTING VATS.—These are best made of poplar wood, and may be of any suitable size, with a capacity of from 100 to 500 gallons. For a larger establishment I would prefer them about 5 feet diameter by 5 feet high, and somewhat narrower at the top than at bottom. They should be well hooped and strong, made of $1\frac{1}{2}$-inch lumber, and worked smoothly inside, so that they can be easily cleaned, with a spigot hole near the botton to draw off the must. Their probable cost is about five to six cents per gallon.

4th. CASKS.—These are wanted, of course, of all dimensions. Large casks save room, and are proportionally cheaper; fermentation progresses rapidly in them, but it takes longer for the wine to fine and clear after fermentation is over, than in small casks. They should be of good, well seasoned white oak wood ; if steamed before using, so that the tannin is drawn out, so much the better. Larger casks should also have a so-called "manhole," so that a man or boy can slip in and thoroughly clean them when used. I do not advise larger casks than 500 gallons, as it takes too long to fill them, and they are, therefore, unhandy, except for very large establishments. These are about 5 feet long by 5 feet diameter, and should

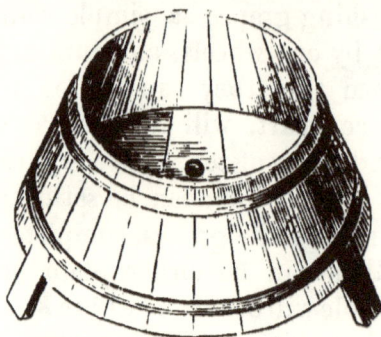

be placed on strong beams in the cellar, about 18 inches above the floor and 15 to 18 inches from the wall, so as to enable you to examine them at any time and clean them of mould or cobwebs. Their cost at present is about 7 cents per gallon. Imported Rhenish wine casks, holding from 80 to

Fig. 14.—WOODEN FUNNEL.

160 gallons each, are also very good if they have not been allowed to sour or become mouldy, but, of course, they take up more room in proportion than do large casks.

5th. A STRONG WOODEN FUNNEL.— This is oblong, with a copper pipe in the bottom, and has two short wooden legs, so that it will set firmly on the cask. Any good cooper can make one. See figure 14.

6th. TUBS TO BE USED IN PRESSING. —Any good pine or cedar tubs will do for the purpose. Also clean tin or wooden pails should be provided in abundance.

7th. A SACCHAROMETER OR MUST SCALE.—This is important and you can not do without, as they are the only sure guides as to quality of the must, and you can not make wine rationally or with certainty of success, unless you know what amount of sugar and acid the must contains. Oechsle's is the one most commonly

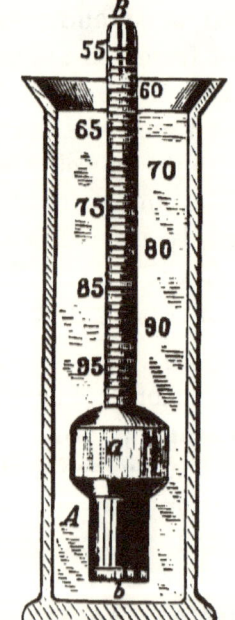

Fig. 15.

used, and can be had in any optical establishment. They are made of glass, platina, or silver, at prices ranging from $3 to $10.

Figure 15 shows must scale (silver) and test tube. With the scale you should also have a long glass, or tin tube made for the purpose of holding the must while testing it.

AN ACIDIMETER.—The one invented and patented by Henry Twitchell is simple, and can be used with accuracy

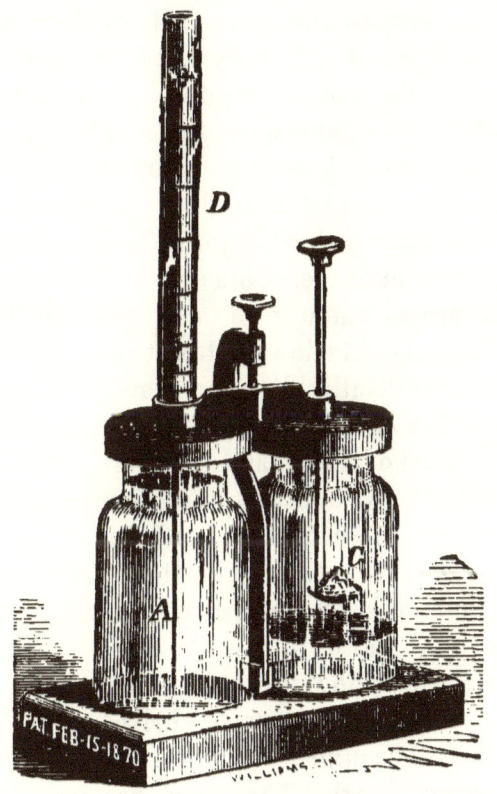

Fig. 16.—ACIDIMETER.

by beginners. It is a timely invention, as it took long practice to work correctly with either Otto's or Geissler's. It is accompanied with full directions for its use. Figure 16 gives an illustration of the Acidimeter.

GATHERING THE GRAPES.

Having our cellar built, and stocked with the necessary
implements, we can now proceed to gather the grapes.
The proper time to do this depends very much upon
the varieties. The *æstivalis*, and most of the *cordifolia*
class, in short, all grapes which have an agreeable flavor—
one which we wish to have in its fullest development in
the must or wine—we ought to have thoroughly ripe.
The riper the grapes, the more fully will their peculiar
flavor be developed, the less acid and the more sugar will
they contain. We must, therefore, learn the nature of
our grapes before we know when to gather them. In the varieties of *Labrusca*, at least in most of them, their peculiar
flavor is not desirable in its highest development, and is
generally characterized as "foxy." A good many of
them also, for instance, Concord and Martha, do not
contain the proper amount of acid when fully ripe, to
bear the necessary dilution of this strong, foxy taste, and
as they must be "Gallized" at any rate, to be palatable, it
is not advisable to let them get over ripe. I would advise,
therefore, to take these, and, in short, all the varieties
with a strong, foxy, and disagreeable aroma, when fully
colored, and let those varieties with an agreeable aroma
hang long, in order to obtain their flavor in its full
perfection and delicacy ; and also to develop the greatest
amount of sugar and diminish the acid. The best evi-
dences of a grape being thoroughly ripe are : 1st. The
stem turns brown and begins to shrivel. 2d. The berry
begins to shrivel around the stem. 3d. The skin is thin
and transparent. 4th. The juice becomes very sweet,
and adheres to the fingers like honey or molasses.

It is often advisable to gather twice, as many bunches will
ripen later than others. If the ripest are gathered first, the
remainder will ripen quicker, and a uniform product can
thus be obtained. The first implements needed for the

gathering are clean wooden or tin pails, and sharp knives, or better still, the small shears spoken of in a former part of this work. Each gatherer is provided with a pail, or two may go together, having a pail each, so that one can empty and the other keep filling. If there are a good many unripe berries on the bunches, these may be put into a separate pail, and also all that are soft, as they will make an inferior wine. The bunch is cut with as short a stem as possible, as the stems contain a great deal of acid and tannin ; every unripe, dry, or decayed berry is to be picked out, so that none but per-·fectly sound, ripe berries remain.

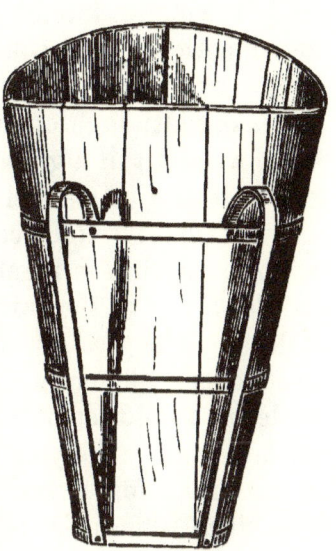

We also need a carrying vat, to carry the grapes to the mill or wagon, if the vineyard is any distance from the cellar. This is made of half-inch pine lumber 3 feet high, 10 inches wide at bottom, 20 inches at top, being flat on one side, where it comes against the back ; it is bound with thin iron hoops. It is carried by two leather straps

Fig. 17.—CARRYING VAT.

running over the shoulders, as shown in figure 17, and will contain about 8 or 10 pails, or 2 to 2½ bushels of grapes. The carrier can easily take it through the rows and lean it against a post until filled, and then carry the grapes directly to the press room, if close by, if too far, place tubs or vats on the wagon, into which the grapes may be emptied. The utmost cleanliness should be observed in all the apparatus, and no tub, vat, or pail should be used which is in the least mouldy, as the must will at once acquire any foreign taste. Everything should be perfectly clean and sweet, and a strict supervision

kept up, that the laborers do not drop crumbs of bread,
etc., among the grapes, as these will cause acetous fermentation. The weather should be dry and fair, and the
grapes dry when gathered.

MAKING THE WINE.

The apparatus being all ready, we can commence operations, and here we must know, first and foremost, what
kind of wine we intend to make, whether light-colored
and smooth, or dark-colored and astringent. The character of the wine depends chiefly on its fermentation on
the husks, although of course we cannot make an entirely
white wine out of a grape with very dark juice, nor a red
wine, except by artificial coloring, out of a white grape,
or one with very light-colored juice. The general rule
is, however, that fermentation draws acid, tannin, color,
and flavor out of the skins and stems, so that if we desire
to develop the greatest amount of these, we must let the
must remain longer on the husks ; if, on the contrary,
we desire a mild, smooth wine, it should not ferment long
on the husks. Many of the red wines of Europe are left
on the husks for several months, and the wine is drawn
from them when it is about finished.

To make white, or light-colored, smooth wine, the
grapes which were gathered and mashed during the day
can be pressed and put into the cask during the following
night. The mill is placed above the fermenting vat,
and the grapes are mashed as soon as they are carried in,
or hauled to the press house. The vat is covered with a
cloth during the day. If the season has been good, and
you have a perfect grape to deal with, such a one as has
all the ingredients of a good wine in the proper proportions, it will make good wine without any other addition.
If not, sugar, or sugar and water, must be added, but I
will speak of this in a separate chapter. With the Concord grape, many make both a white and a red wine. The

white is made by simply pressing very lightly as soon as the grapes are mashed, so as to drain off the first run of the juice before it has acquired any color from the skins. The husks are then thrown into the fermenting vat, water and sugar added, and fermented several days; then pressed, and thus a red wine is produced. I must say that I prefer the wine gained by fermenting, say 24 hours, in a temperature of 65° to 80° on the husks, and all pressed together. It generally contains all the ingredients in better proportions, while the white wine seldom has the due proportion of acid and tannin, and the red generally has an excess of acid, tannin, and flavor. Of course the temperature has a great influence on fermentation, as in warm weather it progresses much more rapidly, and the pressing should be done sooner than in cool weather. It is entirely optional with the wine-maker what kind of wine he produces; he can make it to suit himself, and soon learns how to do it. The longer he ferments his must, the more astringent and rough his wine will be; and the sooner and lighter he presses, the less character will the wine acquire, though it will be much more delicate and smooth.

Before filling the casks they should be well prepared. They should be perfectly clean and sweet without the slightest mouldiness. If new, they should be steamed, or filled with pure water, and allowed to soak for several days, then emptied, and scalded with two or three gallons of boiling wine. This quantity is for a cask of say 500 gallons. Or, if this is not convenient, put in, say a peck of unslaked lime, and about five gallons of water, then put in the bung and turn the cask about, so that all parts of it are touched by the mixture. Then pour out the lime water, and wash with water, then rinse with a decoction of vine leaves, or warm wine, or better still, pour in a pint of pure alcohol or grape brandy, and light it by a match. The fumes of the burning brandy will penetrate the wood, and make you secure against any taint in the wine. But do not bung the cask while the brandy is burning, or you may have an explosion before you know it. The same may be done with mouldy casks, to make them fresh and serviceable again.

The casks can then be filled with the must, either completely, if it is intended that the must should ferment above, as it is called, or under, when the cask is not completely filled, so that the husks, scums, etc., which the must will throw to the surface during fermentation, will remain in the cask. Both methods have their advantages, but after long practice, I now follow the latter, leaving empty space enough until rapid fermentation is over, so that all remains in the cask. As long as fermentation lasts, and the gas escapes, all goes right, and a few vine leaves over the bung-hole, on which a small sack of sand is laid, are sufficient to close it. Of course it must be closely watched, and the bung closed as soon as fermentation ceases, when the casks must be filled with wine kept for that purpose in a separate cask. If, during fermentation, cool weather should set in, and the temperature fall below 60°, the fermenting cellar should be warmed by a stove. But this will rarely be the case, as the vintage should be over before cold weather sets in.

When violent fermentation has ceased, and the must has become quiet, the cask should be closed with a tight bung of white oak or poplar wood. To make dark-red wine, the treatment differs, as it is the object, as before remarked, to get a wine of the darkest color, highest flavor, and of a certain astringency, which it will only attain by fermenting on the husks. The must is, in that case, allowed to ferment on the husks for from three to six days, when the husks which rise to the surface should often be pressed down and stirred through the must, to prevent their souring. The must is then drawn off below, by a faucet, and the husks pressed. If it is desired to make only a dark-colored wine, without so much astringency, and of great body, the grapes are allowed to hang until they are very ripe, even shrivelled ; and stemmed, as the stems contain a large amount of acid and tannin, and give the wine a rough and bitter taste. In this manner the celebrated red wines of Burgundy, and the best brands of France and Germany, are made. Many of them are even allowed to go through the whole process of fermentation before pressing, and the husks are filled into the cask with the must, through a door above, and remain there until the clear wine is drawn off. This is generally not desirable here, however, as our red grapes contain sufficient astringency and color without this process. After the wine has become quiet it is looked after frequently, and the casks filled to the bung. As there is more or less evaporation, this should be done every two or three weeks, always using wine of the same or similar character. In two to three months the wine ought to be clear and bright, and should then be racked, *i. e.*, drawn from the lees by means of a faucet, and put into clean, sweet casks. It is very important here, again, that the casks into which it is drawn, are sweet and clean, or " wine green." For must, fresh brandy or whiskey casks may be used ; but after the wine has fermented, it will not do to use such, as the wine acquires the smell and taste of the liquor. When a cask has been emptied, it should be carefully cleaned, as before described, by entering at the door or man-hole, or, with smaller casks, by taking out the head, as the lees are very adhesive, and will not wash out readily, but should be brushed off. After it is thoroughly cleansed it may be fumigated slightly, by burning a small piece of sulphured paper, or a nutmeg in it, and then filled. To keep empty casks in good condition, they should, after cleaning, be allowed to become thoroughly dry, when they are sulphured, closed tightly, and laid away in the cellar. The sulphuring should be repeated every six weeks. When wanted for use, they are rinsed with cold water.

For racking the wine we should have : 1st. A large, brass or wooden faucet. 2d. Pails of a peculiar shape, narrow at the top, to prevent wastage. 3d. A wooden funnel, as described before, to hold about six gallons.

In racking, first loosen the bung of the cask. Then, after loosening the wooden peg, and closing the tap hole, let your assistant hold the pail opposite the hole. You hold the faucet with your right hand, and with the left withdraw the plug, inserting the faucet quickly ; drive it in firmly and you are ready for the work.

Do not fully open the faucet at first, because the first pailful is generally not quite clear, and should run slowly. This, and the last from the lees, are generally put into a cask together, and allowed to settle, when, in a few weeks, it will become clear, and make a good wine. As soon as the wine runs clear and limpid, it can be put into the cask, and you can let it run as fast as the faucet will allow, opening it to its fullest capacity. When the wine has run off down to the tap hole, the cask may be carefully raised at the other end, one inserting a piece of board or a brick under it, while the other lifts slowly and gently. This may be repeated several times, as long as the wine runs clear, and when it becomes slightly cloudy, keep the cloudy wine to put with what ran out first. As soon as it becomes thick and muddy it is time to stop. The door is then taken out of the cask and the lees emptied out. They will, if distilled, make a fine flavored and strong brandy. If your cellar is built according to the plan already given, you can attach a hose to the faucet and run your wine from the fermenting cellar into the cellar and casks below, which is a great saving of time and wastage. The must can also be run from the press-room into the casks in the fermenting cellar in the same manner.

We should keep in mind, in all operations, the kind of wine we intend to make. In white and light-colored wines, we desire delicacy of bouquet and smoothness of taste ; in red wines for medicinal or stomachic use, we desire astringency, body, and a decided and characteristic flavor. White and light-colored wines should, therefore, be racked as soon as they are clear, while red wines may remain longer on the lees. Both can be modified, by treatment, to meet the peculiar taste ; a red wine may be made smoother, and a white wine more astringent, by longer or shorter fermentation on the husks and lees. We can thus conform to the taste of the consumer. If the prevailing taste is for light-colored, smooth and delicate wines, we can make them so, by pressing soon, and racking soon and frequently. If a dark-colored, astringent wine is desired, we can ferment on the husks, and leave it on the lees a longer period. There is a medium course in this, as in all things, and the intelligent wine-maker will soon find the rules which should guide him, and with a little practice discover the method which will give him the best results with a certain variety.

Among the varieties suited for white wines, and which should be treated as such, I will name the Elvira, Gœthe, Herbemont, Martha, Massasoit, Uhland, Catawba, Delaware, and Taylor, and among the varieties for dark-red wines, Cynthiana, Norton's Virginia, Lenoir, Alvey, Clinton, and Ives' Seedling. The Concord can be used for both, or can be made light-red. For Sherry wine, use the Hermann, Rulander, and Cunningham. These latter require a sort of medium treatment ; it is desirable to develop their peculiar flavor ; it is not desirable to have them astringent or dark-colored. Fermenting on the husks 24 to 36 hours, in a temperature of 60° to 70°, will be about right for them. It is very important that the temperature should not vary much during fermentation, and that the first fermentation on the husks, and for the first week following, should be rapid and uninterrupted. If the wine goes into the next summer fully fermented and finished, clear and limpid, there is little danger of its becoming cloudy and diseased afterwards, even if it must be kept in a changeable temperature.

AFTER TREATMENT OF THE WINE.

Even if the wine was perfectly clear when drawn off, in February and March, when it should be racked for the second time, it will go through a second fermentation, however slight this may be, as soon as warm weather sets in, say in June and July. The clearer and better developed the wine was when last racked, the slighter this will be, for only the lees yet remaining in it which the young wine has not entirely deposited will act as the ferment. It is not safe or judicious, therefore, to bottle the wine before this second fermentation is over. As soon as the wine has become perfectly quiet and clear again, generally about September, it can be bottled, or sold by the cask. For bottling wine we need : 1st. Clean bottles. 2d. Good corks, which must be scalded with hot water first, to draw out all impurities, and soften them, and then be soaked in cold water. 3d. A small funnel. 4th. A small faucet. 5th. A light, wooden mallet to drive in the corks.

After the faucet has been inserted in the cask, fill your bottles so that there will be about an inch of room between the cork and the wine. Let them stand a few minutes before you drive in the cork, which should be of full size, and made to fit by compressing at one end. Then drive in the cork with the mallet, and lay the bottles, either in sand on the cellar floor, or on a rack made for that purpose. They should be so laid that the wine covers the cork, to exclude all air. The greater bulk of the wine, however, can safely be sold now, or kept in casks. All the wine to be kept should be racked once about every six months, and the casks kept well filled.

DISEASES OF WINE AND THEIR REMEDIES.

Wine properly made, and with all ingredients in right proportion, will seldom suffer from any disease. Cases may arise, however, which may make it necessary to give it a different treatment, or fine it by artificial means.

TREATMENT OF FLAT AND TURBID WINE.

The cause of flat wine is generally lack of tannin. If the wine has a peculiar flat, soft taste, and looks cloudy, this is uniformly the case. Draw the wine into another cask, which has been well sulphured, and add some pulverized tannin, which can be had at any drug store. The tannin may be dissolved either in water or wine, about an ounce to every two hundred gallons of wine, and poured in at the bung, after which the wine should be well stirred with a stick inserted through the bung-hole. Should it not become clear in about three weeks, it must be fined. This can be done by adding about an ounce of powdered gum arabic, or isinglass, to each forty gallons. The gum arabic will dissolve in cold water, but isinglass requires hot water ; stir the wine well when it has been poured in. Or take some wine out of the cask, and, for each forty gallons of wine, add the whites of ten eggs, whipped to foam with the wine taken out ; pour this mixture into the cask, stir well, and bung tightly. After a week the wine will generally be clear, and should then be drawn off. An easier and speedier method to fine is to put it through a filter filled with paper pulp, but the apparatus is somewhat costly. As it is accompanied by directions for use to those who purchase it, it would be superfluous to describe it here. As stated before, if the wine has been properly made and fermented, such procedures will seldom be necessary, and the wine will be sound and clear without any artificial means. The observant and rational wine-maker will seldom be troubled by any mishaps, and his wines will be palatable and bright without any such treatment.

USES OF THE HUSKS AND LEES.

These can be distilled, and will make a very strong, fine flavored brandy. The husks are stamped down into empty barrels or vats, as close as possible, with a cover of clay made over them, to exclude the air. They will then undergo a fermentation and be ready for distilling in about a month. They should be taken fresh from the press, for if they remain exposed to the air they become mouldy. The lees can be distilled immediately. Good fresh lees or husks from rather astringent wines or grapes, are also an excellent remedy when the wine becomes flat, as described before. If such wine is fermented on the husks again for a day or two, it will generally become sound and bright.

CHAPTER XXXII.

DR. GALL'S AND PETIOL'S METHODS OF WINE MAKING.

So far, I have only spoken of the handling of the raw product of Nature, taking for granted that we had a fair must in good condition to work with. But this unfortunately is rarely the case, and the natural juice of the grape seldom contains all the elementary constituents of a good wine in the proper proportions. In fact, very many of our American varieties are very imperfect even in the best seasons, and contain generally a superabundance of acid and flavoring matter or aroma. What then is the intelligent operator to do? Shall he use them as they are, although he is aware they are imperfect, and produce a poor, undrinkable, unsalable, and even unhealthful article? Or shall he, with the reason and knowledge God has given him, seek to remedy Nature's imperfections, dilute the acid and aroma, add sugar, if necessary, and thus make a salable, pleasant, and healthful beverage? I think the intelligent wine-makers —and it is only for them I am writing, can not hesitate which course to take.

I am aware that I am treading on dangerous ground, that I have been severely censured for my advocacy of Dr. Gall in my former little book, but truth remains truth, whether assailed or not, and the laws of chemistry will not change to please any of the "Simon Pure Naturalists," who rail against Gallizing, because they do not know anything about its true principles. But let me put myself right before my readers, before entering upon the details of the operation. I advocate Gallizing only so far as it is the best means of improving otherwise imperfect must, not as an indiscriminate means of increasing the quantity at the expense of quality. Only so far as by the addition of water and sugar, an imperfect must can be made the most perfect, is Gallizing not only justifiable, but a necessity. As soon as it aims only at increasing the quantity without regard to quality, it is reprehensible, and should be frowned down. This may be called *gallonizing*, not Gallizing ; and that these gallonizers have done a great deal of mischief by bringing their trash before the public, and calling it wine, can not be denied. But those who, from a mistaken idea that a wine to be good and healthful, must be natural, as they call it, have made it as Nature gave it, and have, therefore, disgusted the palates of refined wine connoisseurs by their pure, but weak, foxy, and acid Concords, and Ives, etc., thus doing even more to bring American wines into discredit than the gallonizers. Both of these, the natural wine-makers and the gallonizers, have been the curse and bane of our wine markets ; those who, in the innocent belief that they were tasting fair samples of American wines, swallowed their compounds and were disgusted, and when they met with good productions, were deterred from tasting again. The true course lies in the middle, as usual. The wine-maker has certain unerring guides, which teach him, with a little practice and experimenting, "thus far shalt thou go, but no farther."

Having thus defined what we intend to do, which is simply to improve our must, if deficient, let us, to see our way clearly before us, examine as to the constituent parts of must or grape juice. A chemical analysis of must shows the following result :

Grape juice contains water, sugar, free acids, tannin, gummy and mucous substances or gluten, coloring matter, fragrant, or flavoring substances (aroma, bouquet).

A good or normal must should contain all these ingredients in due proportion. If there is an excess of one, and a lack of the other, it can not make a perfect wine. This would seem apparent to every reasoning wine maker. Must which contains all of these in exactly the right proportion we call a perfect or normal must; and only by determining the amount of each of the ingredients in this so-called normal must, can we gain the knowledge that will enable us to improve must which has not the necessary proportion of each. The frequency of unfavorable seasons in Europe, set intelligent men to thinking; their grapes were sadly deficient in sugar, did not ripen fully, and also lacked in flavor. How then could this defect be remedied, and a grape crop which was almost worthless from its want of sugar and excess of acids, be made to yield at least a fair article, instead of the sour and unsalable wine generally produced in such seasons? Among the foremost who experimented with this object in view I will here mention Chaptal, Petiol, but especially Dr. Ludwig Gall, who has at last reduced the whole science of wine making to such a mathematical certainty, that we are amazed that so simple a process should not have been discovered long ago. It is the old story of the egg of Columbus, but the poor wine-makers of Germany and France, and we in this country also, are none the less indebted to those intelligent and persevering men for the incalculable benefits they have conferred upon us.

The production of good wine is thus reduced to a science; though we cannot, perhaps, in a bad season, produce as high flavored and delicate wines as in the best years, we can now always make a fair article, by following the simple rules laid down by Dr. Gall. Nay, as most of our grapes, in a good season, contain flavor in excess, we can often make fully as palatable wine in a poor season, when that flavor is not so fully developed, by merely adding water and sugar to dilute the acid. In this respect we can make a more uniform product from our strongly flavored varieties, than the Europeans can from their delicately flavored varieties of *vinifera*, which are deficient in flavor in bad seasons.

When this method was first introduced, it was calumniated and despised, called adulteration of wine, and even prohibited by the governments of Europe, but Dr. Gall fearlessly challenged his opponents to have his wines analyzed by the most eminent chemists. This was repeatedly done, and the results showed that they could find nothing but such ingredients as pure wine should contain; and since men like Von Babo, Dobereiner, and others, have openly endorsed and recommended Gallizing, prejudice is giving way before the light of scientific knowledge. The same will be the case here. Intelligent men will see that there is nothing reprehensible in the practice, and the public will, in time, prefer the properly Gallized, and, therefore, more palatable and more healthful wines, to the foxy and acid productions of the sticklers for natural wines.

To determine the amount of sugar and acids in the must, we need a few necessary implements. The first is the must scale, or Saccharometer, already mentioned in the necessary implements for wine making (see fig. 29.) The most suitable one now in use is Oechsle's Must Scale, constructed on the principle that the instrument sinks the deeper into any fluid the thinner it is, or the less sugar it contains. It is generally made of silver, or German silver, although it is also made of glass. *A* represents a hollow cylinder, best made of glass, filled with must to the brim, into which place the must scale, *B*. This is composed of the hollow float, *a*, which keeps it suspended in the fluid; of the weight, *b*, for holding it in a perpendicular position, and the scale, divided by small lines into from 50° to 100°. Before the scale is placed in the must, draw it several times through the mouth to moisten it, but allow no saliva to adhere to it. When the scale ceases to descend, note the degree to which it has sunk, after which, press it down with the finger a few degrees further, and on its standing still again, the line to which the must reaches, indicates its so-called weight, expressed by degrees. The must should have a temperature of 65° to 70°, be weighed in an entirely fresh state, before it shows any sign of fermentation, and should be free from husks; if strained through a piece of mosquito bar, or small sieve all the better.

This instrument, which is indispensable to every one who intends to make wine rationally, can now be had from prominent opticians in nearly every large town. It indicates the amount of sugar in the must, and its use is so simple, that every one can soon become familiar with it. The next step in the improvement of must was to determine the amount of acids it contained, and this problem has also been successfully solved by the invention of the Acidimeter.

As remarked before, Twitchell's Acidimeter is the best now in use, and as it is accompanied by full directions for use, I need not repeat them here, further than to say that to ascertain the acidity of must, it should be tested when pressed, as many of our pulpy grapes contain nearly all their acid in the pulp, and the instrument will, therefore, not give a fair indication until fermentation has drawn out the acid.

A normal must, to suit the prevailing taste here, should contain about four-thousandths parts of acids, while in Europe it varies from four and a half to seven-thousandths, as the taste there is generally in favor of more acid wines. I cannot do better here than quote from Dr. Gall, who gives the following directions as a guide to distinguish and determine the proportion of acids which

11

a must should contain to be still agreeable to the palate, and good :

" Chemists distinguish the acids contained in the grape as the vinous, malic, grape, citric, tannic, gelatinous, and para-citric acids. Whether all of these are contained in the must, or which of them, is of small moment for us to know. For the practical wine-maker it is sufficient to know, with full certainty, that, as the grape ripens, while the proportion of sugar increases, the quantity of acids continually diminishes, and hence, by leaving the grapes on the vines as long as possible, we have a double means of improving their products, the must or wine.

" All wines, without exception, to be of good and agreeable taste, must contain from four and a half to seven-thousandths part of free acids, and each must containing more than seven-thousandths part of free acids may be considered as having too little water and sugar in proportion to its acids.

" In all the wine-growing countries of Europe, for a number of years past, experience has proved that a corresponding addition of sugar and water is the means of converting the sourest must, not only into a good drinkable wine, but also into as good a wine as can be produced in favorable years, except in that peculiar and delicate aroma found only in the must of well-ripened grapes, and which must, and will, always distinguish the wines made in the best seasons from those made in poor seasons.

" The Saccharometer and Acidimeter, properly used, will give us the exact knowledge of what the must contains and what it lacks, and we have the means at hand, by adding water, to reduce the acids to their proper proportions, and by adding sugar, to increase the amount of sugar the must should contain ; in other words, we can change the poor must of indifferent seasons into the normal must of the best seasons in everything, except its bouquet or aroma, thereby converting an unwholesome and disagreeable drink into an agreeable and healthful one."

THE CHANGE OF THE MUST INTO WINE.

Let us glance for a few moments at this **wonderful,** simple, and yet so complicated process, to give a clearer insight into the functions which man has to perform to assist Nature, and have her work for him, to attain the desired end. I cannot do better than to quote again from Dr. Gall. He says: " To form a correct opinion of what may, and can, be done, in the manufacture of wine, we must be thoroughly convinced that Nature, in her operations, has other objects in view than merely to serve man as his careful cook and butler. Had the highest object of the Creator, in the creation of the grape, been simply to combine in the juice of the fruit nothing but what is indispensable to the formation of the delicious beverage for the accommodation of man, it might have been still easier done for him by at once filling the berries with wine already made. But in the production of fruits, the first object of all is to provide for the propagation and preservation of the species. Each fruit contains the germ of a new plant, and a quantity of nutritious matter surrounding and developing that germ. The general belief is that this nutritious matter, and even the peculiar combination in which it is found in the fruit, has been made directly for the immediate use of man. This, however. is a mistake. The nutritious matter of the grape, as in the apple, pear, or any similar product, is designed by Nature only to serve as the first nourishment of the future plant, the germ of which lies in it. There are thousand of fruits of no use whatever, and even noxious to man, and there are thousands more, which, before they can be used, must be divested of certain parts, necessary, indeed, to the nutrition of the future plant, but unfit, in their present state, for the use or nourishment of man. For instance, barley contains starch, mucilaginous sugar, gum, adhesive matter, vegetable albumen, phosphate of lime, oil, fibre, and water. All these are necessary for the formation of roots, stalks, leaves, flowers, and the new grain ; but for the manufacture of beer, the brewer needs only the first three substances. The same rule applies to the grape.

"In this use of the grape, all depends upon the judgment of man to select such of its parts as he wishes, and by his skill he adapts and applies them in the manner best for his purposes. In eating the grape he throws away the skins and seeds ; for raisins, he evaporates the water, retaining only the solid parts, from which, when he uses them, he rejects the seeds. If he manufactures must he lets the skins remain. In making wine he sets free the carbonic acid contained in the must, and removes the lees, gum, tartar, and, in short, everything deposited during and immediately after fermentation, as well as when it is put into casks and bottles. He not only removes from the wine its sediments, but watches the fermentation and checks it as soon as vinous fermentation is over, and the formation of vinegar about to begin. He refines his wine by an addition of foreign substances; if necessary, he sulphurizes it, and, by one means or another, remedies its diseases.

"The manufacture of wine is thus a many-sided art, and he who does not understand it, or knows not how to guide and direct the powers of Nature to his own purposes, may as well give up all hopes of success in it."

So far Dr. Gall ; and to the intelligent and unbiased mind, the truth and force of these remarks will be apparent. How absurd then are the blind ravings of those who speak of "natural" wines, and condemn as adulteration and fraud every addition of sugar and water to the must by man, in seasons when Nature has not fully done her part. There is no such thing as "natural wine," for wine, especially good wine, is the product of art, and an artificial process from beginning to end. An all-wise Creator gave us the raw materials for our sustenance and convenience, but gave us also reasoning powers to convert them to our use, and make them more wholesome and palatable. Shall we eat the raw potato simply because it is a natural production, or are we justified in cooking and roasting it, to make it more palatable and wholesome? How would the "naturalist" stare if some fine morning his good wife would set a cup filled with raw coffee beans and some water before him, instead of his usual fragrant beverage, and a dish of raw wheat instead of the usual light rolls which tempt his appetite? Yet the making of coffee and bread are even less natural, more artificial, than the addition of sugar and water to the must. Would not the wine-maker act as foolishly as the housewife who puts raw coffee and wheat upon the table, instead of the fragrant cup and white roll, if he has it in his power to remedy the deficiencies of Nature by such means as she herself supplies in good seasons, and which ought, and would be in the must, but for unfavorable circumstances over which we have no control? Wine thus improved is just as pure as if the water and sugar had naturally been in the grapes in the right proportions, just as beneficial to health, and only the fanatical numskull can call it adulterated. But these prejudices will disappear before the light of science and truth, and have disappeared already, until there is not a single establishment of any consequence, either here or in Europe, where it is not followed, either secretly or openly, and to the manifest improvement of their wines.

Yet, strange to say, these same "naturalists" will enjoy sparkling wines with a great deal of gusto, although they are a still more artificial product. And many of them will smack their lips over some rare so-called, "Old

Port," which has never seen a grape, but is some skillful concoction of logwood, spices, tartaric acid, syrup, alcohol, and tannin. "Oh, consistency, thou art a jewel!"

Let us now observe the change which fermentation makes in converting the must into wine. The nitrogenous compounds—vegetable albumen, gluten—(which are contained in the grape, and which are dissolved in the must as completely as the sugar), under certain circumstances turn into the fermenting principle, and so change the must into wine. This change is brought about by the fermenting substance coming in contact with the air, and receiving oxygen from it, in consequence of which it coagulates, and shows itself in the turbid state of must, or young wine. The coagulation of the lees takes place but gradually, and just in the degree that the exhausted lees settle. The sugar generally turns into alcohol. The acids remain partly as tartaric acid, are partly turned into ether, or settle with the lees, crystallize, and adhere to the bottom of the cask. The etheric oil or aroma remains, and develops into bouquet, as does the tannin, to a certain degree. The albumen and gluten principally settle, although a small portion of them remains in the wine. The coloring matter and extractive principle remain, but change somewhat by fermentation.

Thus it is, that must containing a large amount of sugar, needs a longer time to become clear, while that containing but a small portion soon becomes clear. Many southern wines retain a certain amount of sugar undecomposed; such are called sweet, or liqueur wines, whereas wines in which the whole of the sugar has been decomposed in the fermentation, are called sour or dry wines.

I have thought it necessary to be thus explicit to give my readers an insight into the general principles which should govern us in wine making. I have quoted freely from the excellent work of Dr. Gall. We will now see how we can reduce these principles to practice. I will illustrate by an example.

NORMAL MUST.

Experiments continued for a number of years have proved that, in favorable seasons, grape juice contains on an average in 1,000 pounds :

```
Sugar.............................240 pounds.
Acids.............................  6    "
Water............................754    "
                                 -----
                                 1,000
```

This proportion would constitute what I call a normal must. But suppose that in an inferior season the must contains, instead of the above, as follows :

```
Sugar.............................150 pounds.
Acids.............................  9    "
Water............................841    "
                                 -----
                                 1,000
```

What should we do to bring such a must to the condition of a normal must ? We calculate thus : If, with 6 lbs. of acids in a normal must, there is 240 lbs. of sugar, how much is wanted for 9 lbs. of acids ? Answer.—360 lbs. Our next problem is : If, with 6 lbs. of acids in a normal must, 754 lbs. of water appear, how much water is required for 9 pounds of acids ? Answer.—1,131 lbs. As, therefore, the must which we intend to improve by neutralizing its acids, should contain 360 lbs. of sugar, 9 lbs. of acids, and 1,131 lbs. of water, but contains already 150 lbs. of sugar, 9 lbs. of acid, and 841 lbs. of water, there remain to be added, 210 lbs. of sugar, no acids, and 290 lbs. of water.

By ameliorating a quantity of 1,000 lbs. of must, by 210 lbs. sugar, and 290 lbs. of water, we obtain 1,500 lbs. of must, consisting of the same properties as the normal must, which makes a first class wine.

This is wine making in Europe, according to Dr. Gall's

method. Now let us see how we can adapt it to American grapes and wines.

THE MUST OF AMERICAN GRAPES.

If we closely examine the musts of most of our American grapes, we find that they not only contain an excess of acids in inferior seasons, but even a greater superabundance of flavor or aroma, and of tannin and coloring matter. There is such an abundance of flavor in many of them, that, were the quantity doubled by addition of sugar and water, there would still be an abundance. With some varieties, such as Concord and Ives, if fermented on the husks, it is so strongly foxy, as to be disagreeable, and as the pulp of them is very tough and slippery, they can not be pressed clean without fermentation. We must, therefore, not only ameliorate the acid, but also the flavor and astringency, of which the tannin contained in the stems is the principal cause. Therefore, it is even more important to us than to European wine-makers, to gain the knowledge to Gallize our wines properly. By proper management we can change must, which would otherwise make a disagreeable wine, into one in which everything is in its right proportion, and which will thus suit a customer to whose fastidious taste it would otherwise be repugnant. True, our grapes will ripen better here, so that we can, in most seasons, produce a wine without a great excess of acids, but the American taste requires a less acid wine any way, and we must dilute the aroma to make our wines salable. Here another difficulty presents itself. The riper a grape is, the more of its peculiar aroma will it develop, and if we would let our Concords hang until they are so ripe that the acid has been reduced to the proper proportion, the aroma becomes so strong that it is very repugnant to a refined taste. What course remains then for us to take? Shall we let our grapes hang until the acid is reduced, and make an abominably, foxy wine, which no one will buy? Or shall we gather our grapes when well colored, Gallize the must until the acid and flavor are reduced to the proper amount, and thus produce a very fair, light-red wine, palatable to most, and a refreshing and in-vigorating beverage to all? I think the latter is the best course, and the only reasonable one.

At that time the must of Concord grapes will gener-ally weigh about 65° to 70° on Oechsle's Scale, and the Acidimeter will indicate about 6°. Now we make our calculation as follows: A normal must, to suit the palate here, should indicate about 80°, and show 4° on the Acidimeter. To reduce the acid to 4° we must add one-third water, or, in other words, if we have 480 lbs. of Concord grapes, which would make 40 gallons of pure juice, we must add 20 gallons of water. To these 20 additional gallons of water, we must add 40 lbs. of the best crushed sugar, to bring the water up to the ratio of normal must, 80°. But we have also a discrepancy of 15° in the must if it indicated 65°. To bring this also up to 80° we must add three-eighths pound of sugar to every gallon of must, or 15 lbs. to the 40 gallons. The addition to 480 lbs. of grapes would then be as follows: 20 gallons of water, 55 lbs. of sugar, and no acid, making 60 gallons of must of normal proportions, instead of 40 of pure juice. These will be about the right proportions for a pleasant and hand-some wine, of good color, pleasant flavor, and not too acid to suit the general taste, with also the proper pro-portion of tannin, which will be marketable sooner, and at a much higher price, than if we had allowed the grapes to hang a month longer, and then pressed the natural must, which would, perhaps, not contain an excess of acid then, but certainly an excess of foxy flavor and tannin.

Different grapes will, of course, require different treat-

ment. It is only by experimenting that we can find how
much each variety should be Gallized to produce the
best possible wine. Nor are the grapes alike in all seasons, and one season's product of the same grape may require different treatment than the other. To illustrate a
case in point : While experimenting with varieties, I
had, in the summer of 1866, enough of Rulander grapes,
then a new variety, to make 5 gallons of pure juice,
which, when tried by the saccharometer, showed 104°.
This was pressed and put into a 5-gallon cask. The
husks were thrown back into the fermenting vat, and 5
gallons of water, with 15 lbs. of sugar added, bringing
the water up to 100°, and fermented 48 hours, then
pressed and put into another 5-gallon cask. When pressing these my vintner thought that there was too much
flavor and character in the husks left to be thrown away,
and he once more added 5 gallons of water, with 15 lbs. of
sugar, and fermented this three days and three nights,
then pressed, and put into a third 5-gallon cask. The
wines became clear at about the same time, had nearly
the same color, and when tested by several connoisseurs,
they pronounced all good, but No. 2 the smoothest and
finest wine ; No. 1 rather the fullest, but somewhat
more astringent, while No. 3 was but little inferior to
No. 2. This verdict was given without knowing how
the wines had been made. We then mixed the three
wines, equal parts, in a tumbler, and upon testing, found
the mixture a better wine than either was separately.
The three, after this trial, were put together, and made
a wine like very fine Golden Sherry, which took the first
premium as best light-colored wine of any variety, at the
Combined Exhibition of the Longworth Wine House and
the American Grape Growers' Association, at Cincinnati,
in 1867, in competition with over 30 samples of the finest
Catawbas, Delawares, and Herbemont, as well as numerous other first premiums wherever exhibited. I have

made hundreds of such experiments, modifying the treatment with the character of the variety. I know, therefore, whereof I speak. Of course the above is an extreme case ; but few varieties have so much flavor and character as the Rulander, and the treatment which produced so fine a wine from this grape, would have made a very flat "Maxatawney," a grape which has but little character. When making such experiments I made it a rule always to keep some of the pure juice by itself, for comparison, and the tests were, therefore, made with the greatest fairness, and with but one aim, that is, to ascertain how the best possible wine could be made from any variety. Were I to give more of these experiments here, my readers would, perhaps, be even more astonished than I was, at the results ; but facts are stubborn, and can not be controverted. Seeing, and in this instance, tasting, is believing, and as I kept a very careful record of all cellar operations, there could be no mistakes.

I will here quote one of my first experiments made with very imperfectly ripened Catawba grapes, made in 1865, when that grape ripened very poorly, on account of mildew and rot. I found, on testing the must, that it would only show from 52° to 70°, while a normal Catawba must should weigh at least 80° in good seasons. My calculations for making the additions which I knew were imperatively necessary, were based upon the following reasons : If normal must weighs 80°, and this averages but 60°, there is a deficiency of half a pound of sugar to the gallon of must. But there should also be an excess of acid of at least one-third, as the Catawba has a superabundance of acid in even the most favorable seasons. I must, therefore, add at least one-third more water to dilute the acid, and to this water add 2 lbs. of sugar to each gallon, so that the whole mixture will weigh 80°. I did so, fermented all on the husks 36 hours, and the result was a very fine, golden-colored Catawba, which I sold before it was six months old, at the highest figures Catawba wines were then bringing, to the first buyer who came and tasted it.

As the Catawba constitutes yet, to a great extent, the product of Eastern and Northern vineyards, it may be well to give a few more hints to my readers on the management of Catawba must. This variety contains, as already mentioned, a very large amount of acids, as well as a great deal of tannin and flavor. This must be apparent to every one who has ever eaten well-ripened Catawba grapes. It has besides a very tough and acid center or pulp, of which every one can convince himself when eating even the most thoroughly ripened Catawba grapes. The first taste is delightful, but let him press the pulp and skins closely and he will find that the after taste is sour and rough. Of course fermentation extracts all this, and while the Catawba contains all the ingredients for a palatable wine, these two are present to a very great excess, and make the wine sour, astringent, and unpalatable. What then is necessary? We must simply add water and sugar, even in the best vintages, to ameliorate this, and much more in inferior seasons, and we will make better wines than are now in the market and much more wholesome, than the so-called "Sweet Catawbas," which are villainous compounds of unripe grape juice, raw spirits, and syrup added after fermentation, and afford an excuse for the habitual tippler to say that he drinks only wine, not whiskey. It would be better if he did take spirits so far as the effects on his system are concerned, for such mixtures intoxicate nearly as much, and the deleterious stuff they contain is only glossed over by the syrup. If Catawba wine is rationally Gallized, it makes a very pleasant, high-flavored wine, and those who prefer to have it still sweeter, can add sugar when drinking it, to suit their taste. If this were done, we would have no need of these "Sweet Catawbas" which now disgrace the wine trade of the country, and pure, light wine would have a better chance to become the universal beverage of the people. I do not pretend to give fixed rules to do this ; even were I competent, the product varies too much with the locality and the season. I merely attempt to show the way. Let every one experiment, and note the results, and he will soon see how far he should go to make the best wine, for he should not go farther. Let the best product always be his aim, not quantity.

The Concord, now so generally grown, is another variety which is immensely improved by Gallizing, and, as before remarked, to make the most palatable wine, should not be allowed to get too ripe. When the grapes are fully and evenly colored on the bunch, it is time to gather it, and I would rather add more sugar, than wait until it is fully ripe, as then its flavor becomes too strong and apparent. The same rule may be applied to the Martha, which is best when fairly ripe, but when over-ripe loses its sprightliness, and becomes foxy, while its wine is, when made in time, fully as good as the best Catawba. The addition of from one-third to one-half water and sugar, or in other words, from two-thirds to one gallon of water and sugar to every 12 ℔s. of grapes, and the whole mixture brought to 80° on Oechsle's Scale, fermented about 36 to 48 hours on the husks, in a temperature of 75°, will generally make the most palatable wine, from most of the *Labrusca* class and their hybrids. The Gœthe, under the same treatment, will make an excellent white wine, sprightly and pleasant, with just enough of its fine Frontignan flavor to make it agreeable.

Those who wish to satisfy themselves, can easily make the experiment, as I did, cautiously, and step by step. Let them make a small quantity of pure juice-wine, so-called, and compare it with wines made at the same time, of the same grapes, but Gallized more or less, and keep a careful record of the operation. This was my method, and I aimed always at improving the quality; so soon as I found the quality diminished, I considered it time to stop, while so long as the quality improved, I thought it safe to advance. Consider each variety a separate subject for experiment, it will not do to trust to surmises and guess work, nor can any rule be given that will apply to all varieties alike.

So far I have spoken mostly of the *Labruscas* and their hybrids. When we come to the *æstivalis* class we have entirely different material to deal with, and while we may, and can, by judicious Gallizing, improve some of them, and make them smoother and more palatable, yet with those which are used chiefly for medical purposes [as Norton's Virginia, which has become a great remedy for dysentery, bowel complaints, and cholera infantum], it will be better to let the grapes hang until they are dead ripe. Stem them before crushing, add very little or no water, and ferment on the husks for a week, or even longer. Their flavor is not objectionable, and the object here is, to make an astringent and heavy wine, and develop all the medicinal qualities which that grape possesses in such an eminent degree. To make simply a good Claret from it, of course it can be Gallized, and will make even a more pleasant wine for every day use. This class, however, also differs as much in its varieties as the *Labrusca.* I have already cited an example of the Rulander, which has a decided Sherry flavor. The Hermann, a seedling of the Norton's, is another with a strong Sherry character, so marked that the pure juice has too strong a flavor, yet when properly Gallized it makes a delightful deep-yellow wine, equal to any Golden Sherry, and the white seedling from it seems to be a still greater improvement, as it is much more delicate and juicy than its parent. And here let me make a prediction, to which long years of careful observation have led me, and which is shared by all of the prominent grape-growers of the State, so far as I know. It is this, that the grape-growers of the State, if they turn their attention chiefly to the best of the *æstivalis*, the Cynthiana, Norton's Virginia, Neosho, and others, which have not been so fully tried, will, at no distant day, excel the products of the choicest vineyards of the European Continent, and may safely challenge the world in the production of the choicest Burgundies, Clarets, and Sherries, and the sooner we turn our attention to them the better. California, and even the East, may excel us in the quantity, and rival us in the quality of white wines, but from all the information I can obtain, they can not come near to our red wines, which are even now the equals of the best wines of Burgundy. This is our proper field, and the sooner we concentrate our energies upon it, the better will it be for us. They are, at the same time, Phylloxera-proof, and we need not fear that they will "go back" upon us.

In the *cordifolia* we have still another material. The grapes of this class may be said to occupy a position between the *Labruscas* and the *æstivalis* class. Nearly all contain considerable acid, and an abundance of flavor, and are much improved by judicious Gallizing; but as their skin and pulp is tender, they need not be fermented on the husks for any length of time. Twenty-four hours of lively fermentation will generally be sufficient for the Elvira, Taylor, and Clinton. They promise to furnish us another class of wines, and as they are also Phylloxera-proof, we may consider these two classes as the foundation of future grape growing. We have but just commenced experimenting with this class, but the great success achieved by Mr. Rommel and others justify the most sanguine hopes. I was particularly struck with some wines shown me by Mr. James Ricketts, from several Clinton seedlings, foremost among which are the

Bacchus and Ariadne. They show a new class of wines, light red in color, of great body, and very peculiar flavor. Should these varieties prove to be adapted to more general culture, we may expect some remarkable wines from them.

Of course these are only general hints, which are calculated to show my wine-making friends the way they must go, to make palatable and wholesome wines. I shall not attempt to go into details about varieties, as even these differ so much in different localities that no rules for their treatment could be given to apply in all cases. Nor do I pretend to be perfect, but I am convinced more and more every day, how little I yet know, and how much I have to learn.

In all my experiments I aimed to come as near the normal must of the variety I experimented with as possible, in the specific gravity of the water and must, when mixed. I have no doubt that we also have much to learn yet in the judicious mixing of several kinds of grapes. Experiments in that line have already shown astonishing results, and the art of blending and cutting wines, so well understood and practised in the best cellars of Europe, is yet in its infancy here, but will, no doubt, have a great influence upon our future products. But this art can only be based upon a thorough knowledge of the characteristics of each individual variety, and he who undertakes the task must bring to it a peculiar talent and highly developed taste, as well as the nicest discrimination of the traits of each variety. If our grape growing and wine making had the experience of several centuries to look back upon, we could base our operations upon certain knowledge. Now we are feeling our way. The pioneers who first made the clearings in our woods, greatly rejoiced when they could eat the first hoe-cake from the corn their industry had planted in the wilderness, and still more enjoyed the rolls made of their first wheat. Like them are we overjoyed at what we have achieved, and know that the grape, so lately but the child of these same forests, is susceptible of as much improvement and as great a change, as that which converted the old time clearing, with its simple log cabin, into the pleasant homestead with its smiling and tasteful lawn and orchard, rich with golden fruits. And those who intend to be the winners in this race, must have the pluck and perseverance of the old frontier pioneers, hoping always, even in the most gloomy times, for brighter days, and never doubting of the end.

Dr. Gall recommended grape sugar as the best to be used for Gallizing. This is made from potato starch, but all the samples I have yet tried are not pure enough, and leave an unpleasant, bitter taste in the wine. I have, therefore, used the best and purest cane sugar, and as it also dissolves more readily in water, I prefer it, and have found it to answer every purpose. I have lately tasted a sugar made from the Minnesota or Early Amber cane, which seems to be well adapted to the purpose, and if the production of its sugar assumes the dimensions it now promises, we may have an important advantage over our former method, in a cheaper and better article of sugar. The best cane sugar when dissolved in water in the proportion of 2 lbs. of sugar to the gallon, will show upon the scale about 80°. In making additions to Catawba, Goethe, Martha, Elvira, and all the lighter wines, it takes about 2 lbs. of sugar to the gallon of water, to produce the weight of normal must of these varieties. For Norton's Virginia, Cynthiana, Rulander, and all the heavier wines, it will take, at least, 2¹/₂ lbs. of sugar to the gallon of water, as their normal must ranges from 100° to 110°, and sometimes 120°, in the product of the best seasons.

As a general rule it may be assumed, however, that our native grapes, with their strong flavor and abundance of tannin and coloring matter, will admit, nay, require, much more Gallizing than the more delicate and finer flavored grapes of Europe. How far we can go with each variety I do not presume to say, and only experience can safely guide us here. It must be apparent to every one who is ever so slightly acquainted with wine making, how widely different the varieties are in their characteristics and constituents. I have tried only to give an outline of the necessary operations, as well as the principles underlying the science of wine making, have quoted facts, only so far as I have become familiar with them through long practice and observation. No one can be better convinced than I am, how much we have yet to learn, and how wide the field that lies before us. I have been severely censured for the open advocacy of the method of Dr. Gall, even by those who have practised it as zealously and not always confined themselves as much to its true limits as I have tried to do. Many of our best wine-makers think that we should keep the knowledge we have gained to ourselves, and profit by it in secret, instead of openly facing a prejudice which we know to exist. But it has always been a deep-seated conviction with me that knowledge, like God's sun, should be the common property of all ; that it is a duty every citizen owes to the community in which he lives, to impart freely what he may know, to every one. Only thus can we progress in this fast age, where progress is the watchword. Truth and justice need never fear the light, they can only gain by close investigation.

And here let us look at the probable effects these methods of improvement are likely to have upon grape culture, and ask ourselves : Is there anything reprehensible in them, any reason why they should not become generally known ? I think the answer is easily found. Gallized wines contain nothing, which fermented grape juice, in its purest and most perfect condition, does

not also contain. They are, therefore, as pure as any
grape juice can be, with the consideration in their favor,
that they contain all the ingredients in their proper proportion.

It is a matter of course that careless and slovenly work-
ers have failed, and will continue to fail, in making good
wine by this, or any other method, but this cannot be
used as an argument against it. To make a good article
the peculiarities of each variety must be closely studied,
and we must not think that water and sugar will accomplish everything. Its use should be limited, and becomes abuse as soon as it oversteps that limit.

But I will hope that I have contributed my mite to the
fund of universal knowledge, and if this little volume
only aids every farmer in the land, who can grow grapes,
to make a few barrels of pure, light wine for family use,
to take the place of poor whiskey and brandy, now the
bane and curse of so many households, I am more than
repaid for the labor of many a lonely early morning hour
it has cost me. Mine has been an incessantly busy life,
and the time for these scribblings has been stolen mostly
from the "small, still hours." I know of no holidays,
and have often had to force exhausted nature to the
task. This must be my excuse for its many imperfections. But I flatter myself that I am not entirely mistaken, when I think I send it on a temperance mission,
perhaps more true and, therefore, more effective than any
Murphy movement. I have always looked upon the general use of pure, light wine as the best temperance measure that could be adopted. A glass of wine, used early
in the morning, I have found to be the best preventive
against malaria, and nothing revives the sinking energies
of the worn out laborer better during a hot summer day,
as I know from actual experience. I have known it to
save life in dangerous diseases, and could cite many instances did time and space permit.

Let us all then further the cause of grape-culture. The laborer by producing fruit, the mechanic by inventions, the scientist by improving our methods, the lawgiver by wise laws in its favor, and all others by using its products in moderation, as one of the best gifts from the fountain of all that is good, pure, and beautiful.

CHAPTER XXXIII.

WINE MAKING RENDERED EASY.

Perhaps it may have seemed as if I was only writing for the benefit of those who can follow grape growing and wine making on a larger scale, with abundant means at their command, to build commodious cellars, plant large vineyards, and hire laborers to do the work. This is not the case, however. If I have given the outlines of larger operations it is because our object should always be to attain perfection in everything ; I have never for a moment lost sight of the interests of those, who, like myself, have to commence at the lowest round of the ladder, who have to make a small beginning, and work their way up through untold difficulties. There is not an operation in the vineyard, from the clearing of the unbroken forest and prairie, to the finishing touch given to the wine at its last racking, which I have not performed and am not thoroughly familiar with, and I can, therefore, fully sympathize with the poor laborer, who has nothing but his industrious hands, and an honest intention to succeed.

While it may hardly be advisable now, in these days of low prices and light demand for wine, to begin grape growing as a means of support, with the hope of realizing a handsome income from it in the course of a few years, yet there is no reason why every farmer should not have a small vineyard, grow his own grapes, and make his barrel or two of wine, or why every owner of a garden should be without enough grapes for the use of the family.

Grape-vines of the more common varieties are very cheap now, and an outlay of $5 to $10 will buy one hundred to two hundred vines—enough to make a start with. Plant these, at any rate, if you cannot do more, and grow your own vines hereafter to enlarge your vineyard. Wire for trellis is also very cheap now, and it is not needed the first year or two. A few hundred vines can be easily kept in order before breakfast; let the children help you, they can do a great deal of the lighter work, and will learn to take a delight in it. And when your first crop of grapes ripens, and you can make a few barrels of wine, if you have no press or commodious cellar, you can find a cider press somewhere, and room in the cellar of one of your neighbors to store it. One of our most successful wine-growers commenced his operations with a simple hole in the ground, dug under his house, and his first wine-press was merely a large beam, let into a tree, which acted as a lever upon the grapes, with a press bed, also of his own making. His vineyard and wine cellars are now among the best in the county, and although he no longer lives to enjoy it, his family are left in affluent circumstances, and grape growing alone has made them wealthy. Besides, we have got down to the lowest prices, and as the prospects for the grape-growers of the Old World, and even of California, darken on account of the Phylloxera, our own begin to brighten. We know that we have something we can depend upon, and feel that better days will come again for the grape-growers and wine-makers of the country.

Of course it is not advisable to keep the wine over summer in an indifferent cellar, but if it is good, as it

ought to be, you can easily dispose of it as soon as clear.
Or you can dispose of your grapes, if you can not or will
not make them into wine, to some neighbor, or market
them yourself. Nearly all of our small country towns
afford a ready market for a small quantity, indeed often
a better one than do the large cities.

Another way to make grape growing and wine making
easy, is to form grape and fruit colonies. There are locations enough in all the States of the Union, where suitable lands for this purpose can be had cheap. The advantages of such colonies can be easily seen. If each one
has a small piece of suitable land (and he does not need a
large tract for this business), they can assist each other in
plowing and sub-soiling, and will thus be able to do with
fewer animals, by preparing the soil first for one, then for
the other, the ravages of birds and insects will hardly be
felt, the neighbors can join together in building a cellar,
where all can store their wine, and of which one can take
the management. They can market their product easier,
obtain better prices, and lower rates of transportation to
large cities, than single individuals, and also make a better and more uniform product.

There are thousands of acres of land well adapted for
the purpose, in Missouri and other States, which could be
had at very low prices, where the virgin soil waits only the
bidding of intelligent and combined labor, to bring forth
the richest fruits. There is room for thousands—may it
soon be filled with willing hearts and hands to undertake
the task.

CHAPTER XXXIV.

CONCLUDING REMARKS.

I have little to add regarding wine making in all those sections where American grapes are the basis of the wine industry. The principles remain the same, though some of the many new varieties may need more or less modification in their treatment to make palatable wine from them. Some of the new varieties recently introduced by Professor Munson, Hermann Jaeger and the late John Burr, will probably yield better wines, if properly handled, than the old sorts. The seedlings and crosses from the Herbemont and *lincecumii* types will furnish specially valuable material.

Here on the Pacific coast, where I have followed grape growing for the last fifteen years, and introduced many of our American varieties with high hopes of success, the outcome has in most cases been disappointing. The Norton and Cynthiana were total failures, not alone in amount of production, but also in the quality of the wine made from them. The fruit was only half the normal size and almost destitute of juice, so that here, where gallizing is not practiced, they were wholly unprofitable. The only American varieties which succeed, to any extent, are the Herbemont, Lenoir, Louisiana and Rulander. These make a fair natural wine, without any addition. The Herbemont, if pressed lightly, makes a good white wine, sprightly, and of good aroma. The Lenoir makes an exceedingly dark wine, which is considered valuable as a so-called "doctor wine," to blend with *vinifera* wines, and to impart color to claret and burgundies. The Louisiana and Rulander make a natural sherry, about 160 gallons of which, made in my vineyard last year, are of high promise as a natural liquor wine. But the varieties do not all yield the same quality as similar *vinifera* varieties, and as they are, besides, more costly to train and cultivate, they will hardly become popular, except, perhaps, as stocks to graft upon. Even for this purpose the wild *riparia* is generally preferred, as it has proved entirely resistant, and takes the graft easily. The Elvira, and others of its class, were also failures as direct producers, for the grapes are much smaller, drop worse from the bunch, and are more foxy than in the Eastern States. Still, they make good stocks for grafting.

The progress made since the first edition of this work was published may be gathered from the "Experience of Other Growers," in Part II. I can only thank the gentlemen who have so kindly contributed to those pages. They are, naturally, better guides than I can be in estimating the value, for wine making, of the newly introduced American varieties,—who have observed their growth and can judge of their quality better than any person who is working, as I am, in an entirely different field, with *vinifera* sorts as a basis for natural wine. Their detailed experience shows that there is an intermediate region in Western Texas and New Mexico where both American and *vinifera* varieties succeed equally well; where the latter ripen as early as the last of May and all through June, and large tracts are being planted with them for early markets. Their wine-making qualities remain to be tested.

PART IV.

GRAPE CULTURE AND WINE MAKING
IN CALIFORNIA.

CHAPTER XXXV.

THE VINE IN CALIFORNIA.

Grape culture in California differs so materially from Eastern methods that there is hardly any comparison to be made. That the vine has here found the most congenial climate, there can be no doubt. All the choicest *vinifera* varieties flourished here with a luxuriance unknown in Europe until the phylloxera made its appearance and began its ravages. So far, no remedy has been found, save grafting the *vinifera* on the American resistant stocks. This method has been tested for fifteen years, and the results are all that can be desired. Not only do the *viniferas* flourish as well as formerly on their own roots, but they are greater and more abundant bearers, while the fruit produced is fully as good, if not of superior quality. We have now fairly passed the experimental stage, and know pretty well what to plant and what to graft. With these introductory remarks, we can proceed to the first stage of the work, which will be the foundation of the vineyard and the choosing of the different classes of grapes.

RESISTANT STOCKS.

VINIFERA.—Of European or Asiatic origin. By far the greater part of our vineyards, where they have not been destroyed by the phylloxera, consist of these on their own roots. It comprises nearly all the valuable varieties for wine, table or raisins, and as all grow from cuttings with the greatest ease, the establishment of a vineyard was an easy and inexpensive task. Such planting is no longer safe—the phylloxera has destroyed thousands of acres of vineyards already, and the only safe way is to plant resistant vines. These we will consider in the order of their value and general adaptability, ease of propagating and facility for grafting.

VITIS RIPARIA.—This is at present the most popular and preferred class, both in its wild form and some of its cultivated varieties, of which the Elvira is perhaps the most prominent. They have proven entirely resistant, adapt themselves to the greatest variety of soil and location, grow easily and rapidly from cuttings, and take the graft readily, forming a complete junction. Objection has been raised to the Riparia on account of its slender growth, and it has been claimed that the graft would outgrow the stock, but so far this has not been the case, and vineyards grafted twelve years ago are yet perfectly healthy and more productive than when on their own roots. For a minute description of all classes, the reader is referred to the first part of this book.

VITIS ÆSTIVALIS.—This is perhaps next in value, although the different varieties do not grow so readily from cuttings, and it is also claimed by some writers that they are not entirely resistant. This impression, I think, had its origin in the method formerly employed, of grafting below the surface. Thus grafted, the graft made strong roots of its own, causing the stock to dwindle and die, and as the roots of the graft were non-resistant they were attacked and destroyed by the phylloxera. I am not afraid to risk Æstivalis stock, if grafted above the surface, as being entirely resistant, and as it is a heavier grower than the *riparia*, it makes a good stock. An impression prevails that it succeeds best on rich, deep soils. It suckers less than any other American class, which is another point in its favor.

VITIS RUPESTRIS.—This class has somewhat disappointed the high expectations once entertained of it, when it was thought it would prove specially adapted to dry, shallow soils, as it is found on the dryest hillsides in Southern Missouri, Arkansas and Texas. It does not flourish in dry locations here, and as it suckers profusely and does not take the graft as readily as the two former classes, it is not largely propagated.

VITIS LABRUSCA.—This can hardly be called entirely resistant, as the insect feeds on its roots to some extent, though not to the extent that it does on the *vinifera*. In the Simonton vineyard were some Catawbas and Isabellas mixed in a block of old Mission vines, which remained, to all appearances, healthy and produced fair crops after the Mission had entirely succumbed to the phylloxera. I would not, however, recommend it as a resistant stock, as the whole class roots shallow, and is, therefore, apt to suffer from drouth.

VITIS CALIFORNICA.—This, our native wild grape, found all along our creeks and ravines, was at one time considered entirely resistant, although it was suspected that its soft, spongy roots would be as subject to the attacks of the insect as those of the *vinifera*, which they strongly resemble. This surmise proved correct, and it is not considered a resistant to-day, though its vigor and strong growth will doubtless enable it to resist longer than the *vinifera*, the attacks of the phylloxera. Neither will it flourish in dry, shallow soils. It takes the graft readily, perhaps more so than any other class, but does not make so good a junction as *riparia*.

VITIS ARIZONICA.—This seems to be an intermediate between *riparia* and *Californica*, of upright growth and shining leaves. It never seemed to flourish well and has not been fully tried.

The Solonis, Vialla, Berlandieri or Monticola, Doaniana, Champini and Lavata have their admirers in France, and Professor Munson thinks highly of them as resistants, but they have not been fully tried in this State. I believe, from experience up to date, that the *riparia* will be safest to plant and graft. ·Cuttings of the *riparia* can now be had at from two to three dollars per thousand, and rooted plants at about twelve dollars per thousand. Hence there is but little gained here, by growing young plants in a nursery.

CHAPTER XXXVI.

LOCATION, ASPECT AND SOIL.

Vineyards are more easily planted and cultivated in valleys than on hillsides, and on the rich bottom lands are generally more productive; yet to those who desire fine quality, the hillsides are to be preferred. Vineyards in the valley are more liable to damage from late frosts in the spring and early frosts in autumn, and the fruit is naturally inferior. Our best wines, in the future, will have to come from the hillsides, from light, rich, warm soils, and from small growers, not the immense wholesale cellars where hundreds of tons are crushed in a day, handled pellmell and mixed up without regard to quality. But it would be equally unreasonable to suppose that fine wines could be made from vines planted on the bed rock, or in locations which will not support even a moderate growth of grass, as we often see them on our southern hillsides. What the vine wants, here as elsewhere, is a deep, moderately rich soil, which will enable it to send its roots down to elaborate its food. This is generally found on the hillsides sloping to the north or northwest and southwest, where the redwood, manzanita, mountain laurel and hazel form the natural growth. If such a hillside is not too steep, there is the location for the vineyard—not on the southern slope, where the soil is generally shallow and poor, and where the vines are subjected to the rays of the afternoon sun, the dews of the night having already been dried up. We must remember that our vines are expected to do without rain from May to September, and when they are constantly exposed to the afternoon sun, they are apt to become sun-scalded, while on the northern slopes they have the full benefit of the sun in the forenoon, when the foliage is fresh from dew, which enables them to remain fresh all day. Only from a vine in full vigor can we expect to get its most perfect product—not from starved specimens. There are exceptions to every rule, and we have southern slopes with deep soil where vines will do well; but the hot afternoon sun is always an objection to the best of these locations, and where they are finally chosen, the varieties planted or grafted should be such as are least subject to sun-scald. The Zinfindal will hardly do in such situations, as its foliage and fruit are very tender. Steep hillsides should always be avoided, as cultivation and fruit gathering on them are more expensive.

The foregoing applies only to wine grapes. For market and for raisins, the rich bottom lands may be preferable, as they will produce larger and more showy fruit. But if even for these purposes, the frost question should be carefully considered. Any one who has closely observed the effects of frost, will have noted the great difference existing between the lowlands and the hillsides above them.

CHAPTER XXXVII.

PROPAGATION.

By reason of our rainless summers, cuttings, or even rooted vines, do not make much growth the first season, but they become established, and after the rains of the following winter and spring, start into vigorous growth. Many, therefore, plant cuttings at once in the vineyard, taking the precaution to put two at each stake, somewhat diverging at the base, so that if both grow, one can be removed to fill vacancies where both have died. Here, I think this is perhaps the best method, as it saves the labor of planting cuttings in the nursery, digging and transplanting; in addition, the cutting has made its roots and sent them into the most congenial soil, and it receives no check by transplanting. If care be taken to plant only the best cuttings, made of medium, well-ripened wood, if possible with a heel of the old wood attached, there will be but few failures, and it saves a great amount of work. I have seen vineyards, lately, partly planted with rooted *riparias* and partly *riparia* cuttings, and the difference was scarcely perceptible after two years. Both were grafted the same spring, about 95 per cent. of the grafts living, and some of the grafts produced from eight to ten clusters of fruit. This very gratifying result was reached under the personal supervision of the proprietor, on a rich piece of soil carefully prepared, and he may expect a crop of three tons to the acre the fourth season after planting, with grafting intervening. That cuttings planted in the vineyard where they can occupy the space alone, instead of being crowded in nursery rows, will develop better and make a stronger growth, is self-evident. The main condition to this success is clean cultivation and frequent stirring of the soil to induce moisture. Without this, it is impossible.

As to making the cuttings, the rules given in the first part of the book will hold good here. It may be well, however, to make them somewhat longer, say thirteen to fifteen inches, and have about two buds above the ground. To prevent suckering after grafting, the lower buds may be cut off with a sharp knife, leaving the upper three buds, when there will be no further trouble. To plant in nursery, the same rules as to length of cuttings, cultivation, etc., will apply, with the single exception that the cuttings are slanted more in planting, to facilitate digging, while in the vineyard they are planted almost perpendicularly. Cuttings can be procured for three dollars per thousand, but it is safer to prepare them yourself. This can be done at any time during the winter, as long as the wood is dormant, but they should be kept fresh ·from the time the wood is taken from the vines. They can be prepared during rainy days, tied in convenient bundles and heeled in in a shady place to keep them dormant until wanted for planting, which is generally in March or the early part of April, by which date ample opportunity will have been given for preparing the soil in the best manner and allowing it to be warmed up by the rays of the sun.

If it is convenient to irrigate the nursery, it can be made a great help, but do not do it until July or August. To irrigate earlier is unnecessary, as the soil contains enough moisture for growth, whereas irrigation cools the ground below the surface so much that the formation of callus and roots is retarded. Warmth is needed then, as well as moisture. But whether planted in vineyard or nursery, do not fail to keep the lower ends moist. This is best done by keeping them in a bucket of water while planting, and when planted, by firming the soil well around their base by trampling it down

13

compactly after filling with well-pulverized earth. When covered and firmed to the depth of three inches, the remainder of the earth may be pulled in loosely, but should also be well firmed.

CHAPTER XXXVIII.

VINEYARD PLANTING.

This is generally done in the spring. as soon as the. ground is dry and warm enough, the time varying in different parts of the State. We prefer to plant in blocks of two and a half acres, with avenues intervening, to facilitate hauling the grapes. In the old plantations the vines were planted in squares, 7x7 or 8x8 feet, which admitted of cultivation both ways, but planting at a greater distance one way and a lesser space the other is of late more generally preferred. It is urged for the latter method, and no doubt justly, that it admits of more thorough cultivation. At the old distance only two or three furrows could be plowed between rows, while by the latter, five can be made with double teams. The latter method also facilitates picking and hauling, as teams can pass between the row, and it gives more air and light to the vines, thereby making them more healthy and luxuriant. In most plantations vines are now set 6x10 feet, which gives the same number of vines to the acre as when set 8x8, with the wider rows running parallel with the hillside, if hillside there be, making it more convenient to haul on fertilizers and to remove grapes and brush from the vines.

The ground should be deeply plowed and pulverized, as described in Part I. After the ground has been thoroughly evened by rolling, or dragging, it must be marked off. For that purpose, about 1200 markers are needed, small redwood sticks a foot in length, and lines, two to reach lengthways and one crossways. First mark the avenues one way, to the most convenient location for delivering the grapes, twelve feet wide, then the intersecting or cross avenues, by placing a marker along the outside line every six feet and every ten feet on the intersecting line. After thus laying off into blocks, or squares, each containing about two acres, we can mark all the squares. This is most accurately and quickly done by four men (two of whom stretch two lines, one on each side of the block, commencing at the second marker), who also take charge of the cross line, the other two doing the marking. The cross line is now stretched from the second marker, drawn tightly and straight, and markers are placed at each intersection. The line is then moved to marker three, which is similarly marked, and so on to the end of the block.

When the marking is finished, planting is in order, assuming that the ground has been well prepared. Small holes are dug with the spade, always on the upper side of the marker, toward the hill, if hill there be, as nearly perpendicular as possible, and about a foot in depth. The vines or cuttings, as the case may be, should be kept in water while planting. The planters follow the diggers, placing the plant or cutting at the bottom of the hole, the upper end above ground just at the marker. The roots must be covered with well-pulverized, moist earth, firmed around them by pressure with the foot. This is quickly done if the ground has been well prepared. All that now remains to be done during the first summer is to keep the ground loose and moist by a frequent use of the cultivator, plow and hoe.

CHAPTER XXXIX.

CULTIVATION OF THE YOUNG PLANTS.

GRAFTING.

Little pruning will be needed on the young vines the following year, as we suppose they are all resistant stocks—it would be the hight of folly to plant any other. Cultivation should be thorough—by deep plowing in early spring, and frequent stirring of the soil during summer. The young plants need no staking or tying until grafted, and no pruning unless they grow extra strong; in that case the growth of last year may be cut back to three or four buds, and the stronger growth used for cuttings.

Opinions vary widely as to the proper season for grafting. Some contend that grafting should be done early in order to make a complete junction. The French have carried this theory so far as to graft the cuttings in the shop. After forty years' experience in grafting the grape, I have reached the following conclusions:

1. There is no time gained by grafting when the stock is too small to hold the graft firmly. On the contrary, grafts, to succeed at all, must be firmly tied, as otherwise there is danger of moving the cion. The operation materially retards the growth of the stock, and without a vigorous stock to start with, there can be no complete success. A stock of an inch or an inch and a half in diameter is preferable, and this is not often obtained before the third year after planting.

2. The cions should be prepared through the winter, of medium sized, short jointed, well ripened wood, and carefully stored away in a cool, shady place to retard their growth. They should be at least fifteen inches in length, and from an inch to an inch and a half of wood

should be left below the lowest bud. Too much care cannot be exercised in their selection.

3. In grafting *viniferas* on resistant stocks, the operation should be performed above ground, at a smooth place nearest or above the surface. This will prevent the graft from forming roots, which would be non-resistant. The ground should be well drawn up around the graft to prevent drying out.

4. The best time for the operation is when the sap is in rapid motion, which will vary with the locality. If the cions have been kept dormant, it may be performed in California as late as May, but any time in April is preferable. Grafting too early is apt to cause stagnation and souring of sap.

Having laid down the general principles, the operation itself is next in order. This is best done after the first plowing, when the soil is turned away from the vines and it can be conveniently divided between three, or even four men. The first clears the earth away from the vine, cuts off the stock with a pair of sharp pruning shears about one or one and a half inches above a joint or node, and if cleft grafting is the mode practiced, he can make the longitudinal cleft or cut, taking care not to bruise the bark on the side where the cion is to be inserted.

The grafter comes next, with his tools and cions in a basket, and should be the most careful man of all. He needs a sharp, thin-bladed knife to cut the cions to a long, sloping wedge, just below the bud, as already explained in Part I, and if the stocks are too large to be split with shears, a grafting chisel and wooden mallet should be used. Generally these are not necessary in young vineyards. The cion is pushed down firmly into the cleft, and if the stock closes well around it, needs no tying or bandaging. It is wise for the grafter to carry tying material with him, as it will be needed in occasional cases where the split in the stock extends so far down that it will not hold the stock firmly. The success of the operation depends mainly on a close junction of stock and cion from the top to the bottom of the cleft.

The third man follows, drawing well-pulverized earth around the base of the cion, or the junction, pressing it on and around the cleft and the top of the stock, and then drawing well-pulverized earth around the cion, leaving only the two upper buds exposed. This finishes the operation. It is wise to drive a stake at each graft soon after the operation. It serves as a protection to the young graft, and the young, tender growth, when it appears, should at frequent intervals be tied to the stake. Suckers from the stock should be promptly removed.

CHAPTER XL.

SELECTION OF VARIETIES.

The whole success of the vineyard may depend on a proper selection of varieties. It is, however, almost impossible to give general rules, as some soils are especially adapted for producing the choicest red wines, while others will give that delicacy of flavor, that sprightliness and fullness especially admired in the Hocks and Sauternes, of which the Riesling and the Semillion may be considered the leading types. Generally we expect the finest red wines from soils rich in iron, to give them the fine, violet color, the tannin and fine bouquet, while the finest white wines are generally produced on lighter colored, gravelly soils. That there is an immense difference in soil and location goes without saying. The cultivator who comes into an unfamiliar locality would be wise to consult neighbors with similar soil, who have had experience with it, as to what varieties to plant. Unfortunately there has been too little of that reciprocity among growers. A tendency to ape French and Italian methods has also unwisely prevailed, presumably because grape growers have so often been told that California is the France or Italy of America, forgetting that entirely different conditions here prevail. The varieties of the *vinifera* in California are almost without number—they may reach 500 or more, imported from all parts of the globe. That many of these have proved comparatively worthless is but natural. In a book like this, it is impossible to describe any except the most prominent, classifying them under their uses, for red wine, white wine, sherry, port, brandy, for table and market and for raisins.

GRAPES FOR RED WINE.

The demand for red wines exceeds that for white, and descriptions here follow, taking first those which produce red wines of the highest grades but which are moderate bearers, following with varieties used for the more common wines, but which are very productive.

CABERNET SAUVIGNON. Synonym Carbenet.—The highest type of Bordeaux wines, but a rather shy bearer. Vine a rather thin, straggling grower, with deeply lobed and serrated foliage, downy beneath. Clusters rather small, loose, shouldered ; berry small, round, black, covered with blue bloom, juicy and sweet, with a peculiar aroma, somewhat resembling the frost grape. This flavor is strongly perceptible in the wine, so as to become almost disagreeable, although it becomes milder with age. Its true province is in blending with other and softer varieties, such as the Carignane and Mataro, which are abundant bearers, but lack sprightliness.

CABERNET FRANC.—This is closely related to the Sauvignon, but the leaves are not so deeply lobed and it is rather more productive, though perhaps not so high in quality. Grafting on the *riparia* has improved the bearing of both of the Cabernets, many who thus grow them reporting yields of three tons to the acre. As these grapes are always worth double the price of common varieties, such a yield would be satisfactory.

BECLAN.—Makes one of the choicest red wines, smooth and of delicate flavor. Vine a fair grower and bearer; cluster rather small, shouldered and compact; berry rather small, long, black, rather thick skin, fine flavor.

VALDEPENAS.—A Spanish grape of high character, making a true claret wine of the sprightly type. Vine vigorous and productive; cluster long and loose, shouldered; berry medium, round, black, with blue bloom; very valuable.

PETIT SYRAH. Synonym Scrine.—Strong grower and productive, making a fine claret wine of high character. Cluster rather long and loose, shouldered; berry slightly oblong, medium, black, with blue bloom.

GAMAY TEINTURIER.—A moderate grower, with dark foliage; very productive. Cluster compact, shouldered; berry below medium, oblong, black, with very dark juice; very refreshing and sprightly. It is one of the coloring grapes, and can be used to great advantage to ferment with other varieties which lack color, though it makes a fine, sprightly wine by itself. It would make a fine blend with the following:

BLACK PINOT. Synonyms, Chauche Noir, Blauer Burgunder.—Vine a strong grower but moderate bearer, subject to coulure sometimes. Cluster and berry rather small, compact, ripening early and developing a high percentage of sugar; black, with rather thick skin, and very agreeable flavor. Makes a very full, smooth wine, but lacks color and sprightliness, both of which would be imparted by the Gamay, which ripens at the same time.

MEUNIER. Synonyms, Miller's Burgundy, Müllerrebe. —Moderate grower and bearer, as most of the Pinots are, but makes an excellent wine. The foliage is a light green, covered with a white bloom, looking as if dusted with flower, hence its name. Cluster small, slightly shouldered; berry rather small, slightly oblong, also covered with white bloom; delicate and sprightly.

REFOSCO. Synonym, Crabb's Black Burgundy.—This is a strong grower, very productive in some locations, subject to coulure in others. Leaf heart-shaped, covered with gray furze beneath. Cluster medium, shouldered; berry medium, slightly oblong, with thick skin and dark juice, making an excellent, full-bodied wine.

The following I would classify not as high as the foregoing, but as making very good red wines in their proper location: St. Macaire, Spanna or Nebbiolo, Tannat, Carignane, Fresa, Petit Bouschet. The last is especially cultivated because it contains a great amount of color and tannin, which makes it very valuable for blending.

ZINFANDEL.—As this was the first grape of which good red wine was made here, and it yet occupies a large part, if not a majority, of our vineyards, a more complete description of it is given—its good qualities and its faults. If planted on soils rich in iron, along our hillsides, especially on northern slopes with deep soil, it will develop abundance of sugar and fine flavor. Such Zinfandel wine will reach perfection in about two years, and should not be kept over three, as it will then lose that fine raspberry flavor and sprightliness which characterize it when young. Grown on rich valley lands, it is a wine of little color and character, and becomes a very indifferent beverage. Its good qualities are early productiveness, easy training and sure crops, which have given it the name of the "poor man's grape." Its faults are, uneven ripening, some of the berries drying up long before the others are ripe, which makes fermentation very difficult; liability to sunscald of foliage and fruit; liability to frost and over-productiveness. It is not satisfied with producing one crop, but will sometimes produce two or three more from the laterals on the bearing shoots. "With all its faults, we love it still," and a Zinfandel claret from locations best adapted to it, carefully made, is good enough for any one. Unfortunately there is much made not up to these standards, hence the many complaints about inferior red wines. The three following are very productive and make very fair wines:

Mondeuse, or Gros Syrah, Mataro, and Charbonneau. The last makes a wine of very deep color, but of very rough character, and the color fades with age. Grenache may also be classified with these, being very productive, even on poor soil, and makes a fair wine. Of course there are other varieties which have their merits, for instance Grosse Blaue or Koelner, Blauer Portugieser, and a host of others, but not all have been sufficiently tried, and it is not well to cultivate too many varieties. The above are some of the best, and comprise both quality and quantity.

Among the varieties which make the finest port, but which are rather unproductive, is the Trousseau or Trussieux.

GRAPES FOR WHITE WINE.

Owing to the importation of many of the best types of vines from the Rhine and from France, the white wines of California won a reputation at an earlier date than did the red wines, a better grade being produced. Hock from the Mission grape, and the white wine made from the first run of the so-called Black Malvasia, were not calculated to raise their reputation. They were too fiery, and lacked the delicacy of flavor and the smoothness of the better wines, now made from the Riesling and some of the French Sauterne types. It may, however, be justly claimed that our white wines average better than our red and are better adapted to our lighter soils.

SEMILLION. Synonym, Colombar.—This is one of the leading Sauterne grapes. In France, it made its record long ago. As a blend with this, the Sauvignon Blanc and the Muscadelle de Bordelais make the most famous of Haut Sauternes—the celebrated Chateau Yquem. The vine is a handsome and vigorous grower with good and persistent foliage, very productive. Cluster long, rather loose, heavily shouldered; berry full medium, round, transparent, white or pale yellow, changing to a light amber when very ripe, juicy, sweet, and high flavored. A perfect grape in every respect, making a very fine, delicate wine by itself, which is easily handled and keeps well.

SAUVIGNON BLANC. Synonym, Panechiou.—This grape naturally follows Semillion, being often used with it. It is only a moderate bearer; cluster rather small, shouldered; berry below medium, pale yellow, round, transparent, very sweet and delicate.

MUSCADELLE DE BORDELAIS. Synonyms, Raisinote, Cadillac.—Vine a strong grower but shy bearer; cluster small, shouldered; berry small, slightly oblong, transparent, pale yellow, sweet, and high flavored, which makes it of great value for the blend above referred to. It is especially cultivated for that purpose, as it would hardly pay otherwise. Only a small proportion of it is needed in a blend to impart its peculiar flavor.

WHITE BURGUNDY. Synonyms, Chablis, Melon Blanc, Chardenot.—This is the celebrated wine grape of Burgundy, France, from which many of the champagnes are made, and also some of the best dry wines. The vine is a moderate grower, with fine dark green foliage, uniformly healthy and productive. Cluster medium, shoul-

dered, compact; berry roundish oblong, pale yellow,
below medium size, very delicate, sweet and juicy.

SAUVIGNON VERTE.—It is questionable if this is the
true name of this variety, but it has become so well established that it seems fruitless to use any other. It is
supposed to be Pedro Ximenes, and is also known in some
sections as Colombar and White Green Riesling, both
of which are erroneous. It is one of the most productive and hardy of all grapes, a strong grower, and as it
starts late, not much subject to frosts. These qualities
have made it one of the leading grapes, but its wine,
though agreeable and of fine flavor, is hard to handle and
keep, needing a blend with some other variety. Cluster
long, rather loose, shouldered; berry medium, greenish-
yellow, very juicy and thin skinned, sweet and luscious.

These are the leading varieties of French origin which
seem to be more perfectly at home here than the Rhenish
varieties. There are many others, such as Roussanne,
Marsanne and Clairette Blanche, but they are not so well
known and esteemed. Of the Chasselas or Gutedel, we
have three varieties of prominence—the Chasselas Fontainebleau, known and cultivated as Gutedel in Germany,
a good and uniform bearer, making a very good, smooth
wine, but not of the highest character; the Chasselas
Violette or Koenigsgutedel, of which the foliage, and
even the berries take on a brown and violet tinge when
small, making a good wine and a great deal of it, as it is
a good and constant bearer; the Victoria Chasselas or
Queen Victoria, a short, stocky grower, with immense
bunches, sometimes weighing six pounds each; berry
round, violet, juicy and fine flavored, making an excellent wine which will improve with age. While these
three varieties are not of the highest excellence, they are
very useful and well deserve cultivation.

RIESLING.—Of the Rhenish type, making the most
famous wines of Germany, the most prominent is the

true Riesling,—Johannisberg Riesling, as it is generally called in California. The vine is a rather slender grower, with thin, deeply lobed foliage, moderately productive with long pruning; cluster small, shouldered; berry small, round, pale yellow, sometimes changing to light violet when very ripe, with peculiar gray dots, very sweet, sprightly and high flavored ; needs long pruning.

TRAMINER. Synonym, Rother Klaevner.—This grape has given high character to the wines of the Palatinate, and produces a high grade wine here, more full and smooth than, though not so sprightly as, the Riesling. The vine is a moderate grower and bearer, needs long pruning to make it productive, but is of such superior quality that it should be in every vineyard. Cluster small, compact, shouldered, resembling the Delaware of the East; berry oblong, small, pale red, with rather thick skin but a honied sweetness.

RED VELTLINER. Synonym, Fleischtraube.—This was disseminated under the name of Traminer, but it is an entirely different variety, requiring different treatment altogether, though the wine resembles very much that of Traminer, in flavor and character. The vine is a very abundant bearer, requiring short pruning; foliage large, dark green with violet points, grayish beneath, a strong grower. Cluster large and heavily shouldered, compact; berry below medium, slightly oval, pale red or violet, rather thick skin, very sweet and of fine flavor. It has not been widely disseminated, but when better known, will become one of the leading white grapes. It makes one of the finest liqueur wines, if allowed to hang on the vines until it is overripe, which its tough skin makes practicable, and it develops such an exquisite flavor that good connoisseurs have said they have tasted no better Haut Sauternes at $3.00 per bottle.

FRANKEN RIESLING. Synonyms, Sylvaner, Oester-reicher.—This variety has been widely disseminated in

California, and its wine is generally called Riesling, but
it is not equal to the true Riesling in quality, lacking
its sprightliness and high flavor.   It is a valuable grape
and a good bearer, if the true variety is obtained.   Unfortunately it is mixed almost everywhere with a sport
very closely resembling it, but which is very unproductive.   The vine is a strong grower, and with long pruning
bears abundantly; cluster medium, compact, generally
shouldered; berry below medium, round, pale yellow,
transparent, sweet and juicy.

ORLEANS RIESLING.   Synonym, Yellow Orleans.—
This variety will hardly class with the true Rieslings,
as it ripens much later and the berry is double the size.
It is, however, known by that name, and as it has many
good qualities and makes a fine wine, it is worthy a
description.   The vine is moderately vigorous, a compact, short-jointed grower, with pale green, deeply
lobed foliage.   Cluster large, shouldered, compact; berry
above medium, oblong, with firm flesh and skin; ripens
two weeks later than the Rieslings; makes a very nice
wine; very productive, needs a warm soil to bring it to
perfection.   There is a variety cultivated in some sections under the name of Moselle Riesling, which as yet
is not identified.   It is claimed to be a good bearer, and
wines tested from it have proven to be very good.

GREEN HUNGARIAN.   Synonyms, Long Green, Verte
Longue.—This is one of the healthiest and most productive varieties, and is very valuable.   Its strong point
is not high quality, which differs greatly in different
localities and soils, but immense productiveness, strong
growth and beautiful foliage, and its great ease of fermentation, which it imparts to other wines more difficult
to ferment.   It requires short, or stool pruning, as it is
apt to overbear.   Cluster long, moderately compact,
heavily shouldered; berry medium, round, pale greenish
yellow; makes a fine wine in some locations, resembling

Riesling in bouquet, while in others the wine is light and indifferent in quality. It requires a high location to develop its best qualities.

FOLLE BLANCHE. Synonyms, La Folle, Enrageat.—This is so called in France because of its extreme productiveness, and it is there especially valued for making high flavored, delicate brandies. It fully sustains its reputation in that respect in California, some of the finest brandies being made from it. It also makes a good delicate, light wine, as it attains a higher degree of sugar than in France. The vine is a moderate grower, leaf medium, thin, pale green; cluster large, with berries of uneven size; berry oblong, small, transparently yellow, very juicy, covered with gray bloom.

BURGER. Synonyms, Putzscheare, White Tokay.—This is another of the quantity grapes—light in saccharine, but immensely productive and valuable in the fermentation of heavier musts. It requires short pruning. Its foliage is very delicate, making it liable to sunscald. In the southern part of California and on the hillsides, its wine improves and becomes very palatable. The vine is a good grower, with thin, light-green foliage, deeply lobed. Cluster very large, shouldered; berry full medium, round, pale yellow, ripens late, with watery juice and very tender skin. It has repeatedly produced seventeen tons to the acre.

GRAPES FOR SHERRY.

The following special sherry grapes of foreign origin also make good dry wines:

PALOMINO. Synonyms, Listan, erroneously called Golden Chasselas in Napa county.—A very valuable grape and a heavy bearer with short pruning. Vine vigorous and hardy, foliage deeply lobed, light green, downy beneath; cluster large and loose, shouldered; berry full medium, round, pale yellow, juicy and sweet; makes a fine dry wine of good flavor, which will develop into a natural sherry in time.

WEST'S WHITE PROLIFIC.—Introduced by Mr. West of Stockton, Cal. Its true name has never been discovered, but it evidently belongs to the Spanish type of grapes. The vine is a good grower, and very productive with short or stool pruning. It makes a delicate, high flavored wine, also an excellent brandy, said to be equal to the best French Cognac.

YELLOW MOSLER.—Synonym, Formit, erroneously called Pedro Ximenes.—This variety evidently belongs to the same class as one previously described. It makes the Tokay, the celebrated Hungarian wine. It has been cultivated with varying success, succeeding well in some seasons, in others subject to coulure. It is a strong grower, requires long pruning, and is certainly a grape of exquisite quality. Cluster long and loose, shouldered; berry full medium, oblong, transparent, pale yellow. It will hang long and dry up on the vine, thus making the famous liqueur wine which is known as Tokay all over the world.

SULTANA.—This is one of the famous seedless grapes of the Mediterranean, and is best known as a raisin grape, though it makes a fine, delicate, white wine, which will develop a sherry flavor. The vine is a vigorous grower, and needs high stakes and long pruning to bring large crops. Cluster long and loose, shouldered; berry small or below medium, pale-yellow and transparent, without seeds.

THOMPSON'S SEEDLESS. Synonym, Lady de Coverly. —This was received from the nursery of Ellwanger & Barry of Rochester, N. Y., by a Mr. Thompson of Sutter county, and was first cultivated by him. As it proved a shy bearer with short pruning, he gave it little attention. Some grafts were given to Mr. Onstott, who disseminated it, after discovering that it bore heavy crops with spur pruning on long canes. It makes a splendid, very delicate raisin, surpassing the Sultana, to which the vine bears a strong resemblance. Excellent wine has been made from it, and it is one of the finest table grapes, bearing shipment to the most distant markets. The vine is a very strong grower of long-jointed yellow wood. The young canes should be pinched when they reach the top of the stake, to develop the laterals, on which it bears the best fruit the following year. The cluster is very large, long and loose, so that every berry can develop fully; berry below medium, oblong, pale golden yellow, transparent, without seeds, of most exquisite flavor, very juicy and sweet, with a mingling of sprightly acid which makes it very refreshing and palatable.

These comprise the most desirable and best known of the varieties for white wine, and make a list comprehensive enough for any one. There are many more which have their admirers and advocates, such as the Chauche Gris, generally called Gray Riesling, the White Elben or Kleinbereger, Clairette Blanche, Steinschiller, Rulander, and many more. One other should be added, the White Muscatelle, of which the French make their most renowned sweet wine. It is also known as German Muscateller and Muscat de Frontignan. This grape has a pronounced Muscatelle flavor, but it is not rank or disagreeable, as in the Muscat of Alexandria. It is a strong grower and good bearer with long pruning. The vine has a light green foliage, downy beneath; cluster long and compact, cylindrical, shouldered; berry round, greenish yellow, medium, very sweet when fully ripe, fleshy, with an agreeable flavor. Will make a good dry wine, which is relished by many, and if allowed to hang long on the vines, a good sweet wine.

14

FOR TABLE, MARKET AND RAISINS.

These are classed together, as some of the best market grapes make good raisins, and vice versa. The growing and shipping of grapes to market, and the curing of them into raisins, are very important branches of the grape industry. Planting vineyards for raisins has alone assumed vast proportions, and especially in Fresno, San Diego, Tulare and other southern counties, so much so as to almost overshadow the wine industry. For those who like grape culture but who have conscientious scruples against wine making, either of these other branches furnishes an ample field.

The shipping of grapes to distant markets, especially to the North and East, has very much increased during the past five years of better facilities and lower freights. Many varieties, excellent for the home, will not answer for long distance shipping. For this business, we must confine ourselves mostly to those varieties which combine an attractive appearance with a tough skin and a firm flesh. Quality is a secondary consideration. Most of our grapes are good for the home table, and in many instances the most delicate wine grapes are also among the choicest eating kinds.

In the choice of varieties, climatic conditions must govern largely in a State where a difference of a month is noticed in the ripening of the same variety, though in localities only a few miles apart.

FOR EARLY MARKET.

The Chasselas Fontainebleau, commonly called Sweetwater, is about the earliest ripening variety, and also carries well to market. Next in ripening comes the Black Malvasia, so called, a strong grower and good bearer; cluster heavy, compact, shouldered; berry large, oblong, black, with blue bloom, tough skin, meaty and juicy and presenting an attractive appearance.

FOR LATE MARKET.

The favorite for this purpose is the Flame Tokay, which combines fine color, handsome appearance, size of bunch and berry and good shipping qualities. Cluster very large, shouldered; berry very large, oblong, pale red, covered with violet bloom, very firm and meaty.

BLACK FERRARA.—A strong grower, and productive. Cluster medium, compact; berry round, black with blue bloom, tough skin, carries well to market.

BLACK DAMASCUS.—Medium grower and fair bearer. Cluster large, loose, shouldered; berry very large, oblong, dark blue, covered with lighter bloom, meaty, thick skin; ripens late.

EMPEROR.—A strong grower but rather shy bearer, better adapted to Southern than Northern localities, as it ripens late. Cluster long and loose, shouldered, very large; berry large, oblong, purplish black, covered with fine lilac bloom, thick skin, firm.

BLACK CORNUCHON. The vine is a strong but stocky grower, leaf large and thick, deeply lobed; cluster very large, loose, shouldered, with long stems; berry large, long, dark blue with lighter dots, fleshy, thick skin; very late.

BLACK MOROCCO.—This is used as a shipping grape in the South, not being adapted to the North, as it ripens late and unevenly. The vine is a straggling grower, with many laterals which bring an abundant second crop. Cluster very large, compact, heavily shouldered; berry very large, black, round, fleshy, of rather poor quality.

MUSCAT OF ALEXANDRIA. Synonym, Muscatelle Gordo Blanco.—There is yet a doubt as to the identity of these two grapes, many claiming that the latter is more round in berry and a better grape. The vine is a low, straggling grower, an abundant bearer, often bear ing more second than first crop; the wood is short and stocky. It is a leading raisin grape, both here and abroad, and it is also an important shipping grape. It carries well, looks well, and many admire its peculiar flavor. It is sometimes used for sweet wines, such as Angelica and Muscat, but its flavor is rather too prominent. Cluster very long and loose, sometimes shouldered; berry oblong, large, light yellow when fully matured, transparent, fleshy, with thick skin, and a very sweet, musky flavor; liked by some and disliked by others.

MALAGA.—Vine a strong grower, productive. Cluster very large, loose, shouldered, long; berry very large, oval, yellowish green, covered with white bloom, thick skin, fleshy. Ripens rather early, and also makes good raisins.

VERDAL.—A strong grower with long joints, leaf large, deeply lobed; cluster rather short, heavily shouldered; berry oblong, yellowish green, covered with white bloom; very late, productive.

WHITE CORNICHON.—The vine is a strong and stocky grower, and very productive; leaf thin, light green, tomentose below; cluster very large, loose, with long, drooping shoulders; berry oblong, golden yellow with light dots, thick skin, fleshy and transparent; ripens late.

The Sultana and Thompson's Seedless have already been described. Both make the finest raisins and both ship well, the latter being the more showy and delicate. As they ripen rather early, they come between the earliest and late varieties.

The black and white Corinths, from which the so-called Zante currants are made, do not succeed generally, and the two foregoing are much preferable for seedless raisins.

CHAPTER XLI.

CULTIVATION OF THE VINEYARD.

IMPLEMENTS.

If the ground has been well prepared, it will need no deep plowing the first summer after planting. Frequent stirring of the surface with cultivator or horse hoe, with an occasional loosening of the soil around the young plants with the hoe, will be all that is required. The first plowing the next spring is done with the two-horse plow, beginning in the center of the row and throwing the two middle furrows together. If the vines were planted 6x10 feet, take the wider rows first, running parallel with the hill, and plowing as many furrows with the two-horse team as can be done without injuring the vines; then follow with a one-horse plow and take the remaining furrows on each side. This will leave a very narrow strip along the vines, which should be loosened with hoe or spade. A harrow is then run over the plowed land, followed with a sled, drag or crusher, so that all the ground becomes well pulverized. For the second, or cross plowing, the operation is reversed—the single plow comes first, throwing a furrow to each side of the row towards the vines, and the middle is finished out the same way with the two-horse plow. This should leave the land in fine condition, so that no more deep plowing will be needed through the summer. The surface must be kept loose and clean by the cultivator, and the hoe must be used to keep weeds from growing about the young vines. The same method is followed every year, except as the vines become larger we must wait until after pruning is finished and the clippings are removed.

Many implements have been invented to facilitate operations, especially in large vineyards on level lands, such as gang plows with two, and even four, shares to stir the middle of the row. The shares are fastened to an iron frame with iron clamps and bolts, so that they can be removed at will, and throw the earth either toward or from the vines. These need more power, especially in heavy soils. They are so constructed that by operating a lever, they can be made to run deep or shallow, as preferred. Mr. H. Hortop of Rutherford, Napa county, has invented several useful implements for this work. Among them is a plow with two shares, running on one side of the row first and returning on the other, with a wheel to regulate the depth; also a one-horse plow with movable beam which can be so set as to run very close to the vines. He has also excellent plows for preparing the ground, as well as cultivators specially adapted to the work.

PRUNING, STAKING AND TRAINING.

If resistant vines have been planted, but little pruning will be needed for the first two or three years—they flourish best when left undisturbed. Should they grow very strong the second year, the growth may be cut back so as to reduce the number of buds, make cultivation easier and make stronger cuttings, if any are needed, but no particular system need be followed. The third spring, if the vines are strong enough, they may be grafted, following which they should be staked to support the growth from the graft. The size of the stakes needed will depend on the varieties grafted. For those adapted to stool or spur pruning, four-foot stakes will answer; for half-long or short cane pruning, five-foot stakes, and for a few varieties requiring long pruning, six-foot stakes will be required. The following prices are paid for stakes at Napa, one and a half inches in diameter, per 1000 : Four foot, $14.25 ; five foot, $18 ; six foot, $21.50. These should be pointed and driven in with a sledge, as close to the graft as is safe and on the side exposed to the prevailing winds in summer, so that the vine has a slight leaning against them. If fifteen-inch cions have been used in grafting, the head of the vine can be formed at once from the three or four upper buds from which the shoots are allowed to grow—all below them should be rubbed off as soon as they appear. These upper shoots are then tied to the stake, very loosely, so as not to hinder their growth. The best and most economical ties are made from the common dracæna, grown very frequently as an ornamental tree, and of which every vineyardist should plant a good supply. The dead leaves can be taken off every spring, scalded in hot water to make them soft and pliable, and then divided into strips, of which each leaf furnishes from three to five. They are stronger and better than the so-called grape twine, and a single tree will furnish material for tying three or four acres of vines. All the dracænas and yuccas furnish excellent material for tying, as well as the *Phormium tenax* or New Zealand flax. The latter is gratuitously distributed by our State university, but requires to be planted near some spring or brook to flourish well, while the dracænas and yuccas will grow on dry soil. These details are given because thousands of dollars are spent annually for twine which may just as well be saved, and further, because the materials named are more convenient and are not so hard on the fingers in tying. The next pruning after grafting, will find the vine established, if it was strong enough when grafted, with the head established where it ought to be, about a foot from the ground. We are now to determine definitely the plan of pruning to be adopted, stool or goblet, half-long or long, though this is supposed to be settled by the length of the stakes used in staking the vines.

STOOL OR GOBLET PRUNING.

This mode of pruning is calculated to make of each vine a small tree or bush, and as soon as the trunk or stem becomes strong enough to be self-supporting, the stakes may be removed to other plantations. Let us suppose these strong branches are grown from the three uppermost buds and in three different directions—if four and sufficiently strong, so much the better. Each of these is cut back to two buds, and after pruning, the vine is tied firmly to the stake. For this purpose, No. 16 annealed wire answers admirably. Cut it into proper lengths with shears or cold chisel, make a hook on each end, then pass it around the vine and hook the ends together, allowing space enough for the natural expansion by growth. When no longer needed they can be removed, and in other places used again and again. Pruning may be done at any time in the winter after the leaves have fallen. The vine has now six or eight buds, from which will grow six or eight branches, diverging from the main head in all directions, but having the center open in the shape of a goblet. Each of these branches will bear from two to three clusters of fruit, according to the character of the vine, which will give us from twelve to twenty-four bunches. The branches or shoots are not tied up, but allowed to droop. The main point is to get the vine well balanced and open to sun and air.

The next winter the vine has the double number of shoots or branches. It would tax too heavily the vine's bearing powers to cut these back to as many spurs of two buds each, unless it should be very strong. Therefore, cut the upper shoot or branch on each original spur entirely away, at or just above the bunch closest to the head, and cut this back to two buds, always having in view the proposed shape and balance of the head. This sort of pruning is followed every year, with variations suggested by the good sense of the pruner, who should be more than a machine. Summer pruning will be treated in a separate chapter.

This sort of pruning is equally adapted to the heavy bearing varieties such as Zinfandel, Portugieser, Carignane, Mataro, Gamay, Charbonneau, Petit Bouschet, Red Veltliner, Chasselas Fontainebleau, Victoria Chasselas, Palomino, Green Hungarian, West's White Prolific and Folie Blanche.

MEDIUM OR HALF-LONG TRAINING.

Many varieties are not adapted to spur or stool pruning, but require a medium course. Some of these are so constituted that they will not fruit well from the first two or three buds at the base of a cane, while they will bear abundantly from the fourth to the tenth, and among these are some of the most valuable varieties. These should be trained to five-foot stakes, commencing just the same as for stool pruning, with three canes the next spring after grafting, but having them from 15 to 18 inches in length. After pruning tie them firmly to the stake, just below the upper bud, leaving all the canes about the same length. When the young growth appears, leave one of the strongest at the base of each cane to form the future cane and one for a spur, rubbing out all the weaker buds below. When you come to the fourth or fifth bud, leave all the strong shoots above. The next spring, the old cane which has borne the fruit is cut off just above that destined for a spur, this reduced to two buds, and the strongest cane from the base pruned back to 15 or 18 inches. This leaves three canes again, which are tied to the stake as before. The canes for the next year's bearing we expect from the three spurs, as well as another spur, cutting the old cane off entirely and thus renewing them every year. A modification of this training is to leave but one cane for bearing but make it somewhat longer, with more spurs around the head of the vine or from the strongest laterals. Wire may be used for the upper tying, and a loose band of dracæna passed around the middle of the canes to prevent their spreading when heavy with fruit.

Varieties adapted for this training are Sauvignon Verte, Semillion, White Burgundy, Chauche Gris, Traminer, Chasselas Violette, White Elben, White Muscateller, Grosse Blaue, Mondeuse, Petit Syrah, Meunier, Tannat, Beclan, Valdepenas, Refosco, Gamay and many others.

Another modification of this training, called the balloon, is sometimes used. Four canes are grown instead of three from opposite sides of the vine, and bent together in the middle, where they are fastened by a wire and thus made self-supporting, with most of the fruit hanging in the middle. This method has its advantages and its disadvantages. The circular form in which the vines are bent distributes the sap more evenly, while in the upright training it goes more into the upper buds on canes and spurs. The disadvantages are that it takes more room in the vineyard, does not permit as close working, and unless the canes are of equal size and equally loaded, they swerve to the heavy side.

LONG PRUNING AND TRAINING.

Some varieties are shy bearers, even with the latter method of pruning, and need still longer training. The method is the same, the difference being only in detail. Six-foot stakes are used and the canes made long enough to reach to the top. Exception must be made of a few varieties which should have the young shoots for canes pinched during the previous summer, when they have reached the tops of the stakes. This forces out the laterals into stronger growth, which are then pruned back to two buds. The varieties bearing best under this treatment are Rie-ling, Sultana, Thompson's Seedless,

Yellow Mosler, Cabernet Sauvignon, Cabernet Franc, Emperor, Trusseaux, Herbemont and Lenoir. Some of these will even bear better if the old canes are left for permanent arms as long as they are healthy and vigorous, and all the strong shoots of the previous year cut back to two or three buds. A little practice and observation will soon show what modifications are needed to make each variety do its best, and no wine grower can succeed who is not a close observer. Practice alone makes perfect.

There are many other methods of training in vogue in Germany, France and other countries, which have been tried in California to some extent, but as they all more or less obstruct cultivation, have found little favor.

The implements used in pruning are the best kinds of pruning shears and a short saw of a semicircular form, with teeth set toward the handle, to cut in drawing. The latter is used to cut out old and dry stumps and very heavy wood, but anyone who understands using pruning shears to advantage will seldom need the saw.

SUMMER PRUNING, OR PINCHING AND SUCKERING.

Much difference of opinion exists as to the value of the practice of shortening in the bearing shoots, many contending that it is injurious, but all agree that suckering should be done as early as possible. This consists in rubbing off all shoots below the head of the vine, and also all the shoots which may grow from the wood of the previous years—shoots in the middle of the head, also called water sprouts, and which seldom bear any fruit, and also all the unfruitful shoots and double buds from the canes or spurs. Each well-developed bud is a triple one, the main or fruit bud being the central or longest one; the two smaller or auxiliary buds will often not develop at all, but if they do, only rob the main bud of strength. The best time to do this work is when the shoots have made a growth of from six to eight inches, when the whole vine can be looked over easily and the superfluous parts removed. If delayed for only a week the work is doubled, and cannot be so well done, as the mass of foliage obscures the work.

I am decidedly in favor of pinching or shortening in the bearing shoots, if it be done early—which is the main point. If delayed until the young growth becomes hard and woody, it is decidedly detrimental. The right time is when the young shoots are about eighteen inches long and are yet tender. It makes the growth more stocky, develops the young fruit which is then forming more evenly, and brings out the laterals to shade it when it most needs shade. It will also prevent the blowing off of the shoots by high winds and make late cultivation easier, the vine being more compact. Those who object to the practice claim that it forces out too much second growth, which is not desirable, and that it prevents the setting of the fruit. These objections mainly arise because the work is done too late—then it is injurious, bringing stagnation of sap and uneven ripening of fruit. But where the vines are topped when the young growth is tender, and no more than six inches taken off, it aids in the even and perfect development of the young fruit, gently checking the sap and leading it into the young fruit and the dormant lateral buds.

CHAPTER XLII.

DISEASES AND THEIR REMEDIES.

The common mildew (*Oïdium Tuckeri*) prevails to some extent, but can be controlled by the use of powdered sulphur dusted over and through the vine by means of bellows or small wire sieves shaken by hand. It commonly appears after foggy weather, and the first application should be made when the young shoots are about eight inches long, or just before the bloom. A second application may become necessary should the disease again appear. This will stop it effectually.

COULURE, or imperfect setting of the fruit.—This often prevails to a considerable extent, but is, I think, the consequence of mildew and, can be prevented, to a great extent, by early and careful sulphuring. It generally follows late rains and damp, foggy weather accompanied by sultry heat. Possibly the copper mixtures may be of service against this, as also the ripe rot, which has attacked our grapes to some extent when rains have set in early in September. The varieties which have very compact bunches and tender skins are most liable to attack. After a rainless summer the autumnal rains swell the berries, and where they grow compactly, crack them, when myriads of fungus spores find lodgment, and speedy decomposition ensues.

THE PERONOSPORA, from which the vineyards of Europe have suffered seriously, and the black rot of the Eastern States are, so far as I am aware, unknown here. The most formidable malady of grapes is the so-called Anaheim disease, but it has not, so far, reached our Northern vineyards. It originated, or rather was first observed, at Anaheim, Orange county, hence the name. This disease is the more to be dreaded, as all researches by experts have failed to find a remedy. In its aspect, its sudden and deadly effects and rapid spread, it resembles the Eastern pear blight, and may originate in a sudden stagnation of sap. Lately, however, it seems to have spent its force, and very little is heard of its ravages.

BLACK KNOT.—This disease, which is also called grape cancer, is caused by sudden stagnation of sap. This may be the result of excessive pruning, late frosts, or other causes which renders the vine powerless to elaborate all the flow of sap from the roots, which therefore ruptures the sap vessels, stagnates and forms black excrescences, frequently causing the death of the vine. The remedies, or rather preventives, are longer pruning and the use of longer cions in grafting. It would be unreasonable to suppose that a vine which is vigorous enough to produce a hundred feet of wood in a season could be restricted to a dozen buds in pruning, or three buds in grafting, and with them perform all the functions which require as many hundred buds. When a vine, otherwise vigorous, is badly affected by black knot above ground, it is frequently saved by grafting it with long cions below the diseased part.

ANTHRACNOSE, OR SPANISH MEASLES.—This does not prevail here to any great extent. The leaves show red spots, wilt and die off. An application or two of Bordeaux mixture is said to check it.

CHAPTER XLIII.

INSECT AND OTHER ENEMIES OF THE VINE.

The most destructive insect is the phylloxera, which is fully described in the first part of this book. We also have most of the other insects injurious to the vine which are common in the East, except the grape curculio, which has never been seen here as yet. Grasshoppers have been very destructive in some sections of the Pacific slope, and had to be combated by the same means employed east of the Rockies. Some dug ditches, in which the grasshoppers were crushed by heavy logs dragged along; others kept heavy rollers moving along the side of the vineyard from which the invading hosts approached. Such visitations are very rare, however, and occur only at long intervals and in certain localities. Cutworms have been very destructive in some of the raisin vineyards, cutting the young shoots at night. Thousands were poisoned by a mixture of Paris green in water and bran, scattered in small doses under the vines.

Of birds, the linnet and California quail are among the enemies of the grape. Ground squirrels are very troublesome and destructive, but may be kept in check by poisoned wheat thrown into their holes. When they are not very numerous a shot gun in hands that can use it, is a sufficient defense. The large California hare, or jack-rabbit, is hard on young vines and grafts. They are not very numerous in the northern counties, but in the southern ones are such a nuisance that it is found necessary to start great "rabbit drives," in which the men of an entire neighborhood take part, and thousands of the rabbits are killed.

CHAPTER XLIV.

FROSTS.

Late spring frosts, when they come, are quite destructive, but they are mostly confined to the low lands, an elevation of a few feet often securing exemption. At times, however, they occur even on the hillsides, striking vineyards that have been untouched by frost for years. They come late in April, and sometimes as late as the middle of May. Raising a dense smoke in the vineyard during the night is advocated by some as a means of protection, but it has few adherents. If a general smudge is created in a large number of adjoining vineyards, so as to fill the air with smoke, it may aid in repelling frost, but small, isolated efforts in this direction are of little or no value.

That frosty situations should be avoided for grape culture, is self-evident. It is very disheartening to see a promising vineyard browned by frost in a night. Late pruning is advocated by some as a remedy, and not without reason, for the upper buds always start first, while the lower ones remain dormant. But if the vine is pruned so late every year as to cause profuse bleeding, it is quite likely to cause more serious injury than is occasioned by the partial loss of the crop once in four or five years. I have found long pruning in winter much preferable—leaving spurs of three or four buds, and also somewhat longer canes. Then if the frost strikes and kills the shoots which have started from the upper buds, the dormant lower ones will start into active growth, as will also the secondary buds on each side of the frost-bitten shoot, and produce a fair crop, though somewhat later and of smaller bunches. Should no frost come, the shoots which bear the fruit must be thinned out in time, the weakest being removed to avoid overloading the vine. In case of frost the removal of the frozen shoots as soon as possible will facilitate the growth from the dormant buds, and also keep the vine in healthier and more vigorous condition. This can be done well and expeditiously by clipping them close to the base of the shoots, with the small shears used in picking grapes. Eight years of experience with this treatment have shown it to be the best I have ever tried to secure a fair crop, even in the most frosty season.

Some varieties are hardier than others and start later in spring. These should be planted or grafted in localities subject to late frosts. Among these varieties are the Sauvignon Verte, Semillion, Mataro, Marsanne and Green Hungarian. The Zinfandel is one of the tenderest, and this, as well as the Pinots, is unsuitable for frosty situations.

CHAPTER XLV.

RESTORING INFESTED VINEYARDS.

When the phylloxera has begun its devastation in a block, it is, in my opinion, best to let it finish its work. Cultivate the vines as long as any of them will yield a fair crop, and then tear them all out. This is easily done by a pair of steady horses or mules in winter, when the ground is soft from rains. Then plow the land deeply and thoroughly the following spring, and sow it to oats or some other grain for a year or two. After it has been thus well mellowed and loosened, prepare it in the same way as for a new vineyard, lay it off and plant, as described heretofore. I regard this as much better

15

than trying patchwork, as many have done, in planting non-resistant vines in place of those killed out by the phylloxera. It cannot reasonably be expected that a young vine would flourish in a soil impoverished by the growth, for fifteen to twenty years, of vines which took from the soil the same elements required by the young vine. There is, in fact, no time gained by replanting among older vines, and it is simply impossible to obtain an even stand where it is practiced. Such management has done much to bring non-resistant vines into bad repute. Let the land rest for a year or two, giving it careful and thorough cultivation, then plant it with first-class roots or cuttings, and they will make better growth in two years than patchwork planting will make in four. Let the new vines attain sufficient strength, then graft them at or near the surface, with the best wood for the purpose. If it is necessary to plant sooner, to keep up a vineyard better, take a new piece of ground, and let the others have a much-needed rest. I write from personal experience, having tried both methods and seen them tried by my neighbors.

CHAPTER XLVI.

MARKETING GRAPES.

The varieties suitable for the market have been described on foregoing pages. The process of picking and packing may be described in few words: The grapes are generally picked one day and packed the next, to give the stems a slight wilting so they will pack more snugly. When picked they are carried to the packing house, where, the next day, all small, imperfect or damaged berries are clipped out with small scissors, and the bunches packed in five-pound baskets, which are put into slatted crates, to admit plenty of air. The grapes must be well colored, and ripe, but not overripe. If they are not fully ripened the stems and berries wilt too much, and will not present the same handsome appearance as fully ripe grapes. The more the natural bloom is preserved in handling, the better the grapes will look and sell.

Judging by the latest advices I have received from parts of Texas, Arizona and New Mexico, I deem it the best policy for California vineyardists to cultivate the late varieties for market, as those regions can bring in ripe grapes in June and July, and thus control the early markets, while some sections of California can furnish grapes fresh from the vines as late as December and even the early part of January. Successful marketing of grapes may be summed up somewhat as follows:

1. Market the grapes when they are in the best condition.

2. Grow the best and most attractive varieties.

3. Handle and pack carefully, and send to market over the best and quickest route.

4. Get them to market at the right time, at home or abroad, and in the most convenient and attractive packages.

5. Supply a fine article throughout and establish a good name.

CHAPTER XLVII.

RAISIN MAKING.

As remarked before, we have but few varieties of grapes with the qualities for making fine raisins. Of those with large berries there are but two : the Muscat of Alexandria, or Muscatelle Gordo Blanco, and the Malaga. Authorities are still in doubt whether the Muscat or Muscatelle, and Gordo Blanco are identical. It is claimed by some that the Muscatelle has a rounder and sweeter berry, sets better, and that the berries are more uniform in size. I do not claim to be an authority in this matter, but leave it as it stands, and refer the readers to the very elaborate work of Prof. Gustave Eisen on the Raisin Industry of California. The Malaga also has a large berry, but without the musky flavor of the Muscat. The latter is, however, the leading variety, from which all the largest and most showy raisins are made, the musky flavor being rather an attraction to most palates. Fresno is the banner county of the raisin industry, where immense vineyards of raisin grapes have been planted within recent years, some parties planting as many as two to four hundred acres in a single season. While Fresno is the leading county, a good many raisin grapes are grown in Tulare, Kern, San Diego, Ventura and Yolo counties, while Yuba and Sutter have more or less. As it is claimed that an average crop is from eight to ten tons per acre, it is difficult to foresee what will be the outcome of this rapid rush into an industry which has scarcely become established or organized. There is reason for grave fears of overproduction and ruinously low prices. For the last two years they have, fortunately perhaps, had only partial crops, yet the market is already glutted. Should all the young vineyards come into bearing and produce full crops, it is difficult to see how prices could be maintained sufficient to cover the cost of production.

The culture of the Muscat and the process of drying into raisins, as pursued in California, are very simple. The vine is, perhaps, the most dwarfish of all varieties and is grown with very low heads, only about one foot high, which when once formed are cut back to spurs, as heretofore described in stool or goblet pruning. Thus the bunches of the first crop hang around the head, or stool, sometimes resting on the ground. In that dry, sandy soil the vines are generally irrigated once or twice during the summer, for which purpose the soil must have been leveled and ditched before planting. The Muscat has a strong tendency to bear a second crop from the laterals—sometimes as heavy as the first, but ripening much later. The first crop is ordinarily ripe about the middle or last of August. The process of curing them is thus described by the late R. B. Blowers, one of the veterans in the business:

"The grapes should be allowed to remain on the vine until quite ripe, showing a yellowish or golden color, and becoming quite translucent. Then they should be carefully picked and placed upon a drying tray, usually two by three feet in size, made of light lattice work, and exposed with an inclination toward the sun, between the rows of the vineyard. After being sufficiently exposed to become about half dry they are turned by two men, who take an empty tray, place it on a full one, holding them together firmly, and with a swinging motion turn them over, replacing the turned grapes in their former position. This should be done in the morning, before the dew is quite dried off; then, when they have become so dry as to lose their ashy appearance, some being a little too green and others quite dry enough, they are, after removing those that are entirely too green, slid from the trays into large sweat boxes, having a thick sheet of paper between every twenty-five or thirty pounds of raisins; then they are removed to the storeroom, where they should remain two weeks or more. When ready to pack, it will be found that those which were too moist, have parted with their surplus moisture, which has been absorbed by the stems and drier raisins. The stems are now tough, and the raisins soft and ready to pack. They are carefully placed in frames made of iron or steel, the large and fair ones being carefully placed in the bottom of the frames and the surplus stems and berries cut away; then the average raisins are arranged in and weighed, placing five pounds in each frame, and pressed, but not enough to break the skins. They are then passed to an inspector, who examines the exposed sides of the raisins, removing all imperfect ones, then placing the wrapper paper on the frame, holds it in place with a wooden or steel plate, turns it bottom up, drops the left end into the box, slides the plate quickly from under the raisins, and they drop into the box; then pressing slightly upon the movable bottom of the frame, the frame is removed. The bottom of the frame is then pressed more firmly, to cause the raisins to fill the space formerly occupied by the sides and ends of the frame; then it is removed, and the face of the latter is exposed, all imperfect or too wet berries are removed, and all vacancies or hollows filled with large, loose raisins. The label of the proprietor is then placed on the face, the ends of the wrapper and the sides are folded over, the box cover is nailed on, and they are ready for market."

There is a difference of opinion yet among raisin growers as to whether irrigation is absolutely necessary. The irrigationists claim that the berries are larger, more uniform and showy; while the other side claims finer flavor, more sugar, and more delicate bloom. Not being a raisin grower myself, I am unable to decide who is right, but most of the raisins so far have been produced under a system of irrigation. Judging from other fruits, I am inclined to the latter opinion; although irrigation may produce more pounds, I would suppose quality to be with the non-irrigated article.

The Sultana and Thompson's Seedless belong to an entirely different class of grapes, and require different treatment. The vines are strong growers, and require long pruning and high stakes to produce well, but under this treatment they are immense bearers, as single vines have been known to produce over one hundred pounds. They have the further advantage of drying much more quickly and easily, having much smaller berries and loose bunches. They are also much more delicate, with a pure flavor, and a slight mingling of acidity, which makes them much more sprightly. They are therefore admirably suitable for cooking purposes, especially as they have thin skins and no seeds. As they are earlier than the Muscat, and will dry in half the time, they may be grown further north than that variety can be expected to succeed. Furthermore, they make an excellent, delicate white wine, and are delightful as table fruit, while the Muscat wine and fruit are too feline to suit all palates. On the whole they are decidedly preferable, at least for Northern localities; and of the two, judging from present experience, the Thompson is the finest and most productive. The little seedless raisins made from these varieties are stemmed, when dry, and packed loosely, either in small sacks or pressed into neat boxes for the trade. If it were not for the American propensity for "big things," I would predict larger and more profitable sales for them as soon as they become better known, than for the Muscat raisins. The little white and black grapes of Zante and Corinth, of which the currants of commerce are made, have not found much favor here, and there is no reason why they should. The varieties referred to above are immeasurably superior to the dirty imported product, which has only the very questionable recommendation of being "far fetched and dear bought."

It is an open question whether it is better to dry by sun or artificial heat in a dryer. Without discussing the question we may rejoice in the undisputed fact that we can make raisins without artificial heat.

Since the beginning of the raisin industry manifold improvements have been made in selecting, curing and packing in an attractive style, and California raisins are now fully equal, if not superior, to the best imported brands, and they can be produced as cheaply. American ingenuity has brought out many machines and appliances, by means of which enough more can be accomplished to overcome the competition of cheap foreign labor. The only apparent danger which threatens the industry is the imminent one that overproduction may force prices down below cost. Whether the combinations which have been entered into by the growers and manufacturers will suffice to avert this, remains to be seen. We can only hope for the best.

CHAPTER XLVIII.

OTHER USES OF GRAPES.

DRIED GRAPES.

When the prices of wine and wine grapes went down so low, a few years ago, that wine making was no longer profitable, the drying of wine grapes for culinary purposes was resorted to, on a somewhat limited scale. It was found that three tons of fresh grapes would make a ton of dried, which could be packed in plain white sacks and shipped for cooking or making wine. Many low-grade grapes were thus dried and shipped to the East, where they were sold for an average of about three cents per pound. Such dried grapes are very nice, and many were thus utilized. But the movement proved to be only a makeshift, as the dried grapes replaced many other fruits in the kitchen, and interfered with their sale, while the wine made from them in the East, where water and sugar were added to increase the wine product, also interfered with the sale of our pure wines made from grape juice alone. Finally, it proved difficult in the North to dry our juicy wine grapes, when a sudden shower would sometimes come at the inopportune time and spoil them. So it has been gradually abandoned, until very little is heard of it to-day.

CONDENSED MUST.

Another of the expedients attempted with a view to making a market for our grapes in seasons of low prices, is to partially evaporate the must and ship the condensed product. The Spring-Muehl system, which is calculated to work up large quantities, is a process for condensing the fresh must of the grapes, especially red varieties, in a vacuum pan, to about one-third of its volume;

then mixed with the fresh pomace of the grapes, in barrels, it is shipped abroad, for wine making. In England and other countries water is added, and the whole refermented into wine. It is claimed that quite as good wine can be made there from this material as from fresh grapes, and this claim would seem to be reasonable. But the first shipments were only partially successful, as the must began to ferment on the way. Later shipments have given better satisfaction, yet the process has not given as good results as were hoped for. The business has not attained any considerable magnitude, though the reduced cost of transportation secured by it, is apparently in its favor.

GRAPE MILK, OR UNFERMENTED GRAPE JUICE.

To those who have conscientious scruples against the use of fermented wine, however pure, this has been offered as a substitute. Fermentation is suppressed by the use of sulphur, salycilic acid, or some other chemical agent, best known to those who make it. None of them are entirely harmless, being more or less injurious to health. For obvious reasons I do not recommend them ; and that pure, fermented wine is far more wholesome, all authorities agree. Yet it is worthy of mention here, for a considerable amount of it is made and consumed by the public under the idea that it is harmless. The product of our vineyards is doubtless as good, and perhaps better than the similar article manufactured at the East as "Sweet Concord" or "unfermented" wine.

GRAPE SYRUP.

This is the pure juice of the grape, simply condensed by boiling, and is certainly far preferable to the last-mentioned article. Moreover, it can be made to serve the same purposes by diluting with water. It has the additional advantage of easier and cheaper transportation, provided it is properly managed in boiling down.

Both products retain, to a certain extent, the pleasant acidity and the sugar contained in the grape, yet neither can compare for refreshing, invigorating qualities, with pure, fermented wine, and are only poor substitutes for it.

THE GRAPE CURE.

The State of California has numerous summer and health resorts, where the wealthy and wearied denizens of the cities go with their families, during the warm months, to recruit their energies, impaired by the activities of business and city life. Yet strangely little has ever been done, either by the managers of the summer resorts or the physicians, to bring grapes into consumption as a hygienic agent. They are the most healthful fruit known, and are universally recognized as such in Europe, and recommended by the most eminent physicians. Yet a hygienic article of diet would seem to be more needed on this dyspeptic continent than in any part of Europe. Thousands flock annually to vine-growing districts of the Rhine, the Danube and the Moselle, for the grapes, which are regarded as a universal remedy for impaired digestion, and diseases of the bowels and kidneys. Each one begins with half a pound daily, eaten fresh from the vines, increasing gradually to four or five pounds a day, before the season is over. Is it not strange that here, where so many suffer from gastric derangement, and the remedy is at their door, pure, fresh and palatable, it is so little used, and so rarely recommended by physicians? If the proprietors of our summer resorts would each have a few acres of vineyard, which would furnish their guests with grapes at all times through the autumnal months, fresh and cool every morning, it would be safe to predict that their mineral waters would enjoy greater celebrity and their resorts more popularity. But as long as Americans subsist on hot biscuit, pies and divers abominations from the frying pan, washed down with scalding tea or coffee, or whisky and poor brandy, so long will it continue to be a nation of dyspeptics. When in place of these, good, simple, wholesome fare is their daily food, and sound, pure, light wines their daily beverage, we may hope for an improvement in the public health. Especially will this be likely if the dietetic change is accompanied by judicious exercise, walking and horseback riding.

CHAPTER XLIX.

WINE MAKING IN CALIFORNIA.

This is quite a different matter from making wine in the States east of the Rocky mountains. The grapes are of a widely different species, and the climate is wholly unlike any other on the continent. Our dry summers mature our grapes and develop a sufficient amount of sugar to make good, sound, dry wine, without resort to the practices of Gall, Petiol and others, so necessary in the East. Our grapes do not contain an excess of either flavor or acids, and usually supply a perfect must, which needs no manipulation aside from being well fermented and kept in a cool cellar, to develop into a good, sound wine. We have suffered more from improper and interrupted fermentation than from all other causes. It is those which have given a bad reputation to our lower grades of wine and led to the hasty conclusions arrived at by some of our *soi disant* experts that "wine could be made anywhere, even under an old shed or an oak tree." Such talk has done more harm to the industry than all the competition it has met with from abroad. In a State where every little valley has its own climate, and where the product and temperature vary so greatly, it becomes necessary to take into account all these differences, weigh them rationally, and conform the treatment of the young must to them.

The construction of the cellar and the fermenting room is the first object for consideration. The cellar for keeping the wine, after it is fermented, should be under ground, so as to maintain an even temperature the year around. Our hillsides afford abundant good and convenient sites for cellars, and the northern slope of a hill inclining toward the south or southeast, would be my choice. If building stone is conveniently attainable, that is, of course, the best and most durable material. In its absence good double walls of redwood or concrete may be used. The entrance to the cellar should be level with the lower side of the slope upon which the house is built, so that any water which may find access in winter can drain off. From this the slope should rise twelve or fourteen feet, so that all but the front of the lower story shall be wholly below the ground. The width and length must depend upon the capacity desired. Forty feet wide by sixty feet long will give ample room for thirty thousand gallons, which may be increased to forty thousand if thousand-gallon casks are used for the lower tier, with smaller casks on top of them. This will admit of four rows of thousand-gallon casks, five on each side, two rows in the middle, and one at the end, with walks in and around the middle, ample room for racking and working, and necessary space to get around the casks next to the walls. These casks should be of oak, as that wood is much better for keeping wine of any kind. New oak casks can be bought for seven to eight cents per wine gallon, though second-hand casks in good condition can often be obtained at much lower rates, and are even preferable to new, provided they have been kept sweet and in good condition.

The second story designed for a fermenting room is of the same length and width as the cellar, and ten feet high in the clear. Stone is the best material for the walls, but if necessary they may be built of redwood, double walls, or filled in with sawdust or some other non-conducting material. The entrance is at the opposite end from that to the cellar, so as to bring it on a level with the upper part of the slope, and thus both may be entered from the ground. The earth excavated from the cellar may be used to bank up against the side walls of the second story. This second floor will afford room for a row of fermenting tanks all around the sides, and one in the middle, with walks between in which to perform the pumping, racking, etc. The fermenting tanks may be of redwood or oak, comparatively shallow for the breadth. Tanks ten feet wide and four feet deep will hold about two thousand wine gallons each. Redwood tanks will cost about two and a half cents a gallon. Of course the capacity can be increased by increasing the depth, but fermentation is much more thorough in shallow tanks with free circulation of air, than in deeper ones, where, besides the retarded fermentation, there is liability of heating the pomace. The floor of the second story should be double, of very strong planks, the sleepers resting on heavy timbers extending lengthwise, with a double row, ten feet from each wall, supported by strong pillars based on broad stones, as they have to sustain all the superincumbent weight. This is as good as arching, and much cheaper. A layer of tarred paper is generally placed between the floors, to prevent leakage to the room below. Ventilation of both stories is secured by holes left in the wall, which may be opened or closed at will from the outside. Strong doors, either double folding doors or one sliding door, wide enough to admit the large casks and fermenting vats, for both rooms, complete the outside arrangements. Inside, large beams of sawed timber, six by eight inches, laid about three feet apart lengthwise, and resting on crosspieces, form the foundations for the casks and vats. There will be room enough under the roof, above the middle of the second story, for the crusher, stemmer, pumps, elevator, and all the machinery needed. Twenty feet wide of flooring extending the length of the building and properly supported, will afford all the space needed. The machinery may be operated by steam or by hand. The two rows of fermenting vats on each side will suffice to receive all the crushed grapes, and a row of casks or tanks with double bottoms may be placed in the center of the fermenting room, into which the young wine can be pumped as soon as fermentation is complete. From these it can be conducted, by means of hose, into the casks below, immediately after the first racking, which should be done as soon as it has deposited most of the lees and become quiet and transparent. There are several establishments in the State which manufacture the machinery for wine making, in sufficient variety to suit a large or small business. One of the most complete is that of Mr. Heald, of Benicia, Solano county.

PICKING THE GRAPES.

The grapes must be fully ripe, but how ripe depends somewhat on the character of the wine to be made. For the common grades of clarets and white wines they are ripe enough when the stems become brown, and the berries evenly colored and translucent. But the best test is the saccharometer, of which Balling's is the scale most commonly used, and of which one degree is about equal to four degrees of Oechsle's, which is generally used in the East and in Germany. Whenever our common grapes show 22° to 24° Balling, they are considered ripe enough to make good dry wine. But when it is desired to make a Haut Sauterne from such varieties as Sauvignon,

Semillion, Chablis or Veltliner, or a high-grade Burgundy, they should be allowed to hang longer, until some of the berries are shriveled, and they show from 26° to 32° Balling. There is a growing taste and increasing demand, among the American public, for full-flavored, heavy wines, retaining a slight degree of sweetness when fermented. Manifestly it costs more to make such wines, but if the consumer is willing to pay for the extra labor, smaller yield and higher quality, we can make them. It is only recently that there has been much inducement offered by the trade or the public for making them. But for about a thousand gallons of this grade, made in 1893, we had no difficulty in obtaining double the price of common dry wines, as they proved equal, in quality and bouquet, to the finest Haut Sauterne. That convinced me that we can fully rival the French in this.

The vintage begins with us, in Napa county, about the 15th of September, and continues, with slight intermissions, until some time in November, or even until the first week in December, if there are no severe frosts, and the second crop of grapes has fair weather in which to ripen. In young, vigorous vineyards, and with some varieties, this crop is almost as heavy as the first, though not as high in quality. We generally have a few showers of rain in September, which have some influence on the crop. A few light rains are beneficial, as they freshen the fruit and promote a more active fermentation. But if the rains continue, ripe-rot is likely to ensue, which is deleterious, especially on the red grapes, though white grapes are little, if any, injured. It is even held, by the best authorities in Europe, that this so-called "noble rot" (*Edelfæule*) improves the quality of white wines, and that the choicest vintages are made from such grapes. Of course they must be picked before any acetic acid has developed in the berries. With black grapes, however, ripe-rot is regarded as injurious, for it diminishes color and tannin. All black grapes stricken with ripe-rot must be carefully removed as they are picked.

Grapes are here picked into boxes holding forty to fifty pounds each, which are carried, as fast as filled, to the avenues dividing the blocks. Thence they are conveyed, in wagons, to the winery, and crushed as soon as they arrive. Most of the larger wineries have stemmers and crushers combined, where the stems are removed first, and drop before they are carried into the crusher. Any attempted description of the different machines used in this State would lead beyond the limits of this book. Suffice it to say that some wineries have apparatus which enables them to prepare the material for millions of gallons of wine, within six weeks. Others are content to make from 10,000 to 25,000 gallons with a common hand crusher, and a screen for a stemmer, upon which the bunches are rubbed, the berries falling below. Some even do the work without stemming. As a general thing the wines made in these smaller cellars are of superior quality, because they are more carefully and skillfully handled than those in the large cellars. In those it is often impossible to grade and watch the product sufficiently to secure the highest quality. It is from the smaller cellars, where the proprietor personally watches and manipulates everything, that we must continue to expect our choicest product.

MAKING WHITE WINE.

The process of making white wine is materially different from that of making red wine. In white wines we desire smoothness and delicacy ; in red wine, color and a certain proportion of tannin and astringency. To make wine from the light-colored varieties, which are the white wine grapes proper, is a very simple matter. In crushing the grapes into a fermenting vat the crusher

16

must be adjusted to break the skins without crushing the stems and seeds, as they would impart too much tannin. The whole mass is then generally allowed to stand from twelve to twenty-four hours, until fermentation sets in, and then pressed as dry as possible. To facilitate this, the juice is drawn off first through a spigot in the bottom of the vat, and the must filled into barrels, puncheons or casks in the fermenting room, which, however, should not be quite full, as a precaution against running over. Some makers, who aim for a very delicate wine, press immediately after crushing, but I regard it as safer to allow it to first begin fermentation. The fermenting room should be kept at a temperature of 60° to 70°, and as soon as violent fermentation is over, which will generally be at the end of four to six days, the casks should be filled up with the same must, kept in a separate cask, which is closed lightly to guard against flies and impurities. As long as carbonic acid gas escapes there is no danger for the young wine, but when it becomes quiet it should be closed, though not firmly at first. In six weeks or two months the sediment will be deposited and the wine become transparent, when it is to be racked off into casks in the cellar, taking care to keep back as much as possible all the lees. Rather put the cloudy wine, which runs last, into a separate package, than run it with the clear wine. From this time on it is important to keep the casks well filled, and closed air-tight with round oak or maple bungs.

MAKING WHITE WINE FROM BLACK GRAPES.

This is not practiced as much as formerly, because the Mission and Malvasia, which formerly occupied a large part of our vineyards, have almost disappeared and are not valued for wine making. We have some other varieties—Zinfandel in the valley lands, for example— and also the Black Pinot, which will hardly give color enough without taking off the first run of the juice. Immediately after the grapes are crushed they are either pressed very lightly, or the juice is run off without pressing and filled into casks to ferment as white wine. The pomace is then thrown into the fermenting vat and treated as red wine. I do not recommend this practice under any other than the exceptional conditions mentioned above. The first run of the juice is generally the best in quality, and while the red wine may gain in color and astringency, it will lose in soundness and quality. Location is all-important for the finest wines. A really fine red wine cannot be expected, save from a soil rich in iron and other essential elements. On such soils there will be no deficiency in sugar, color and tannin, nor in fine flavor, if all the juice is fermented together.

MAKING RED WINE.

The process of making red wine is quite distinct, and from different material, yet the difference is not as great as many suppose. Formerly the public taste was—or was supposed to be—in favor of very dark, astringent wines, containing the greatest possible amount of tannin. This, in the opinion of our wine makers, required long fermentation on the skins, and red grapes were often left for two weeks in the fermenting vat, until they had become entirely quiet, and a heavy crust had formed on the top, sometimes moldy and acid. True, these wines were very rough, provided they did not spoil altogether. The result was loss of bouquet and of all the better qualities a fine red wine ought to possess, and nothing was added to the color, which will be acquired by a fermentation of four or five days. These flat, rough wines have done more to damage the reputation of California wines than anything else. Fortunately a better and more discriminating taste prevails, and the public re-

quirement is for smooth, full-bodied wines, of sprightliness and bouquet. With proper management we can
make them from the varieties of grapes now at our command. Of the processes of fermentation by means of
false bottoms, in closed casks, and others which have
their advocates, I have found none better than the simple treatment of fermenting in open vats, which I have
practiced while I have been in the State. The grapes
are crushed into the vat, and left there until fermentation ensues, which is generally in from twelve to twenty-
four hours, according to the temperature. The entire
mass should be evened out, so that the berries are submerged in the liquid. As soon as active fermentation
appears they should be thoroughly stirred three or four
times a day, so that no crust can form, and they are
kept wholly submerged. This is the main point,—
frequent working, so that no 'part of the mass has a
chance to develop acetic acid. Fermentation will set in
rapidly and violently, but it generally subsides the fourth
or fifth day, when the seething mass will lose its pun-
gency and sweetness, and become quiet and cooler.
Draw some of the young wine, and if it has acquired a
slight bitterness, now is the time to draw off the fluid
from below into fresh casks, and press the pomace.
Even if it should retain a slight sweetness, as is usual
with rich musts, it is better to rack it than to let it become flat in the vat. A slight fermentation will continue in the cask, all the saccharine will be changed to
alcohol, and the fine bouquet and freshness aimed for
will be developed. If it changes its character and color
every week for the next month or so, no harm is done.
This is a peculiarity of young red wines, and they come
out all right if the casks, vats, and everything else have
been kept sweet and clean. It is, in fact, one of the
most important conditions of wine making that everything is kept scrupulously clean.

The after treatment is about the same as for white wines, or like that described in the first part of this book. There is this difference, however, that the California wines, being pure juice of the grape, contain more gluten and albumen than gallized or petiotized wines, and therefore require more time to become clear and matured. This is especially true of our white wines, which do not contain as much tannin, and thus have arisen complaints that they become cloudy when shipped long distances, and do not keep well. The remedy, or rather, preventive, is frequent racking. After the first racking in November or December, there should be another in fair weather in February or March. If they are then perfectly clear and limpid and remain so until the beginning of May, they may perhaps be trusted to lie through the summer, but generally it is best to rack them again early in May. In most cases, however, they are sold to a dealer when six months old, which obviates this necessity. The latter is, perhaps, the best course, if a fair price can be obtained.

Of Haut Sauternes and heavy Burgundies I have already made mention. Their treatment is the same as for other red wines, only we do not wait for all sweetness to disappear. But when violent fermentation is over they are racked from the fermenting vats, and the Haut Sauternes are left in the cask until they have become clear. Such wines are so heavy in alcohol, developed by fermentation from the sugar they contain, that there is less liability of clouding or other trouble.

FORTIFIED WINES.

The so-called "sweet" wines are, in fact, not true wines,—that is, pure fermented juice of the grape. All have alcohol in some form added to them, increasing their strength and keeping them in that sweet condition so palatable to many. As I know little about them, my

notes upon them will necessarily be brief. They are of
four kinds: port, sherry, Angelica and sweet Muscat.
The last two are made in a similar manner. Angelica is
made from the first run of the juice of Mission grapes;
sweet Muscat from Muscat of Alexandria, and a finer
grade from the German Muscatelle or Frontignan. The
grapes are allowed to hang until very ripe, then crushed
and immediately pressed; then a gallon of quicklime is
added to every hundred gallon weight, and about a quart
of grape brandy to each gallon of the must. These additions are made in an open vat, and the liquid is allowed
to stand until it is clear, which, as the wine and brandy
suppress fermentation, is generally in two or three days.
It is then racked into casks, as all the lees have settled
to the bottom, and with another racking in two months
is ready for use, although it becomes more mellow
with age.

Port is commonly made from the red wine of Mission
and Malvasia grapes, though other red wines are also
used. The Trousseau makes the finest port of any.
The fluid is fortified by adding brandy or alcohol up to
23 or 24 per cent. Grape syrup, made by boiling down
sweet must, is also added.

Sherry is made in a similar manner, fortified, but not
made so sweet, and then kept in a room or oven heated
to a temperature of 140° to 160° for about six weeks.
This gives it the peculiar aged taste and flavor which
many admire. This is quite different from the methods
employed in Spain. There, special varieties of grapes
are used and the sherry flavor is acquired from them,
and from being aged in *bodegas*, or storage houses, for a
number of years. It is scarcely to be expected that this
method will ever be generally followed in this country,
as our people have not the patience to wait ten or twelve
years for results. But we have many of the best sherry
grapes which will develop the true flavor in a few years.

Even our common Mission grapes will do so, and the riper the grapes are when crushed the sooner this flavor will appear. We have made a very fine natural sherry from the Louisiana, ripened until the must showed 32°. It retains quite enough sweetness, and is as much superior to the artificial sherries as a fine Haut Sauterne is to the fortified Angelica and Muscat. In this matter, as in many others, there is a wide field for experiment.

SPARKLING WINES.

These are made both after the French method of developing carbonic acid gas in the bottle, which requires age, and also by the speedy method of charging the wine. A third method, now pursued by the California Champagne Company, is the Reihlen process, of creating the gas in the cask, which gives the speediest and best results. All the wines made by this process seem to have a lasting mousseux, a pure flavor and sprightliness, equal to good French or German sparkling wines, and are sold at about half the price. Mr. Arpad Hareszthy has the oldest establishment in the State in which the mousseux is developed in the bottle, and his wines, after long experimenting, seem to give general satisfaction. There are several other establishments in the State, and we may confidently hope that, when proper blending and manipulation have been fully studied, this branch of the business will attain much larger dimensions in the future.

CHAPTER L.

BRANDY.

A great deal of brandy may be made of the wash, lees and pomace, but such is not always of the desired fine quality. The best brandy in California has been made from West's White Prolific and Folle Blanche. The latter forms the basis of all the fine Cognacs of France. Were it not for the revenue laws, which make distilling a perplexing business to engage in, even for the strictly honest distiller, while the rogues do not find it very difficult to circumvent them in one way or another, the manufacture of brandy would afford some relief to those who have a surplus of wines. As it is, after paying ninety cents a gallon and incurring all the risk of evaporation and leakage, while the product is stored in government bonded warehouses, there is little profit left after selling the brandy at $1.35 or $1.40 per gallon. It requires five gallons of wine on an average to produce a gallon of brandy, and besides, there are the labor and fuel. That we can make as good brandy here as anywhere has been repeatedly proved. That our brandy is better than the cheap whiskies and brandies manufactured abroad and brought here is also a conceded fact. But where is the inducement to make it at forty-five to fifty-five cents a gallon above the internal revenue tax? It is the old, old story: that home production is discouraged and suppressed in every possible way; and that "far-fetched and dear bought" find ready demand, while home products go begging for a market. England, Germany and the northern countries are our best customers now. They can appreciate what we make, while our own countrymen turn up their noses at anything which has not a foreign label.

CHAPTER LI.

A FEW NECESSARY CELLAR IMPLEMENTS.

Besides casks, barrels and kegs of various sizes, of which the smaller ones can be placed upon and between the larger to save room, many other appliances are needed. Faucets of different sizes for racking, rubber hose with couplings which can be screwed to the faucets, and pumps, are among the things needed. The pump most commonly in use is the Challenge, which may easily be worked by one man. A small jack-screw for lifting heavy casks, is also a convenience. A few buckets, made of strong tin, smaller at the top than at the bottom, with a spout on one side and a handle on the other; tubs to be used in racking; a filling can, with a long spout bent down at the farther end, used to keep the casks full; and rods to be used in stirring the wine when fining becomes necessary, are required in every cellar. Other implements, which have been described in a previous chapter, are as useful here as in the East.

CHAPTER LII.

CLARIFICATION, FILTERING AND FINING.

If wine has been well fermented, and carefully racked twice, this process will rarely be necessary, and it is never desirable. But it happens with our pure juice wines, that they will not become bright. This is because they contain more tannin and albumen than the wines made at the East. When wine is turbid it must be made bright by some process, as cloudy wine is unsalable, however good it may be otherwise. Filtering is a purely mechanical process, which takes out all the impurities suspended in the wine, without imparting any other foreign matter to it. Paper and paper pulp are very common materials for filtering, and a paper filter invented by Mr. A. Beck, San Francisco, possesses the advantages of low cost, and self-action, by gravity alone, which saves much labor. The wine to be filtered is contained in a cask, which is elevated on a platform a few feet above the filter. The wine flows through a faucet and hose to the bottom of the filter, which contains a number of flannel bags, drawn over spiral springs to keep them suspended. The wine is forced upward in the filter by the pressure of the fluid in the cask above, is pressed through the bags and a false bottom which holds them in position, and flows thence through a hose, into a cask below. It takes about twelve hours, with a filter of ten-gallon capacity, to filter a puncheon of 160 gallons. The apparatus, when once started, needs no looking after until the next morning, when the most turbid wine will have come out bright and clear. The sacks, when they become clotted, can readily be taken out and washed, or rinsed by forcing water through them.

Gelatine and isinglass are the most common and the best finings for white wine. The former is manufactured from the cartilages, skins and tendons of animals, and comes in tablets or sheets. It is one of the most powerful of finings and takes with it a great deal of tannin and color. It should therefore not be used for red wines unless it is desired to relieve them from an excess of color and tannin. It precipitates more sediment than any other fining, and wines treated with it should be racked as soon as they are clear, which will generally be within three weeks. It is generally used to clarify common wines, and if they are somewhat flat, tannin should be added to them. Gelatine is used at the rate of one ounce to each hundred gallons of wine. Soak the gelatine a few hours in tepid water, then dissolve in a dish over a slow fire, in a little water, stirring it constantly, and do not allow it to boil.

Isinglass, or fish glue, is made from the air-bladder of the sturgeon, and comes chiefly from Russia. It is the best fining for fine white wines. One ounce, for each hundred gallons of wine, is broken into small fragments, by pounding it with a hammer on a block of wood. Put into an earthen vessel, and pour over it enough of the wine that is to be fined to cover it. Add a little more after an hour or two, when the first will have been absorbed. In about twenty-four hours it will have become a jelly, and may be thinned by adding more of the wine, and is to be worked with the hands until it is wholly dissolved. Then strain it through a piece of linen, with pressure enough to force all the mucilage through. If too thick it must be whipped or beaten and more wine added, before using. It may be kept in bottles for some time after it is prepared, if a little brandy is added.

FOR RED WINES.

The whites of eggs are the best fining for red wines. The albumen in them coagulates by the action of the alcohol and tannin, and forms a precipitate heavier than the liquid, carrying with it as it falls the matters held in suspension. Only strictly fresh eggs can be used, and the yolks must be carefully kept out, as they discolor the wine. The whites of a dozen eggs are required for each hundred gallons of wine, beaten thoroughly with a small quantity of the wine. For sweet wines, containing so little spirit that the finings will not act, alcohol must be added. But such wines are rarely found here, the deficiency, if any, being in tannin, and that in white wines. This is supplied by adding from half an ounce to an ounce of tannin to every hundred gallons of wine. Dissolve one-half pound of tannin in a quart of strong alcohol, by shaking it thoroughly; let it stand twenty-four hours, then strain through a cloth. One gill of the solution contains about one ounce of tannic acid. After the finings have been prepared as above, two or three gallons are drawn from the bunghole of the cask of wine to be treated, and added to the finings, and the whole well mixed. The mixing may be done by means of a stick split into several prongs, or a wire or bristle brush. The mixture is then poured into the cask until it is full, and left to rest until the wine is bright, which will generally be in two or three weeks. Just as soon as the wine is clear it should be racked off, or it will acquire a bad taste.

CHAPTER LIII.

AGING WINE—BOTTLING.

A great deal has been said about the importance of age for wines, and the evils of selling California wines too young. There is doubtless some foundation for all this, but it is greatly exaggerated. There are great differences in varieties, some ripening in much less time than others, and all depending largely on their treatment. Strong, full-bodied wines require more time to develop their best qualities than light wines, which are bright and clear after a season or two. I regard a wine as old when it is perfectly bright and clear, having deposited all its impurities, developed its flavor and bouquet, and attained its highest degree of perfection. When it has arrived at this stage it should be bottled or sold. In bottles it will retain its good qualities, and we cannot look for further improvement in casks. It is better, under ordinary circumstances, to sell as soon as a reasonable offer can be obtained. It is seldom to the interest of the producer to bottle the wine, for bottling is, in fact, a distinct branch of the business. To age wines is more properly the business of the dealer, but the producer will, under ordinary circumstances, find it better to sell as soon as the wine has reached maturity. It will enable him to prepare for the next vintage, and to save room and cooperage. If he wishes to retain any wines for experiment or other purpose, he can reserve them. If, for any reason, it should become desirable to bottle wine, the one essential requirement is that it shall be perfectly clear. There are differences in varieties and locations. For example, our Zinfandels, even from the choicest locations, are at their best when two years old, and lose their sprightliness and fine bouquet when kept over three years, while Cabernet Sauvignon, Burgundy, Riesling and Traminer will need more time to bring out their best qualities. Wines that had perfect fermentation are in no danger of disease.

CHAPTER LIV.

PURE WINE AS A PROMOTER OF TEMPERANCE.

I have no fault to find with those who honestly believe that they should abstain from everything which contains the least particle of alcohol, yet I desire to enter a solemn protest against denouncing wine as necessarily a source of drunkenness. It is not the moderate use, but the abuse of any article of daily food or drink, which constitutes intemperance, and I am as sincerely and strongly opposed to such abuse of wine as any one can be. I regard wine as one of the best gifts of a beneficent Creator to mankind. The same Being who "causeth the grass to grow for the cattle and herb for the service of man," also gives "wine that maketh glad the heart of man" (Ps. 104; v. 14, 15). This gift is too good to be abused, but is designed to be used, like other good things, in moderation; to promote health and happiness, and not to degrade to the level of the brute. It should drive out of use such fiery, alcoholic drinks as poor whisky, brandy, and those vile decoctions which are sold under the names of sweet Catawba, Angelica, port and sherry, which often contain as much spirit in disguise as the first-named. Pure light wine as a general beverage is one of the most effective promoters of temperance that can be found, and the nations with whom it is in common use are the most sober and temperate. When I mention wine the reference is to "the cup that cheers but not inebriates," such as our Savior Himself created by His first miracle, at Cana in Galilee, consecrated at His holy supper and ordained to be used in the sacrament in loving remembrance of Him. Our total-abstinence friends seem to forget this when they claim to be His followers, and yet denounce the cup which He consecrated and appointed to perpetuate His memory on earth. St. Paul exhorted Timothy: "Use a little wine for the stomach's sake and thine often infirmities." And in many other places the Holy Scriptures show how fallacious is the idea that they forbid its use. Martin Luther, the great reformer and the very highest type of clear-headed independent manhood, wrote:

> "Who loves not woman, wine and song,
> Will be a fool his whole life long."

Surely he did not go down to a drunkard's grave, nor was he ever charged with drunkenness.

Human nature is so constituted that it craves some kind of a stimulant. Why not furnish it the most invigorating, health-giving, pure light wine, instead of enervating tea and coffee. All eminent physicians agree that it assists digestion when taken with the food, and it can now be had as cheaply as tea and coffee. If prohibitory laws have failed to prohibit, it is because their authors do not recognize the inherent wants of human nature, nor the truth of the maxim that "forbidden fruit is the sweetest." If, instead of futile prohibitory legislation, we had laws (and they were enforced) making drunkenness a crime which brings upon the transgressor infamy and punishment, I would heartily rejoice. But I cannot see the justice of laws which prescribe equal punishment for the innocent and the guilty, and forbid everyone to use wine in moderation and with beneficial effects, because another abuses it, or makes a beast of himself by drinking bad whisky.

Wine has become so cheap in California that any family may, by purchasing in five-gallon kegs, have good, sound, light wine at a cost of twenty-five cents per gallon, delivered at their door. This is cheaper than tea or coffee, and should be kept in every house as a daily table beverage with the meals, for lemonades, etc. It would be much better for the community if it were thus made a part of the household supplies, to be drunk only at home, instead of leaving it to be had only in the drinking saloons, where it costs five to ten cents a glass, and where the abominable practice of "treating" prevails. As to this so-called custom of "treating," I hold it responsible for more drunkenness, broken constitutions and moral ruin than any other cause, especially among young men. A party of them will go to a saloon, where one of them invites the others to "take a drink." They do so, and then another one of them feels under a sort of moral obligation to return the compliment. Thus it goes around until every one has, in turn, "stood treat," and spent his money to be even with the others, and the liquor enters their heads. They call this "having a good time," which it may be for the bartender but not for them. It means heavy heads and empty pockets if kept up, and ruins many a promising young man. How much better would it be if each took his glass of light wine at home, with his food, at one-tenth the price. I have labored in the cause of true temperance (as I understand it) all my life, and my dearest wish has been to see this nation the freest and happiest on earth, which it can never be until it is one of the most temperate. I firmly believe that the general use of light wines would be one of the chief agents in bringing this about. I may not live to see it, but after the experience of a lifetime I have no reason to retract a word that I have ever written or spoken in the cause of true temperance.

CHAPTER LV.

EXTENT AND PROSPECTS OF THE INDUSTRY.

It is difficult to give accurate figures showing the acreage devoted to grapes in California. Several years ago the estimated amount was 150,000 acres, of which about 90,000 acres were in wine grapes and 60,000 in table and raisin grapes. I do not think the acreage has changed greatly since then. Thousands of acres have been destroyed by phylloxera and the Anaheim disease, but to make up for this other, thousands of acres have been planted to raisin grapes. The decrease has been in the acreage of wine grapes, and it is still decreasing. The magnitude of the wine industry is shown by the fact that about $60,000,000 are invested in vineyards, cellars and fixtures, giving employment to about 15,000 persons. I am unable to give exact figures, though the State Board of Viticulture has tried hard to collect them every year. They doubtless fall short of the reality, as many of the small vineyards and cellars are hidden away in the mountains or little valleys, where they were over-looked. The following are the estimates, showing the increase since 1876:

YEAR.	GALLONS.	YEAR.	GALLONS.
1876	3,750,000	1885	9,000,000
1877	4,000,000	1886	18,000,000
1878	5,000,000	1887	18,000,000
1879	5,000,000	1888	25,000,000
1880	8,500,000	1889	24,000,000
1881	7,000,000	1890	23,000,000
1882	10,000,000	1891	26,000,000
1883	8,500,000	1892	23,000,000
1884	15,000,000	1893	21,000,000

The extremely low prices which have prevailed during the last few years have discouraged thousands from planting, until it now seems that the acreage of wine grapes would fall off at the rate of 2,000 acres per

17

annum. Many, despairing of its future, have planted
fruit trees among the failing vines, with the intention of
eradicating the latter. This has been more largely done
in the counties of Napa and Sonoma, which produce the
finest light wines, and only a few have replanted with
resistant vines, trusting to the future to bring a change
for the better. As I am one of those few, I will give
the reasons why I still have faith in the eventual success
of the wine industry here. Though there has been an
overproduction of inferior wines for several years, yet the
consumption of wine is increasing. It has increased
in the State to over six million gallons annually, while
the outside demand has also increased in an equal ratio.
A great deal of inferior wine has been manufactured into
brandy, and thus taken out of the market. The quality
of our wines is improving rapidly, as we cultivate better
varieties of grapes and have learned how to handle them.
The time is not very remote in the future when California wines will have to be sold under their own labels,
instead of those borrowed from the French and Germans,
as has so often been done. The phylloxera, great as have
been its devastations, may prove to be a blessing in disguise, as it will destroy our old vineyards of inferior
varieties, which will be replaced, if at all, by the very
best. Thus, while the quantity may be diminished,
the quality will be improved. And when the demand
exceeds the supply, prices must advance, as they did
in 1878–81, when there was not enough sound wine
in the State to meet the demand. When the new and
increased demand comes, we are ready to meet it with
better wines, which will command better prices and
more permanent sales. At the period referred to there
were but few varieties, limited knowledge and imperfect
apparatus. We certainly can do much better now.

One of the most prominent factors in bringing about
a favorable change is, in my opinion, the wine syndicate,

comprising a combination of producers and dealers, which has recently been organized and incorporated under the name of "California Wine Association," with a capital stock of $10,000,000. The directors are, Henry Epstein, Charles Carpy, Henry Kohler, Henry Van Bergen, J. J. Weglein, E. C. Priber, Henry Lachmann, J. Frauenfeld, A. L. Tubbs, Hans H. Kohler and Percy T. Morgan, who have taken stock to the amount of $2,600,-000. Officers of the association : President, C. Carpy ; Vice Presidents, Henry Epstein, Henry Van Bergen, Henry Lachmann ; Treasurer, J. Frauenfeld ; Secretary, Hans H. Kohler. The object of the association is to control the product of the vineyards in the State. With this in view they have entered into contracts with the producers for options on their products—wines on hand, grapes of the coming crops and wines made from them,—for five years. These products are to be delivered at their destination within a stated time, at prices which are gradually increased year by year—one-third to be paid on delivery, one-third with acceptance in three, and the remainder in six months. The wines and grapes are to be graded in four classes at different prices for bottom and hill products, and also for different varieties. Due distinction is thus made as to quality—the first step that has been taken in that direction. This combination was the outcome of an evident necessity for self-defense,—to save the industry, we may say, from ruin. Previously every one had acted for himself. There was no concert; all sold at such prices as they saw fit, underbidding one another in the market. While the dealers were engaged in this cut-throat business, the unfortunate producer was forced to sell to them at such prices as they felt disposed to offer, which was sometimes far below the cost of production. But the dealers saw that this could not continue,—that they were killing the goose which had laid golden eggs for them, and that they must raise prices to a living basis if the vineyards were to be kept up. It was very clear to them that their immense storage houses, casks and machinery, and all the capital it had cost to build up their trade, would be wholly unremunerative if the vineyards died out, and they would be in worse plight than the producers, who had at least their lands, to cultivate in some other crops.

As about eighty per cent. of the producers have entered into contract with the association, it will be able to control the market and fix prices. Most of the other producers will find it to their interest to come in, and the dealers who are not in the syndicate will also join or be compelled, at least, to pay the same prices. In this move I see the dawn of a new and better era in California grape culture. We have the finest climate in the world, and are reasonably sure of a fair crop of salable products every year. There is no apparent reason why this should not again become, as it once was, a leading industry of the Golden State.

My task is ended—perhaps the last of the kind that I shall ever undertake. Whether it is well done is for those to say who read these pages. They may find their way into many a vintner's cottage, and if faults and oversights are found in them it is hoped the readers will think as kindly of the author as he thinks of everyone who grows the noble grape, and that it may prove helpful to them after he has been laid to rest in California's soil. But while life lasts, so long will continue undiminished his predilection for grapes and wine, and for his brothers, the producers.

CHAPTER LVI.

WINE SONGS.

"Wine maketh glad the heart of man." Can it surprise us, therefore, if all nations which produce it have had their poets who glorified it in song, and that singing and merriment prevail during the vintage? But none has more of them than Germany, the fatherland of song; while America, the coming Wineland, is singularly deficient in this respect. Let us hope that, when good wine is more appreciated than it has been so far, some of our poets will also immortalize it in song. My poetic vein has long ceased to flow, or I would try. But at the end of a book devoted to grape culture and wine making, I cannot forego the pleasure of attaching a few translations of German songs, nearly as good as the original in their quaint humor and deep meaning.

FATHER NOAH, THE FIRST WINE GROWER.

1. When Noah left his floating frame,
   Our Lord to Father Noah came.
   He prized his pious offering,
   And said, "Thou'st done a goodly thing,
   And to reward thy piety,
   Thou may'st e'en choose a boon from me."

2. Then to the Lord old Noah said,
   "The water now tastes rather bad,
   The whilst there have been drowned therein
   All beasts and mankind in their sin.
   'Tis therefore, Lord, I even think
   I should prefer some other drink."

3. Thereat the Lord to Eden went,
   And brought him thence the grapevine's plant,
   And gave him counsel and advice
   To tend this shrub of Paradise,
   And bade him nurse it carefully.
   It pleased old Noah wondrously.

4. He made a solemn household call
    And summoned wife and child and all,
    And planted vines where'er they'd grow.
    Forsooth old Noah was not slow.
    He pressed the grape, and built a cave,
    And put it into casks to save.

5. Old Noah, grateful for the boon,
    Cask upon cask did open soon;
    And with sincerest piety,
    Did empty them most willingly;
    And drank yet, since the flood was o'er,
    Three hundred years, and fifty more.

6. This to each prudent man does show,
    From drinking wine no harm can flow,
    And Christian folks it warns, moreo'er,
    No water in their wine to pour,
    The whilst there have been drowned therein
    All beasts and mankind in their sin.

(From the German of Kopish, translated by J. A. Schmidt.)

NOAH'S LEGACY.

1. When Noah felt approach his end
    He said, "I'll make my testament."
    He counted over all his stocks,
    His cattle, donkeys, goats and bucks,
    The sheep, camels, and all the rest
    With which so richly he was blest.

2. This done, he said, "I wish to see,
    At once, my friend the notary."
    To him he spoke, "You shall divide
    My property. Now do it right;
    Let all my children have their share,
    And take, yourself, what's just and fair."

3. Thus they divided all. But still,
    Before the lawyer signed the will
    (He was, as clerks in average,
    Fond of a pleasant beverage),
    He said: "But now, beloved sir,
    Who of your wine shall be the heir?"

4. Said Noah: "In daylight and here
    We can't decide that question, dear!
    Let to the cellar us descend
    And see, how there, the case may stand.

Don't fear pains." "What my duty is,"
The lawyer said, "I never miss."

5. A generous man old Noah was,
And freely filled the lawyer's glass.
They drew a sample everywhere,
They tasted here, they tasted there;
And when they had the stock gone through,
Took an inventory anew.

6. Back came to Noah youth and life,
He thought no more of child and wife.
"Dear friend," said he, "now put that[down,
And head it with a golden crown.
Of all the wine that here you see,
The *human race* the heir shall be.

7. "No death bells! Let the goblets ring,
And jolly boys my requiem sing.
Each cask filled with the golden wine
Shall be a monument of mine.
Write this, and make, dear notary,
Eternal thus my memory."

(*German text by Gruner, translated by J. A. Schmidt.*)

There is a deep significance to me in the following, as I look back through the past, and think of the genial spirit now laid at rest, old "Father Muench," as he was familiarly called by his friends, to the closer circle of whom it was my privilege to belong. One of the pioneers of German descent in Missouri, who served his adopted country in its legislative halls through all the stormy period of the late war, and yet more by his numerous writings in various fields of literature, he was one of the first who followed the then new industry of grape culture; and his earliest beginnings date back to 1846. His "American Vintner's School," a text-book for the beginner, attained a deserved popularity, and was translated from the German into English. Many pleasant hours have we spent together at his homestead and at mine. At my farewell visit in 1881, he expressed the wish to "die in harness," without any previous illness. His wish was gratified by an all-wise Providence. He was found dead among his beloved vines, one fine winter's morning of that year, with the pruning shears still in his hand, in his 84th year. Peace be to his memory. One of the best and most genial of men, he yet lives eternal in the memory of his many friends.

AMERICAN VINTNER'S SONG.

BY FREDERICK MUENCH (FAR WEST).

(Translated from the German by Mrs. Wistar.)

Plant the vine! Plant the vine!
Generous fount of ruby wine!
   In the sunlight gladly playing,
   Richly all your toil repaying,
Will the smiling clusters shine.

Eve and dawn! Eve and dawn!
Still must find us working on,
   Digging, cutting, pruning, binding,
   Round their props the tendrils twining,—
Sweet the mite of labor done.

Sun and air! Sun and air!
Leafy green and odors fair;
   Then the berries, luscious treasure,
   Fill the inmost soul with pleasure,
Leaves and fruit and blossoms fair,—

Then at last! Then at last!
Left below, our labors past,
   Let us, o'er the mountains straying,
   Where the air's mild breath is playing,
Down the vale our glances cast.

Gather in! Gather in!
Let our harvest now begin.
   Now the purple juice, dark glowing,
   Full and free, in streams is flowing.
Young and old, come, gather in.

Hear it foam! Hear it foam!
Surging in its narrow home;
   Let it seethe and bubble rightly
   Till it sparkles, clear and brightly
Here within its narrow home.

Now come on! Now come on!
For our hardest task is done.
    Now we pour the wine's rich treasure,—
    Gods might envy us the pleasure;
Clink your glasses, every one.

Freedom's land! Freedom's land!
Where anon my home I planned;
    Lo, I drink to thee, brave nation;
    Comrades, join in this ovation:
Hail, our chosen Fatherland!

INDEX.

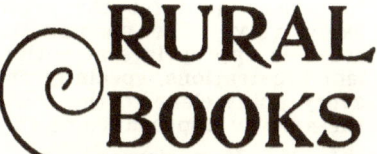

Greenhouse Construction.

By Prof. L. R. Taft. A complete treatise on greenhouse structures and arrangements of the various forms and styles of plant houses for professional florists as well as amateurs. All the best and most approved structures are so fully and clearly described that anyone who desires to build a greenhouse will have no difficulty in determining the kind best suited to his purpose. The modern and most successful methods of heating and ventilating are fully treated upon. Special chapters are devoted to houses used for the growing of one kind of plants exclusively. The construction of hotbeds and frames receives appropriate attention. Over one hundred excellent illustrations, specially engraved for this work, make every point clear to the reader and add considerably to the artistic appearance of the book. Cloth, 12mo. $1.50

Greenhouse Management.

By L. R. Taft. This book forms an almost indispensable companion volume to Greenhouse Construction. In it the author gives the results of his many years' experience, together with that of the most successful florists and gardeners, in the management of growing plants under glass. So minute and practical are the various systems and methods of growing and forcing roses, violets, carnations, and all the most important florists' plants, as well as fruits and vegetables described, that by a careful study of this work and the following of its teachings, failure is almost impossible. Illustrated. Cloth, 12mo. $1.50

Bulbs and Tuberous-Rooted Plants.

By C. L. Allen. A complete treatise on the history, description, methods of propagation and full directions for the successful culture of bulbs in the garden, dwelling and greenhouse. As generally treated, bulbs are an expensive luxury, while when properly managed, they afford the greatest amount of pleasure at the least cost. The author of this book has for many years made bulb growing a specialty, and is a recognized authority on their cultivation and management. The illustrations which embellish this work have been drawn from nature, and have been engraved especially for this book. The cultural directions are plainly stated, practical and to the point. Cloth, 12mo. $1.50

Irrigation Farming.

By Lute Wilcox. A handbook for the practical application of water in the production of crops. A complete treatise on water supply, canal construction, reservoirs and ponds, pipes for irrigation purposes, flumes and their structure, methods of applying water, irrigation of field crops, the garden, the orchard and vineyard; windmills and pumps, appliances and contrivances. Profusely, handsomely illustrated. Cloth, 12mo.   . . $1.50

Landscape Gardening.

By F. A. Waugh, professor of horticulture, University of Vermont. A treatise on the general principles governing outdoor art; with sundry suggestions for their application in the commoner problems of gardening. Every paragraph is snort, terse and to the point, giving perfect clearness to the discussions at all points. In spite of the natural difficulty of presenting abstract principles the whole matter is made entirely plain even to the inexperienced reader. Illustrated, 12mo. Cloth. . $ .50

Fungi and Fungicides.

By Prof. Clarence M. Weed. A practical manual concerning the fungous diseases of cultivated plants and the means of preventing their ravages. The author has endeavored to give such a concise account of the most important facts relating to these as will enable the cultivator to combat them intelligently. 222 pp., 90 ill., 12mo. Paper. 50 cents; cloth. $1.00

Talks on Manure.

By Joseph Harris, M. S. A series of familiar and practical talks between the author and the deacon, the doctor, and other neighbors, on the whole subject of manures and fertilizers; including a chapter especially written for it by Sir John Bennet Lawes of Rothamsted, England. Cloth, 12mo. $1.50

Insects and Insecticides.

By Clarence M. Weed, D. Sc., Prof. of entomology and zoology, New Hampshire college of agriculture. A practical manual concerning noxious insects, and methods of preventing their injuries. 334 pages, with many illustrations. Cloth, 12mo. $1.50

Mushrooms. How to Grow Them.

By Wm. Falconer. This is the most practical work on the subject ever written, and the only book on growing mushrooms published in America. The author describes how he grows mushrooms, and how they are grown for profit by the leading market gardeners, and for home use by the most successful private growers. Engravings drawn from nature expressly for this work. Cloth. $1.00

Handbook of Plants and General Horticulture.

By Peter Henderson. This new edition comprises about 50 per cent. more genera than the former one, and embraces the botanical name, derivation, natural order, etc., together with a short history of the different genera, concise instructions for their propagation and culture, and all the leading local or common English names, together with a comprehensive glossary of botanical and technical terms. Plain instructions are also given for the cultivation of the principal vegetables, fruits and flowers. Cloth, large 8vo. $3.00

Ginseng, Its Cultivation, Harvesting, Marketing and Market Value.

By Maurice G. Kains, with a short account of its history and botany. It discusses in a practical way how to begin with either seed or roots, soil, climate and location, preparation, planting and maintenance of the beds, artificial propagation, manures, enemies, selection for market and for improvement, preparation for sale, and the profits that may be expected. This booklet is concisely written, well and profusely illustrated, and should be in the hands of all who expect to grow this drug to supply the export trade, and to add a new and profitable industry to their farms and gardens, without interfering with the regular work. 12mo. . . . . . $ .35

Land Draining.

A handbook for farmers on the principles and practice of draining, by Manly Miles, giving the results of his extended experience in laying tile drains. The directions for the laying out and the construction of tile drains will enable the farmer to avoid the errors of imperfect construction, and the disappointment that must necessarily follow. This manual for practical farmers will also be found convenient for references in regard to many questions that may arise in crop growing, aside from the special subjects of drainage of which it treats. Cloth, 12mo. $1.00

Henderson's Practical Floriculture.

By Peter Henderson. A guide to the successful propagation and cultivation of florists' plants. The work is not one for florists and gardeners only, but the amateur's wants are constantly kept in mind, and we have a very complete treatise on the cultivation of flowers under glass, or in the open air, suited to those who grow flowers for pleasure as well as those who make them a matter of trade. Beautifully illustrated. New and enlarged edition. Cloth, 12mo. $1.50

Tobacco Leaf.

By J. B. Killebrew and Herbert Myrick. Its Culture and Cure, Marketing and Manufacture. A practical handbook on the most approved methods in growing, harvesting, curing, packing, and selling tobacco, with an account of the operations in every department of tobacco manufacture. The contents of this book are based on actual experiments in field, curing barn, packing house, factory and laboratory. It is the only work of the kind in existence, and is destined to be the standard practical and scientific authority on the whole subject of tobacco for many years. Upwards of 500 pages and 150 original engravings. $2.00

Play and Profit in My Garden.

By E. P. Roe. The author takes us to his garden on the rocky hillsides in the vicinity of West Point, and shows us how out of it, after four years' experience, he evoked a profit of $1,000, and this while carrying on pastoral and literary labor. It is very rarely that so much literary taste and skill are mated to so much agricultural experience and good sense. Cloth, 12mo. . . $1.00

Forest Planting.

By H. Nicholas Jarchow, LL. D. A treatise on the care of woodlands and the restoration of the denuded timberlands on plains and mountains. The author has fully described those European methods which have proved to be most useful in maintaining the superb forests of the old world. This experience has been adapted to the different climates and trees of America, full instructions being given for forest planting of our various kinds of soil and subsoil, whether on mountain or valley. Illustrated, 12mo. $1.50

Soils and Crops of the Farm.

By George E. Morrow, M. A., and Thomas F. Hunt. The methods of making available the plant food in the soil are described in popular language. A short history of each of the farm crops is accompanied by a discussion of its culture. The useful discoveries of science are explained as applied in the most approved methods of culture. Illustrated. Cloth, 12mo. $1.00

American Fruit Culturist.

By John J. Thomas. Containing practical directions for the propagation and culture of all the fruits adapted to the United States. Twentieth thoroughly revised and greatly enlarged edition by Wm. H. S. Wood. This new edition makes the work practically almost a new book, containing everything pertaining to large and small fruits as well as sub-tropical and tropical fruits. Richly illustrated by nearly 800 engravings. 758 pp., 12mo. $2.50

Fertilizers.

By Edward B. Voorhees, director of the New Jersey Agricultural Experiment Station. It has been the aim of the author to point out the underlying principles and to discuss the important subjects connected with the use of fertilizer materials. The natural fertility of the soil, the functions of manures and fertilizers, and the need of artificial fertilizers are exhaustively discussed. Separate chapters are devoted to the various fertilizing elements, to the purchase chemical analyses, methods of using fertilizers, and the best fertilizers for each of the most important field, garden and orchard crops. 335 pp. $1.00

Gardening for Profit.

By Peter Henderson. The standard work on market and family gardening. The successful experience of the author for more than thirty years, and his willingness to tell, as he does in this work, the secret of his success for the benefit of others, enables him to give most valuable information. The book is profusely illustrated. Cloth, 12mo. $1.50

Herbert's Hints to Horse Keepers.

By the late Henry William Herbert (Frank Forester). This is one of the best and most popular works on the horse prepared in this country. A complete manual for horsemen, embracing: How to breed a horse; how to buy a horse; how to break a horse; how to use a horse; how to feed a horse; how to physic a horse (allopathy or homoeopathy); how to groom a horse; how to drive a horse; how to ride a horse, etc. Beautifully illustrated. Cloth, 12mo. $1.50

Barn Plans and Outbuildings.

Two hundred and fifty-seven illustrations. A most valuable work, full of ideas, hints, suggestions, plans, etc., for the construction of barns and outbuildings, by practical writers. Chapters are devoted to the economic erection and use of barns, grain barns, house barns, cattle barns, sheep barns, corn houses, smoke houses, ice houses, pig pens, granaries, etc. There are likewise chapters on bird houses, dog houses, tool sheds, ventilators, roofs and roofing, doors and fastenings, workshops, poultry houses, manure sheds, barnyards, root pits, etc. Cloth, 12mo. $1.00

Cranberry Culture.

By Joseph J. White. Contents: Natural history, history of cultivation, choice of location, preparing the ground, planting the vines, management of meadows, flooding, enemies and difficulties overcome, picking, keeping, profit and loss. Cloth, 12mo. $1.00

Ornamental Gardening for Americans.

By Elias A. Long, landscape architect. A treatise on beautifying homes, rural districts and cemeteries. A plain and practical work with numerous illustrations and instructions so plain that they may be readily followed. Illustrated. Cloth, 12mo. $1.50

Grape Culturist.

By A. S. Fuller. This is one of the very best of works on the culture of the hardy grapes, with full directions for all departments of propagation, culture, etc., with 150 excellent engravings, illustrating planting, training, grafting, etc. Cloth, 12mo. $1.50

Turkeys and How to Grow Them.

Edited by Herbert Myrick. A treatise on the natural history and origin of the name of turkeys; the various breeds, the best methods to insure success in the business of turkey growing. With essays from practical turkey growers in different parts of the United States and Canada. Copiously illustrated. Cloth, 12mo. . . $1.00

Profits i Poultry.

Useful and ornamental breeds and their profitable management. This excellent work contains the combined experience of a number of practical men in all departments of poultry raising. It 's profusely illustrated and forms a unique and important addition to our poultry literature. Cloth, 12mo. $1.00

How Crops Grow.

By Prof. Samuel W. Johnson of Yale College. New and revised edition. A treatise on the chemical composition, structure and life of the plant. This book is a guide to the knowledge of agricultural plants, their composition, their structure and modes of development and growth; of the complex organization of plants, and the use of the parts; the germination of seeds, and the food of plants obtained both from the air and the soil. The book is indispensable to all real students of agriculture. With numerous illustrations and tables of analysis. Cloth, 12mo. $1.50

Coburn's Swine Husbandry.

By F. D. Coburn. New, revised and enlarged edition. The breeding, rearing, and management of swine, and the prevention and treatment of their diseases. It is the fullest and freshest compendium relating to swine breeding yet offered. Cloth, 12mo. $1.50

Stewart's Shepherd's Manual.

By Henry Stewart. A valuable practical treatise on the sheep for American farmers and sheep growers. It is so plain that a farmer or a farmer's son who has never kept a sheep, may learn from its pages how to manage a flock successfully, and yet so complete that even the experienced shepherd may gather many suggestions from it. The results of personal experience of some years with the characters of the various modern breeds of sheep, and the sheep raising capabilities of many portions of our extensive territory and that of Canada—and the careful study of the diseases to which our sheep are chiefly subject, with those by which they may eventually be afflicted through unforeseen accidents—as well as the methods of management called for under our circumstances, are carefully described. Illustrated. Cloth, 12mo. $1.00

Feeds and Feeding.

By W. A. Henry. This handbook for students and stock men constitutes a compendium of practical and useful knowledge on plant growth and animal nutrition, feeding stuffs, feeding animals and every detail pertaining to this important subject. It is thorough, accurate and reliable, and is the most valuable contribution to live stock literature in many years. All the latest and best information is clearly and systematically presented, making the work indispensable to every owner of live stock. 658 pages, 8vo. Cloth. $2.00

Hunter and Trapper.

By Halsey Thrasher, an old and experienced sportsman. The best modes of hunting and trapping are fully explained, and foxes, deer, bears, etc., fall into his traps readily by following his directions. Cloth, 12mo, $ .50

The Ice Crop.

By Theron L. Hiles. How to harvest, ship and use ice. A complete, practical treatise for farmers, dairymen, ice dealers, produce shippers, meat packers, cold storers, and all interested in ice houses, cold storage, and the handling or use of ice in any way. Including many recipes for iced dishes and beverages. The book is illustrated by cuts of the tools and machinery used in cutting and storing ice, and the different forms of ice houses and cold storage buildings. 122 pp., ill., 16mo. Cloth. $1.00

Practical Forestry.

By Andrew S. Fuller. A treatise on the propagation, planting and cultivation, with descriptions and the botanical and popular names of all the indigenous trees of the United States, and notes on a large number of the most valuable exotic species. $1.50

Irrigation for the Farm, Garden and Orchard.

By Henry Stewart. This work is offered to those American farmers and other cultivators of the soil who, from painful experience, can readily appreciate the losses which result from the scarcity of water at critical periods. Fully illustrated. Cloth, 12mo. $1.00

Market Gardening and Farm Notes.

By Burnett Landreth. Experiences and observation for both North and South, of interest to the amateur gardener, trucker and farmer. A novel feature of the book is the calendar of farm and garden operations for each month of the year; the chapters on fertilizers, transplanting, succession and rotation of crops, the packing, shipping and marketing of vegetables will be especially useful to market gardeners. Cloth, 12mo. . . $1.00

The Fruit Garden.

By P. Barry. A standard work on fruit and fruit trees, the author having had over thirty years' practical experience at the head of one of the largest nurseries in this country. Invaluable to all fruit growers. Illustrated. Cloth, 12mo. $1.50

The Nut Culturist.

By Andrew S. Fuller. A treatise on the propagation, planting and cultivation of nut-bearing trees and shrubs adapted to the climate of the United States, with the scientific and common names of the fruits known in commerce as edible or otherwise useful nuts. Intended to aid the farmer to increase his income without adding to his expenses or labor. 12mo. Cloth. . . $1.50

American Grape Growing and Wine Making.

By George Husmann of California. New and enlarged edition. With contributions from well-known grape growers, giving wide range of experience. The author of this book is a recognized authority on the subject. Cloth, 12mo. $1.50

Treat's Injurious Insects of the Farm and Garden.

By Mrs. Mary Treat. An original investigator who has added much to our knowledge of both plants and insects, and those who are familiar with Darwin's works are aware that he gives her credit for important observation and discoveries. New and enlarged edition. With an illustrated chapter on beneficial insects. Fully illustrated. Cloth, 12mo. $1.50

The Dogs of Great Britain, America and Other Countries.

New, enlarged and revised edition. Their breeding, training and management, in health and disease; comprising all the essential parts of the two standard works on dogs by "Stonehenge." It describes the best game and hunting grounds in America. Contains over one hundred beautiful engravings, embracing most noted dogs in both continents, making, together with chapters by American writers, the most complete dog book ever published. Cloth, 12mo. $1.50

Harris on the Pig.

By Joseph Harris. New edition. Revised and enlarged by the author. The points of the various English and American breeds are thoroughly discussed, and the great advantage of using thoroughbred males clearly shown. The work is equally valuable to the farmer who keeps but few pigs, and to the breeder on an extensive scale. Illustrated. Cloth, 12mo. . . . $1.00

Pear Culture for Profit.

By P. T. Quinn, practical horticulturist. Teaching how to raise pears intelligently, and with the best results, how to find out the character of the soil, the best methods of preparing it, the best varieties to select under existing conditions, the best modes of planting, pruning, fertilizing, grafting, and utilizing the ground before the trees come into bearing, and, finally, of gathering and packing for market. Illustrated. Cloth, 12mo. . $1.00

The Secrets of Health, or How Not to Be Sick, and How to Get Well from Sickness.

By S. H. Platt, A. M., M. D., late member of the Connecticut Eclectic Medical Society, the National Eclectic Medical Association, and honorary member of the National Bacteriological Society of America; our medical editor and author of "Talks With Our Doctor" and "Our Health Adviser." Nearly 600 pages. Profusely illustrated. An index of 20 pages, so that any topic may be instantly consulted. A new departure in medical knowledge for the people—the latest progress, secrets and practices of all schools of healing made available for the common people—health without medicine, nature without humbug, common sense without folly, science without fraud. 12mo. 576 pp., 81 illustrations. Cloth. $1.50

Gardening for Young and Old.

By Joseph Harris. A work intended to interest farmers' boys in farm gardening, which means a better and more profitable form of agriculture. The teachings are given in the familiar manner so well known in the author's "Walks and Talks on the Farm." Illustrated. Cloth, 12mo. $1.00

Money in the Garden.

By P. T. Quinn. The author gives in a plain, practical style, instructions on three distinct although closely connected branches of gardening—the kitchen garden, market garden and field culture, from successful practical experience for a term of years. Illustrated. Cloth, 12mo. $1.00

The Pruning Book.

By L. H. Bailey. This is the first American work exclusively devoted to pruning. It differs from most other treatises on this subject in that the author takes particular pains to explain the principles of each operation in every detail. Specific advice is given on the pruning of the various kinds of fruits and ornamental trees, shrubs and hedges. Considerable space is devoted to the pruning and training of grapevines, both American and foreign. Every part of the subject is made so clear and plain that it can be readily understood by even the merest beginner. Cloth, 8vo, 530 pages. Illustrated. $1.50

www.ingramcontent.com/pod-product-compliance
Lightning Source LLC
Chambersburg PA
CBHW020900020726
47497CB00005B/1494